Good Inside

Good Inside

A PRACTICAL GUIDE TO BECOMING THE PARENT YOU WANT TO BE

Dr Becky Kennedy

Thorsons

Thorsons
An imprint of HarperCollins*Publishers*
1 London Bridge Street
London SE1 9GF

www.harpercollins.co.uk

HarperCollins*Publishers*
Macken House, 39/40 Mayor Street Upper,
Dublin 1, Ireland D01 C9W8

First published by HarperCollins*Publishers*, 2022

12

© Dr Rebecca Kennedy 2022

Dr Rebecca Kennedy asserts the moral right to

be identified as the author of this work

A catalogue record of this book is available from the British Library

ISBN 978-0-00-850554-7

The information in this book has been carefully researched by the author
and is intended to be a source of information only. While the methods contained
herein can and do work, readers are urged to consult with their doctor or other
professional advisors to address specific medical or other concerns that may be
causing behavioural and other issues. The author and the publisher assume no
responsibility for any injuries suffered or damages or losses incurred during or
as a result of the use or application of the information contained herein.

Names and identifying characteristics of some individuals
have been changed to preserve their privacy.

Printed and bound in the UK using 100% renewable
electricity at CPI Group (UK) Ltd

To my husband, who is the grounding force in my life,
and my kids, who have taught me more than I will ever teach them.

Contents

Introduction

> "Dr Becky, my five-year-old is in a stage where she's mean to her sister, rude to us, and melting down at school. We feel totally stuck. Can you help?"
>
> "Dr Becky, why is my potty-trained child suddenly peeing all over the house? We've tried using rewards and punishments and nothing is changing. Can you help?"
>
> "Dr Becky, my twelve-year-old never listens to me! It's infuriating. Can you help?"

Yes. I can help. We can figure this out.

As a clinical psychologist with a long-standing private practice, I work with parents who seek me out to problem-solve through the tricky situations that leave them feeling frustrated, depleted, and hopeless. Though on the surface the situations are unique—the smart-mouthed five-year-old, the regressing potty-trained toddler, the defiant preteen—the underlying desire is the same: all parents want to do better. I am essentially told and retold: *"I know the parent I want to be. I don't know how to get there. Please help me fill the gap."*

During our sessions, parents and I start by unpacking a problem behavior together. Behavior is a clue to what a child—and, often, an entire family system—is struggling with. As we investigate behaviors, we get to know the child better, we learn about what this child needs and what skills they're missing, we uncover a parent's triggers and areas for growth, and we move from a place of *"What's wrong with my child and can you fix them?"* to *"What is my child struggling with and what's my role in helping them?"* And hopefully also, *"What's coming up for ME about this situation?"*

My work with parents centers on helping them move from a place of despair and frustration to one of hope, empowerment, and even self-reflection—all without leaning on many of the most commonly promoted parenting strategies. You will not see me recommend time-outs, sticker charts, punishments, rewards, or ignoring as a response to challenging behaviors. What *do* I recommend? First and foremost, an understanding that behaviors are only the tip of the iceberg, and that below the surface is a child's entire internal world, just begging to be understood.

Let's Do Something *Different*

When I was in my clinical psychology PhD program at Columbia and working in the clinic, I did play therapy with kids. While I loved treating children, I quickly grew frustrated by the limited contact I had with parents, often wishing I was also working with the parents rather than working directly with the child and talking to the parent adjunctively. Simultaneously, I was also counseling adult clients, and I became fascinated by an undeniable connection: with the adults it was so clear where, in childhood, things went awry—where a child's needs weren't met or behaviors were a cry for help that was never answered. I realized that if I looked at what adults needed and never received, I could use that knowledge to inform my work with children and families.

When I opened my private practice, I worked solely with adults for therapy or parent guidance. After I became a mother myself, I increased my parent guidance work—both in one-on-one consultations and in ongoing monthly parenting groups. Eventually

I enrolled in a training program for clinicians that proclaimed it offered an "evidence-based" and "gold-standard" approach to discipline and troubling behavior in children. The methods it taught felt logical and "clean," and I walked away having learned about the same interventions that are regularly promoted by parenting experts today. I felt like I had learned a perfect system to extinguish undesirable behavior and encourage more prosocial behavior— basically, behavior that was more compliant and more convenient to parents. Except, a few weeks later, something struck me: this *felt* awful. Every time I heard myself give this "evidence-based" guidance, I felt sick to my stomach. I couldn't shake the nagging suspicion that these interventions—which certainly wouldn't feel good if someone used them on me—couldn't be the right approach to use with kids.

Yes, these systems made logical sense, but they focused on eradicating "bad" behaviors and enforcing compliance at the expense of the parent-child relationship. Time-outs, for example, were encouraged to change behavior . . . but what about the fact that they sent kids away at the exact moments they needed their parents the most? Where was . . . well . . . the humanity?

Here's the thing I realized: these "evidence-based" approaches were built on principles of *behaviorism,* a theory of learning that focuses on observable actions rather than non-observable mental states like feelings and thoughts and urges. Behaviorism privileges *shaping* behavior above *understanding* behavior. It sees behavior as the whole picture rather than an expression of underlying unmet needs. This is why, I realized, these "evidence-based" approaches felt so bad to me—they confused the signal (what was really going on for a child) with the noise (behavior). After all, our goal is not to shape behavior. Our goal is to raise humans.

As soon as this realization crept in, I couldn't shake it. I knew there had to be a way of working with families that was effective without sacrificing the connection between parent and child. And so I got to work, taking everything I knew about attachment, mindfulness, and internal family systems—all theoretical approaches that have informed my private practice—and translating these ideas into a method for working with parents that was concrete, accessible, and easy to understand.

It turns out, switching our parenting mindset from "consequences" to "connection" does not have to mean ceding family control to our children. While I resist time-outs, punishments, consequences, and ignoring, there's nothing about my parenting style that's permissive or fragile. My approach promotes firm boundaries, parental authority, and sturdy leadership, all while maintaining positive relationships, trust, and respect.

Deep Thoughts, Practical Strategies (and How to Use This Book)

In my work with patients, I often say that two things are true: *practical, solution-based strategies* can also promote *deeper healing*. Many parenting philosophies compel parents to make a choice: they can improve a child's behavior at the cost of their relationship, or they can prioritize the relationship while sacrificing a clear path to better behavior. With the approach offered in this book, parents can do better on the outside *and* feel better on the inside. They can strengthen their relationship with their child *and* see improved behavior and cooperation.

This underlying message, that these two things are true, is at the core of so much of what you're about to read. The information is theory driven *and* strategy rich; it is evidence based *and* creatively intuitive; it prioritizes the self-care of a parent *and* the well-being of a child. A client may come to my office looking for a set of strategies to fix their kid's behavior, but they leave with so much more: a nuanced understanding of the child underneath the behavior and a set of tools that puts this understanding into practice. My hope is that after reading this book you will walk away with the same. I hope you emerge with renewed self-compassion, self-regulation, and self-confidence, and feel equipped to wire your children for these important qualities as well.

This book is an initiation into a parenting model that is as much about self-development as it is about child development. The first ten chapters consist of the parenting principles I live by—at home with my own three kids, in my office with clients and their families, and on social media, with the many parents I've connected with over the years. My intention with these principles is to promote healing in children *and* parents, and offer practical strategies for a more peaceful family experience. And at the heart of these principles is the idea that by understanding the emotional needs of a child, parents can not only improve behavior but transform how the entire family operates and relates to one another.

In the second half of this book, you will find, first, tactics for what I call *building connection capital*. These are tried-and-true strategies for increasing connection and closeness in a parent-child relationship. No matter the issue—even if the mood just feels bad at home and you can't figure out why—you can implement one of these interventions to start turning things around. After that, we'll move into tackling specific childhood behavior issues that often drive parents to seek out my help: everything from sibling rivalry, tantrums, and lying to anxiety, lack of confidence, and shyness. Not every single tactic will be applicable to every single kid—only you know your child's individual needs—but these strategies will help you think differently when challenges arise, and empower you to tackle these moments in ways that feel good to you, and safe to your child.

* * *

It probably comes as no surprise that I've never been one for trade-offs. I believe you can be firm and warm, boundaried and validating, focused on connection while acting as a sturdy authority. And I believe that, in the end, this approach also "feels right" to parents — not just logically, but deep in their souls. Because we all want to see our children as good kids, see ourselves as good parents, and work toward a more peaceful home. And every one of those things is possible. We don't have to choose. We can have it all.

PART I

DR BECKY'S
PARENTING PRINCIPLES

CHAPTER 1

Good Inside

*L*et me share an assumption I have about you and your kids: you are all good inside. When you call your child "a spoiled brat," you are still good inside. When your child denies knocking down his sister's block tower (even though you watched it happen), he is still good inside. And when I say "good inside," I mean that we all, at our core, are compassionate, loving, and generous. The principle of *internal goodness* drives all of my work—I hold the belief that kids and parents are good inside, which allows me to be curious about the "why" of their bad behaviors. This curiosity enables me to develop frameworks and strategies that are effective in creating change. There is nothing in this book as important as this principle— it is the foundation for all that's to come, because as soon as we tell ourselves, "Okay, slow down . . . I'm good inside . . . my kid is good inside too . . . ," we intervene differently than we would if we allowed our frustration and anger to dictate our decisions.

The tricky part here is that it's remarkably easy to put frustration and anger in the driver's seat. While no parent wants to think of herself as cynical or negative or assuming the worst of her kids, when we're in the throes of a tough parenting moment, it's common to operate with the (largely unconscious) assumption of *internal badness*. We ask, "Does he really think he can get away with that?" because we assume our child is purposefully trying to take advantage of us. We say, "What is wrong with you?" because we assume there's a flaw inside our kid. We yell, "You know better!" because we assume our child is purposely defying or provoking us. And we berate ourselves in the same way, wondering, "What is my problem? I know better!" before spiraling into a puddle of despair, self-loathing, and shame.

Plenty of parenting advice relies on perpetuating this assumption of badness, focusing on controlling kids rather than trusting them, sending them to their rooms instead of embracing them, labeling them as manipulative rather than in need. But I truly do believe that *we are all good inside*. And let me be clear: seeing your child as good inside does not excuse bad behavior or lead to permissive parenting. There's a misconception that parenting from a "good inside" perspective leads to an "anything goes" approach that creates entitled or out-of-control kids, but I don't know anyone who would say, "Oh well, my kid is good inside, so it doesn't matter that he spit at his friend," or "My kid is good inside, so who cares that she calls her sister names." In fact, the opposite is true. Understanding that we're all good inside is what allows you to distinguish *a person* (your child) from *a behavior* (rudeness, hitting, saying, "I hate you"). Differentiating who someone is from what they do is key to creating interventions that preserve your relationship while also leading to impactful change.

Assuming goodness enables you to be the sturdy leader of your family, because when you're confident in your child's goodness, you believe in their ability to behave "well" and do the right thing. And as long as you believe they are capable, you can show them the way. This type of leadership is what every child craves—someone they can trust to steer them down the right path. It's what makes them feel safe, what allows them to find calm, and what leads to the development of emotion regulation and resilience. Providing a safe space to try and fail without worrying they'll be seen as "bad" is what will allow your children to learn and grow, and to ultimately feel more connected to you.

Perhaps this sounds like an obvious idea. Of course your kids are good inside! After all, you love your children—you wouldn't be reading this book if you didn't want to encourage their goodness. But operating from a "good inside" perspective can be harder than it seems, especially in difficult or highly charged moments. It's easy—reflexive, even—to default to a less generous view, for two main reasons: First, we are evolutionarily wired with a negativity bias, meaning we pay closer attention to what's difficult with our kids (or with ourselves, our partners, even the world at large) than to what is working well. Second, our experiences of our own childhoods influence how we perceive and respond to our kids' behavior. So many of us had parents who led with judgment rather than curiosity, criticism instead of understanding, punishment instead of discussion. (I'd guess they had parents who treated them the same way.) And, in the absence of intentional effort to course correct, history repeats itself. As a result, many parents see behavior as the *measure of who our kids are*, rather than using behavior as a *clue to what our kids might need*. What if we saw behavior as an expression of needs, not identity? Then, rather than shaming our kids for their shortcomings, making them feel unseen and alone, we could help them access their internal goodness, improving their behavior along the way. Shifting our perspective isn't easy, but it's absolutely worth it.

Rewiring the Circuit

I want you to reflect on your childhood and imagine how your parents would have responded in a few scenarios:

- You're three years old, with a new baby sister everyone is oohing and aahing over. You're struggling in this transition to siblinghood, even though your family says you should be happy about it. You're having lots of tantrums, grabbing toys from your sister, and you finally let it all out: "Send my baby sister back to the hospital! I hate her!" What happens next? How do your parents respond?
- You're seven years old and you really want an Oreo that your dad explicitly said you couldn't have. You're sick of being dictated to and being constantly met with no, so when you're alone in the kitchen, you grab the cookie. Your dad sees you with the Oreo in hand. What happens next? What does he do?
- You're thirteen years old and you're struggling with a writing assignment. You tell your parents it's done, but later they get a call from the teacher saying you never handed it in. What happens next? What do your parents say when you get home?

Now let's consider this: We all mess up. We all, at every age, have difficult moments when we behave in ways that are less than ideal. But our early years are especially powerful, because our bodies are beginning to wire how we think about and respond to difficult moments, based on how our parents think about and respond *to us* in our difficult moments. Let me say that another way: how we talk to ourselves when we are struggling inside—the self-talk of "Don't be so sensitive" or "I'm overreacting" or "I'm so dumb," or, alternatively, "I'm trying my best" or "I simply want to feel seen"—is based on how our parents spoke to or treated us in our times of struggle. This means that thinking through our answers to those "What happens next?" questions is critical to understanding *our body's circuitry.*

What do I mean by "circuitry"? Well, in our early years, our

body is learning under what conditions we receive love and attention and understanding and affection, and under what conditions
we get rejected, punished, and left alone; the "data" it collects along
those lines is critical to our survival, because maximizing attachment with our caregivers is the primary goal for young, helpless
children. These learnings impact our development, because we
quickly begin to embrace whatever gets us love and attention, and
shut down and label as "bad" any parts that get rejected, criticized,
or invalidated.

Now, here's the thing: no parts of us are *actually* bad. Underneath "Send my baby sister back to the hospital! I hate her!" is a
child in pain, with massive abandonment fears and a sense of threat
looming in the family; underneath the defiance of taking that cookie
is probably a child who feels unseen and controlled in other parts
of her life; and underneath that incomplete school assignment is a
child who is struggling and likely feels insecure. Underneath "bad
behavior" is always a good child. And yet, when parents chron-
ically shut down a behavior harshly *without recognizing the good
kid underneath*, a child internalizes that *they are bad*. And badness has to be shut down at all costs, so a child develops methods,
including harsh self-talk, to chastise himself, as a way of killing
off the "bad kid" parts and instead finding the "good kid" ones—
meaning the parts that get approval and connection.

So what did you, as a child, learn comes after "bad" behavior?
Did your body learn to wire for judgment, punishment, and aloneness . . . or boundaries, empathy, and connection? Or, put more
simply, now that we know a person's "bad behavior" is really a sign
that they're struggling on the inside: Did you learn to approach
your struggles with criticism . . . or compassion? With blame or
curiosity?

How our caregivers responded to us becomes how we in turn
respond to ourselves, and this sets the stage for how we respond to

our children. This is why it's so easy to create an intergenerational legacy of "internal badness": my parents reacted to my struggles with harshness and criticism → I learned to doubt my goodness when I am having a hard time → I now, as an adult, meet my own struggles with self-blame and self-criticism → my child, when he acts out, activates this same circuitry in my body → I am compelled to react with harshness to my child's struggles → I build the same circuitry in my child's body, so my child learns to doubt his goodness when he struggles → and so on and so forth.

Okay, let's pause. Place your hand on your heart and deliver yourself this important message: "I am here because I want to change. I want to be the pivot point in my intergenerational family patterns. I want to start something different: I want my children to feel good inside, to feel valuable and lovable and worthy, even when they struggle. And this starts . . . with re-accessing my own goodness. My goodness has always been there." You are not at fault for your intergenerational patterns. Quite the opposite—if you're reading this book, that tells me that you're taking on the role of cycle-breaker, the person who says that certain damaging patterns STOP with you. You are willing to take on the weight of the generations before you and change the direction for the generations to come. *Wow.* You are far from at fault—you are brave and bold and you love your kid more than anything. Being a cycle-breaker is an epic battle, and you are amazing for taking it on.

The Most Generous Interpretation (MGI)

Finding the good inside can often come from asking ourselves one simple question: "What is my *most generous interpretation* of what just happened?" I ask myself this often with my kids and my friends, and I'm working on asking it more in my marriage and with myself. Whenever I utter these words, even internally, I notice my body soften and I find myself interacting with people in a way that feels much better.

Let's walk through an example: You're planning to take your older son out to lunch, solo, for his birthday, and you decide to gently prepare your younger son a few days ahead of time. "I wanted to let you know about Saturday's plan," you say. "Daddy and I are going to take Nico out to lunch for his birthday. Grandma will come over and stay with you while we're out for an hour or so." Your younger son responds: "You *and* Daddy are going out with Nico without me? I hate you! You're the worst mom in the world!"

Wow, what just happened? And how do you respond? Here are some options: 1) "The worst mom? I just bought you a new toy! You're so ungrateful!" 2) "When you say that, it makes Mommy sad." 3) Ignore. Walk away. 4) "Wow, those are *big* words, let me take a breath . . . I hear how upset you are. Tell me more."

I like option 4, because it's the intervention that makes sense after considering the most generous interpretation of my child's behavior. The first option interprets my son's response as simply spoiled and ungrateful. The second teaches my son that his feelings are too powerful and scary to be managed, that they harm others and threaten attachment security with a caregiver. (We'll get into more detail about attachment in chapter 4, but the short of it is this: focusing on a child's *impact on us* sets the stage for codependence, not regulation or empathy.) The third option sends the message that I believe my son is unreasonable, and his concerns are unimportant to me. But my MGI of my child's response is this: "Hmm. My son really wishes he was included in this special lunch. I can understand that. He's sad. And jealous. Those feelings are so big in his small body that they explode out of him in the form of big hurtful words, but what's underneath is a raw, painful set of feelings." The intervention that comes next—the empathetic statements based on seeing my child as *good inside*—acknowledges his words as a sign of overwhelming pain, not as a sign of his being a bad kid.

Finding the MGI teaches parents to attend to what is going on inside of their child (big feelings, big worries, big urges, big sensations) rather than what is going on outside of their child (big words, or sometimes big actions). And when we put this perspective into practice, we teach our children to do the same. We orient them to their internal experience, which includes thoughts, feelings, sensations, urges, memories, and images. Self-regulation skills rely on the ability to recognize internal experience, so by focusing on what's inside rather than what's outside, we are building in our children the foundation of healthy coping. Choosing the most generous interpretation of your child's behavior does not mean you are "being easy" on them, but rather you are framing their behavior in a way that will help them build critical emotion regulation skills for their future—and you're preserving your connection and close relationship along the way.

Here's another reason I like thinking in terms of MGI: at all times, but especially when our kids are *dysregulated*—meaning their emotions overwhelm their current coping skills—they look to their parents to understand, "Who am I right now? Am I a bad kid doing bad things . . . or am I a *good kid having a hard time*?" Our kids form their own self-view by taking in their parents' answers to these questions. If we want our kids to have true self-confidence and to *feel good about themselves*, we need to reflect back to our kids that they are good inside, even as they struggle on the outside.

I often remind myself that kids respond to the version of themselves that parents reflect back to them and act accordingly. When we tell our kids that they're selfish, they act in their own interest. When we tell our son that his sister has much better manners than he does, guess what? The rudeness continues. But the opposite is true as well. When we tell our kids, "You're a good kid having a hard time . . . I'm here, I'm right here with you," they are more likely to have empathy for their own struggles, which helps them regulate and make better decisions. I remember once watching my older son wrestle with whether he would share his snack with his sister. I felt myself wanting to say, "Your sister would share with you! Come on, do one nice thing!" but I also heard another voice crying, "Most generous! Most generous!" and instead I said to him, "I know that you have just as much sharing capacity and generosity as anyone else in this family. I'm going to leave the room; you and your sister can work this out." I heard him tell his sister that she couldn't have the cracker she asked for, but she could have a few of his pretzels. Perfect outcome? No, but if I look for perfect, I'll miss growth . . . and I'm a pretty big fan of growth. My son chose to make a small sacrifice. I'll take it.

There's nothing more valuable than learning to find our goodness under our struggles, because this leads to an increased capacity to reflect and change. All good decisions start with feeling secure in ourselves and in our environment, and nothing feels more secure than being recognized for the good people we truly are. So if you remember nothing else from this book, remember that. You are good inside. Your child is good inside. If you return to that truth before you begin all your attempts at change, you will be on the right path.

Two Things Are True

When Sara, *a mom of two boys, walked into my office, she* expressed feelings of frustration, self-blame, and resentment. She had great kids and a loving partner, but she was sick of constantly disciplining her children at the expense of having any fun with them. "I wish I could be silly, but someone has to enforce rules and make things happen," she told me. What Sara and I worked on—what I work on with so many parents—is acknowledging the idea that she could be two things at once: fun and firm, silly and sturdy. And not only that she *could* be both, but that maybe she would feel better—and her family system would operate better—if she *would* be both.

This idea underlies so much of my parenting advice: We don't have to choose between two supposedly oppositional realities. We can avoid punishment and see improved behavior, we can parent with a firm set of expectations and still be playful, we can create and enforce boundaries and show our love, we can take care of ourselves and our children. And similarly, we can do what's right for our family and our kids can be upset; we can say no and care about our kids' disappointment.

This idea of multiplicity—the ability to accept multiple realities at once—is critical to healthy relationships. When there are two people in a room, there are also two sets of feelings, thoughts, needs, and perspectives. Our ability to hold on to multiple truths at once—ours and someone else's—allows two people in a relationship to feel *seen* and feel *real*, even if they are in conflict. Multiplicity is what allows two people to get along and feel close—they each know that their experience will be accepted as true and explored as important, even if those experiences are different. Building strong connections relies on the assumption that no one is right in the absolute, because *understanding*, not *convincing*, is what makes people feel secure in a relationship.

What do I mean by understanding and not convincing? Well, when we seek to understand, we attempt to *see* and *learn more about* another person's perspective, feelings, and experience. We essentially say to that person, "I am having one experience and you are having a different experience. I want to get to know what's happening for you." It doesn't mean you agree or comply (these would imply a "one thing is true" perspective), or that we are "wrong" or our truth doesn't hold; it means we are willing to put our own experience aside for a moment to get to know someone else's. When we approach someone with the goal of understanding, we accept that there isn't one correct interpretation of a set of facts, but rather multiple experiences and viewpoints. Understanding has one goal: connection. And because connecting to our kids is how they learn to regulate their emotions and feel good inside, understanding will come up over and over again as a goal of communication.

What's the opposite of understanding? For this argument's sake, it's convincing. Convincing is the attempt to prove a singular reality—to prove that "only one thing is true." Convincing is an attempt to be "right" and, as a result, make the other person "wrong." It rests on the assumption that there is only one correct viewpoint. When we seek to convince someone, we essentially say, "You're wrong. You are mis-perceiving, mis-remembering, mis-feeling, mis-experiencing. Let me explain to you why I am correct and then you'll see the light and come around." Convincing has one goal in mind: being right. And here's the unfortunate consequence of being right: the other person feels *unseen* and *unheard*, at which point most people become infuriated and combative, because it feels as if the other person does not accept your realness or worth. Feeling unseen and unheard makes connection impossible.

Understanding ("two things are true") and convincing ("one thing is true") are two diametrically opposed ways of approaching other people, so a powerful first step in any interaction is to notice which mode you're in. When you're in "one thing is true" mode, you're judgmental of and reactive to someone else's experience, because it feels like an assault on your own truth. As a result, you will seek to prove your own point of view, which in turn makes the other person defensive, because they need to uphold the realness of their experience. In "one thing is true" mode, exchanges escalate quickly—each person thinks they're arguing about the content of the conversation, when in fact they're trying to defend that they are a real, worthy person with a real, truthful experience. By contrast, when we're in "two things are true" mode, we are *curious about* and *accepting of* someone else's experience, and it feels like an opportunity to get to know someone better. We approach others with openness, and so they put down their defenses. Both parties feel seen and heard, and we have an opportunity to deepen connection.

Research on marriage, business, and friendship has shown, time and again, that relationships do better when we are in understanding—"two things are true" mode. For example, a core pillar of the Gottman Method, a research-backed approach to successful marriage developed by psychologists John and Julie Gottman, is accepting that two perspectives are valid. In a study of two types of listening, clinical psychologist Faye Doell demonstrated how people who listen in order to *understand* versus listen in order to *respond* have higher across-the-board relationship satisfaction.[*] And neuropsychiatrist Daniel Siegel, coauthor of *The Whole-Brain Child*, often refers to the critical importance of "feeling felt" in relationships. He describes this as "our minds being held within another's mind," but ultimately he's talking about connecting to someone else's experience.[†] Studies have even found that the best business leaders listen to and validate their employees more than they talk to them—in other words, they get to know their employees' truths instead of trying to convince them that management is always right.[‡]

We also do better, as individuals, when we approach our own internal monologue with a "two things are true" perspective. Multiplicity is what allows a person to recognize that I can love my kids *and* crave alone time; I can be grateful to have a roof over my head *and* feel jealous of those who have more childcare support; I can be a good parent *and* yell at my kid sometimes. Our ability to experience many seemingly oppositional thoughts and feelings at once—to know that you can experience several truths simultaneously—is key to our mental health. Psychologist Philip Bromberg may have said it best: "Health is the ability to stand in the spaces between realities without losing any of them—the capacity to feel like one self while being many."[§] We are at our best when we no-

---

[*] Faye Doell, "Partners' Listening Styles and Relationship Satisfaction: Listening to Understand vs. Listening to Respond" (graduate thesis, University of Toronto, 2003).

[†] Daniel J. Siegel and Tina Payne Bryson, *The Whole-Brain Child* (New York: Random House, 2012).

[‡] J. H. Zenger and J. Folkman, *The Extraordinary Leader: Turning Good Managers into Great Leaders* (New York: McGraw-Hill, 2002).

[§] P. M. Bromberg, "Shadow and Substance: A Relational Perspective on Clinical Process" *Psychoanalytic Psychology* (1993), 10: 147–68.

tice the multiple feelings, thoughts, urges, and sensations inside of us without any of them "becoming" us, when we can locate our *self* amid a sea of experiences ("I notice a part of me is feeling nervous and a part of me is feeling excited," or "I notice a part of me wants to scream at my kids and a part of me knows to take a deep breath"). In other words, we are our healthiest selves when we can see that two (or more!) things are true.

Parenting in "two things are true" mode can help guide us to becoming sturdier adults. I am always looking to hold two realities at once: I can parent in a way that feels good to me and to my kids, that involves firm boundaries and warm connection, that gives my kids what they need today and sets them up for resilience in the future. On a more micro level, "two things are true" always seems to be the answer to our problems: I can say no to screen time and my child can be upset about it; I can be angry that my child lied and be curious about what felt too scary to tell me; I can see my child's anxieties as irrational and still be empathic around what she needs. And perhaps most powerful of all: I can yell and be a loving parent, I can mess up and repair, I can regret things I've said and do better in the future.

"Two things are true" can help anyone make sense of a world that often feels contradictory, but it's especially critical for kids, who need to feel that their parents recognize and permit their feelings *and* that their feelings do not take over and bleed into decision-making. And, for most of us, that's the goal. As parents we can make decisions that we think are best *and* care about our kids' feelings about those decisions. These are two totally separate things. Working on holding both truths, working on allowing both realities—this is essential to building understanding, and in turn connection, with our kids.

Let's explore this idea within the context of an adult relationship. You've had a great year at work and you were promised a long-overdue raise at your year-end review. But at the meeting, your boss shares this news: "Our budget has been cut drastically, and we have to let some people go. You still have your job, but there's no way I can give you that raise this year. Hopefully next year!"

Pause and check in with yourself. How do you feel toward your boss? Disappointed? Grateful? Happy? Angry? It's confusing, right? Here's my take: two things are true. "I'm happy to still have a job *and* I feel disappointed not to get the raise I was promised." Let's separate what's happening for your boss and what's happening for you. Your boss has made certain decisions: I can maintain employment for this employee but cannot give her a raise this year. You have certain feelings: disappointment, betrayal, anger, some relief too. Your anger won't change your boss's decision. Also, your boss's logic won't change your feelings. Both make sense. Both are true.

We don't have to choose a single truth. In fact, in most areas of life, we have multiple realities that don't exactly add up. They simply coexist, and the best we can do is acknowledge all of them. Your gratitude for still having a job doesn't have to overpower your disappointment about not getting a pay increase. Your anger about your salary doesn't invalidate your relief that you still have a job.

Let's keep going. Your boss sees you looking a bit downtrodden the next day and is only able to hold on to *one thing being true.* She approaches you and says, "It wasn't possible to give you that raise. Come on! Be grateful that you still have a job." How does that feel? What's happening inside? You might notice a spike in internal blame ("What's wrong with me, I'm so self-centered!") or external blame ("What's wrong with my boss, she's so self-centered!"), or you might be seething or feeling undervalued. If left unattended, these feelings will likely lead to resentment of your job and your boss, and eventually, you'll become less motivated to do your best work. Why does one thing being true feel so bad? Why does one thing being true set off a chain reaction of less-than-ideal behaviors?

At our core, we all want someone else to acknowledge our experience, our feelings, and our truths. When we feel seen by others, we can manage our disappointment, and we feel safe and good enough inside to consider someone else's perspective. Had your boss *seen* your experience and said, "I just couldn't make the raise happen . . . and still, I get that you're disappointed. I'd feel the same way," the emotional tenor of the moment would have changed entirely. Your boss doesn't even have to apologize for not giving you the raise; as long as she holds and explicitly acknowledges both truths—that the raise isn't possible and your negative feelings about it are legitimate—you can move on.

"Two things are true" is a foundational parenting principle because it reminds us to see our child's experience, or a coparent's experience, as real and valid and worthy of naming and connecting to. And it also allows us to hold on to our own experience as real and valid and worthy of naming and connecting to. It reminds us that logic doesn't overpower emotion: I may have a valid reason for doing something . . . *and also* someone else has a valid emotional reaction. Both are true.

"Two things are true" comes up in so many of the parenting struggles we'll discuss: how to hold boundaries with kids in the face of protest, how to get out of power struggles, how to handle rudeness from your child, how to ground yourself when parenting feels hard, and so much more. I'll walk through a few examples here, but my hope is that you'll start applying this concept to other areas of your life as well. In fact, that broader application is my ultimate goal for you. Yes, this is a parenting book, but at its core it's a relationship book. The principles I'm sharing with you apply to your relationship with your kids but also your relationship with your partner, your friends, your family, and perhaps most important . . . yourself. So as you read the examples below, pause and ask yourself: "Where else in my life is this idea useful?" Trust yourself to experiment, to put the "two things are true" idea into action wherever it is needed.

"Two Things Are True" While Holding Boundaries in the Face of Protest

Here's a common point of conflict: Your child wants to watch a show or movie that you deem inappropriate for his age. He's very upset, insisting that all his friends have seen it, that you're the worst parent ever, that he'll never talk to you again.

Your Decision: My child cannot watch this show/movie.

Your Child's Feelings: Upset, disappointed, angry, left out.

If only one of these things can be true, then your child's feelings will probably overrule your decision. And if you tell yourself that *caring* about your child's feelings has to be linked to your decision-making, then you will definitely change your mind to prove to yourself that you're a good, loving parent.

But what if two things are true? Now you can do both: I am holding my boundary that my child cannot watch this movie *and* validating that my child feels upset, disappointed, angry, and left out.

When you make a decision you believe in but you know will upset your child, you might say as much to your kid: "Two things are true, sweetie. First, I have decided that you cannot watch that movie. Second, you're upset and mad at me. Like, really mad. I hear that. I even understand it. You're allowed to be mad." You don't have to choose between firm decisions and loving validation. There's no trade-off between doing what feels right to you and acknowledging the very real experience of your child. Both can be true.

And, of course, there's another example of two things being true here: you can feel great about your "two things are true" approach—"Yeah! I did it! I'm winning at parenting!"—and your child can still be upset. After all, these aren't magic words that will immediately solve the problem or deescalate the situation, but they *are* words that will help you acknowledge the humanity of your kid and build a connection that has long-term benefits. Still, good parenting isn't always rewarded with good behavior. So, what then?

Let's say you deliver the "You're allowed to be mad" line, and your son screams, "Well I *am* mad! I hate you!" First: ground yourself and internally validate your perspective ("I know I am making a good decision here. I trust myself"). Then, continue to acknowledge your child's perspective—his truth: "Ugh, I know you are. I know you're really mad. I get it." Now, hold your boundary. Feel free to add on when you feel an opening. "There are lots of other movies we can watch, let me know if you want to pick one of those," or "I wonder if there are any other things we can do tonight that would feel fun?" But remember, you've already done what's necessary, for both of you.

"Two Things Are True" to Get Out of a Power Struggle

Power struggles almost always represent a collapse of the "two things are true" principle. They are me-versus-you moments—

you against your child. Take a battle about getting ready to go outside:

> PARENT: *"You must put on your jacket before you go play in the backyard!"*
> CHILD: *"No! I'm not cold, I want to go out like this!"*

You may think you're each talking about the problem—wearing a coat—but really, you're both searching to feel *seen*. You, as the parent, want to be acknowledged for your concern about your child's well-being; your child wants to be seen as independent and in charge of their own body. When we feel like we're not being acknowledged, we can't solve problems. So, in this power-struggle moment, your foremost goal should not be to solve the problem. The first goal is to re-find your "two things are true" mentality, because as soon as we feel truly seen in our experience and our desires, we can let our guard down—after all, as humans, we are less invested in any specific decision than we are in feeling seen. This is almost always what matters most.

In this scenario, once we return to the idea that two things are true, we can switch from a me-versus-you mentality to a me-and-you-against-a-problem mentality. Ah . . . This is everything. Now we are on the same team, gazing at a problem, wondering what *we* can do about it.

Let's revisit that example:

> PARENT: *"You have to put a jacket on before you go outside. It is freezing!"*
> CHILD: *"I don't get cold! I'll be fine, let me go outside!"*
> PARENT: *"Okay, one second. Let me take a breath. Let me see if I understand what's happening here . . . I'm worried about*

you being cold, because it's pretty windy outside. You're telling
me that you feel your body doesn't get that cold and you're
pretty sure you'll be okay, huh? Did I get that right?"
CHILD: *"Yeah."*

Now there are lots of possibilities. There's an opening in the
conversation. Let's continue with two different options.

PARENT: *"Hmm . . . what can we do? I'm sure we can come up*
with an idea that both of us feel okay about . . ."
CHILD: *"Can I bring my jacket with me and if I'm cold, I'll*
put it on?"
PARENT: *"Sure, what an awesome solution."*

When children feel seen and sense their parent is a teammate and
not an adversary, and when they're asked to collaborate in problem-
solving . . . good things happen. Now, let's say you're insisting your
child wear the jacket—it's two degrees outside with fifty-mile-per-
hour winds. This isn't a control thing but a true safety thing.

PARENT: *"Hmm . . . what can we do? As your parent, it's my*
job to keep you safe, and right now safety means wearing a
jacket. And also, you like to make your own decisions and it
feels bad to have a parent tell you what to do."
CHILD: *"I'm not wearing that jacket!"*
PARENT: *"I hear you. Two things are true: you have to wear a*
jacket if you're going outside . . . and also, you're allowed to be
mad at me about it. You don't have to like wearing it."

Even in my unilateral decision, I acknowledge my child's experience. I am not trying to convince my child that one thing is

true, that it is freezing and that the only thing that "makes sense" is to wear a jacket. I convince myself that the jacket is important to wear, I set a boundary that the jacket has to be worn outside, and then I name my child's feelings and give permission for them to have them. I made the decision, my child is having their feelings. No one is right. Two things are true.

"Two Things Are True" in Response to Your Child's Rudeness

Here's another common scenario I hear about from my readers and clients. You tell your child there's no screen time before dinner/bedtime/school. "I hate you!" he yells. "You're the worst!"

Okay, deep breath. First, let's understand what's happening. If a child's behavior on the surface is a window into how he's feeling on the inside, then his out-of-control words are a sign he feels out of control. Remember, your child is good inside. Bad behavior comes from dysregulated feelings that we cannot manage. What helps us manage the unmanageable? Connection.

Take two:

CHILD: *"I hate you! You're the worst!"*
PARENT: *Takes a deep breath. Says to self, "My child is upset inside. His outside behavior is not a true indication of how he feels about me. He's a good kid having a hard time." Then says aloud: "I do* not *appreciate that language . . . you must be really upset, maybe about some other things too, to be talking to me like this. I need a moment to calm my body . . . maybe you do too . . . then let's talk."*

Here, you're naming the behavior that upsets you—but you're not letting it take over as the truth. You recognize the feeling underneath as valid even if it comes out in a dysregulated way.

"Two Things Are True" to Cope with Bad Feelings

Perhaps most powerfully, "two things are true" is useful when we start to spin into our "bad parent" thoughts: the guilt, the self-blame, the worry that we're messing up our kids.

When things feel tough, I remind myself of this ultimate "two things are true" statement: I am a good parent having a hard time. It's so easy to slip into a "one thing is true" mentality here: "I'm a bad parent, I'm messing everything up, I can't to do this, I'm the worst." This self-talk fills us with guilt and shame, and when we're in that mindset, change is impossible. We will discuss shame in more detail later, but here's what you need to know now: shame is a sticky emotion that makes us feel unsafe, so the more we convince ourselves that *one thing is true and that thing is that I'm a bad parent*, the more we dig ourselves into a hole, act in ways that don't feel good, and become even more convinced of our unworthiness.

So what's an alternative? As always, we have to separate *behaviors* (what we do) from *identity* (who we are). This does not mean letting yourself off the hook or making excuses for yourself. It means recognizing that you are good, *and* that you can do the hard work to improve. So commit this principle to memory and tell yourself, over and over and over again: "Two things are true: I am having a hard time and I am a good parent. I am a good parent having a hard time."

CHAPTER 3

Know Your Job

I n any system, *clearly defined roles and responsibilities are critical* to ensuring things run smoothly. The opposite is true as well: systems break down when members are confused about their roles or when they start impinging on other people's functions. Family systems (yes, family units are also systems) are no different, and every member of a family has a job. Parents have the job of establishing safety through boundaries, validation, and empathy. Children have the job of exploring and learning, through experiencing and expressing their emotions. And when it comes to jobs, we all have to stay in our lanes. Our kids should not dictate our boundaries and we should not dictate their feelings.

In a family system, some roles are prioritized over others. Safety comes before happiness and before our kids' being pleased with us. First and foremost, our job is to keep our children safe, physically and psychologically. There's nothing as scary to a child as noticing when their parent fails at this job (especially when that failure stems from a parent's fear of their kid's reaction). The child receives the subconscious message: when you are out of control, there's no one capable of stepping in and helping you. Of course, your kid won't thank you for stepping in and keeping them safe, but I promise you, that's what they're looking for, because it's what allows them to build the emotion regulation skills they need to grow into a healthy adult. So the next time you pull your child away from their sibling when things get rough between them, when you hold your child's wrist to stop them from hitting, when you carry your child to their room to sit *with them* because they are out of control and need containment, remind yourself: "I am doing my job of keeping my child safe. My child is doing their job of expressing feelings. We are both doing what we need to do. I can handle this."

If safety is our primary destination, boundaries are the pathway we use to get there. Boundaries, when created with intention, serve to protect and contain. We set boundaries out of love for our children, because we want to protect them when they're unable to make good decisions for themselves. We don't let our toddlers walk too far from us on the sidewalk, because we know they might not be able to resist the urge to dart toward the street. We don't let our young kids watch horror movies, because we know they could spark fears our kids can't yet handle. Our children need us to set firm (that doesn't have to mean scary!) boundaries, because they need to know that we can keep them safe when they are developmentally incapable of doing so themselves.

Why are they unable? Well, to put it simply: children are more able to *experience* strong feelings than they are to *regulate* those feelings, and the gap between experiencing strong feelings and regulating those feelings comes out as dysregulated behavior (think hitting, kicking, screaming). In their book *The Whole-Brain Child*, neuropsychiatrist Daniel Siegel and psychotherapist Tina Payne Bryson describe why children so often become dysregulated. They use the analogy of a two-story house: The downstairs brain is responsible for our most basic functions, like breathing, as well as our impulses and emotions. The upstairs brain is responsible for more complex processes, like planning, decision-making, self-awareness, and empathy. Here's the kicker: The downstairs brain, marked by intense emotions and sensations, is fully built and functioning in young children. But the upstairs brain is under construction *well into a person's twenties.* Talk about lag time! No wonder children often struggle with future planning, self-reflection, and empathy—these are all part of the upstairs brain. It's important to remember: When kids are overwhelmed with emotion and unable to regulate and make good decisions, this is developmentally normal. Exhausting and totally inconvenient for parents, yes, but normal.

In this two-story-house analogy, the parent is, basically, a staircase. Their primary function is to start linking a child's downstairs brain (overwhelming feelings) to their upstairs brain (self-awareness, regulation, planning, decision-making). Knowing your job is fundamental to this goal. We want our kids to feel their wide range of feelings and have new experiences, and our job is to help them build resilience by teaching them to cope with whatever the world throws at them. The goal isn't to shut down their feelings or teach kids to turn away from what they notice. The goal is to teach our kids how to *manage* all of their feelings and perceptions and thoughts and urges; we are the primary vehicle for this teaching, not through lectures or logic, but through *the experiences our children have with us.*

Helping our kids regulate their feelings is an important—though perhaps underappreciated—part of keeping them safe. Think of it as containing the emotional fires that are blazing inside your child. If there were a fire in your home, your first job would be to contain it. Yes, you need to fireproof your home better, but that can't happen until the fire is managed and you feel safe again. When parents struggle to set boundaries or regulate their own strong emotions, it's as if a fire is burning and we've opened up all the doors, poured on extra fuel, and spread the fire through the house. Containment first. Boundaries first.

Parents express boundaries with both our words and our bodies. When I say "bodies," I'm not suggesting you use physical force to assert power or intimidate—hurting or scaring your child is never okay. Never never never. But physicality, sometimes, is needed to keep our child safe. If I tell my daughter she cannot hit her brother, I may also need to hold her wrist to prevent the hitting from happening again. If I tell my son that he needs to get off the counter and he struggles to listen, I will have to pick him up—yes, even if he is crying and screaming—and put him back in a safe place. If I need to buckle my child into a car seat on a day she's screaming, "No no no!," a boundary will involve my buckling it and maybe restraining her body as I do so. Do I *want* to have to physically enforce boundaries? No, I'd rather not—I'd prefer working on the core issue of connection and regulation so that my child is more likely to cooperate in the first place (more on this later—lots more). But when things don't go that way, when things get messy and we have a safety matter at hand, we have to do our job and keep our child safe.

Just because we know our job doesn't mean it's always easy to do our job. The other day, a mother in my private practice told me this story: "I walked into the playroom to see Reina and Kai playing nicely with their toys—they set up a whole scene of trucks and blocks and little figures. Then, of course, it was too good to be true, and they got into an argument about what should go where, and Reina picked up one of the figures and threw it at Kai. And then she threw another. I told her, 'Reina! Stop throwing right now!' But she didn't listen. She took another and then another. It was such a mess!"

Nothing is wrong with this parent. Nothing is wrong with Reina (or Kai). What's going on here? Well, a boundary was never set. **Boundaries are not what we tell kids *not* to do; boundaries are what we tell kids we *will* do.** Boundaries embody your authority as a parent and don't require your child to do anything. In the case of Reina and Kai, a productive intervention might have looked like their mother stepping between them, moving the figures from

Reina's reach, and saying, "I won't let you throw these toys." Or maybe, if she didn't want to upset the thoughtfully laid-out figures in the playroom, she would pick Reina up and go sit with her in another room. These are boundaries. Saying, "Stop throwing right now!"—though a natural reaction for most parents—is not.

Some other examples of boundaries:

- "I won't let you hit your brother" as you walk between your daughter and her brother and position your body in a way so the hitting doesn't happen again.
- "I won't let you run with scissors" as you place your hands around your child's hips so that movement isn't possible.
- "Screen time is over now, I'm going to turn off the TV." You turn off the TV and place the remote somewhere it cannot be reached by your child.

Here are examples of *not* boundaries, but instead ways we essentially ask our kids to do our jobs for us. In these scenarios, despite our attempts to shut down a behavior, it usually escalates further—not because our kids "don't listen," but because their bodies feel a lack of containment. The absence of a sturdy adult keeping them safe is more dysregulating to them than the original issue.

- "Please stop hitting your brother!"
- "Stop running! I said to stop running! If you keep running with those scissors, you're not going to get dessert!"
- "Didn't we say you'd be done after this show? Can't we be done? Why do you have to make this so hard?"

In each of these examples, parents are asking their kids to inhibit an urge or desire that, frankly, they are developmentally incapable of inhibiting. We cannot tell a child who is hitting someone to stop hitting, or a child who is running to stop running, or a child who is complaining about wanting more TV to stop complaining. Well, we *can* (I am someone who says all these things too!), but these pleas won't be successful. Why? Because we cannot control someone else—we can only control ourselves. And when we ask our child to do our job for us, they are more likely to get further dysregulated, because we are essentially saying, "I see that you're out of control. I don't know what to do here, so I'm going to put you in charge and ask you to get yourself back in control." This is terrifying for a child, because when she is out of control, she needs an adult who can provide a safe, sturdy, firm boundary; this boundary is a form of love. It's a way of saying, "I know you're good inside and you're just having a hard, out-of-control time. I will be the container you need, I will stop you from continuing to act in this way, I will protect *you* from your own dysregulation taking over."

Isn't this what we all want when we're out of control? Someone who will stay calm and take charge and help us feel safe again?

Of course, our jobs don't stop at protecting our children's physical safety—we are also their emotional caretakers. This is where two other important job duties come in: validation and empathy.

Validation is the process of seeing someone else's emotional experience as real and true, rather than seeing someone else's emotional experience as something we want to convince them out of or logic them away from. Validation sounds like this: "You're upset, that's real, I see that." *Invalidation*, or the act of dismissing someone else's experience or truth, would sound like this: "There's no reason to be so upset, you're so sensitive, come on!" Remember, all human beings—kids and adults—have a profound need to feel seen in who they are, and at any given moment, **who we are is related to what we are feeling inside**. When we receive validation from others, we start to regulate our own experience because we "borrow" someone's communication of realness; when we receive invalidation, we almost always get further dysregulated and escalated, because now we have the experience of being told we are not real inside. Very few things feel as awful as this.

Empathy, the second part of a parent's emotional caretaking job, refers to our ability to understand and relate to the feelings of another person, and our desire to do that comes from the assumption that someone else's feelings are in fact valid. So, validation comes first ("My child is having a real emotional experience") and empathy second ("I can try to understand and connect with these feelings in my child, not make them go away"). Empathy comes from our ability to be curious: it allows us to explore our child's emotional experience from a place of learning, not judgment. When a child receives empathy—in fact, when any of us receives empathy—it makes them feel like someone is on their team, almost as if that person is taking on some of their emotional burden; after all, feelings come out in behavior only when those feelings are unmanageable inside, when they are too big to regulate and contain. When someone greets us with empathy ("Ugh, that feels so hard!"), we have that experience that Daniel Siegel described as feeling felt. Our bodies also sense that someone else is present in our emotional experience, which makes the experience more manageable—thereby building our ability to regulate the feelings. And as kids strengthen that ability to regulate their feelings, those feelings are less likely to manifest as behavior: this is the difference between your child's saying, "I'm so mad at my sister!" (regulating anger) and your child's hitting her sister (dysregulation); the difference between your child's saying, "I want to run!" (regulating an urge) versus your child's grabbing a pair of scissors and running down the hallway (dysregulation); the difference between your child's saying, "I wish I could watch another show right now" (regulating disappointment), and having a meltdown (dysregulation).

While empathy and validation certainly make kids feel good inside, their functions actually go much deeper. One of the primary goals of childhood is to build healthy emotion regulation skills: to develop ways to have feelings and manage them, to learn how to find yourself *amid* feelings and thoughts and urges, rather than have feelings and thoughts and urges *overtake* you. Empathy and validation from parents are critical ingredients in helping a child develop regulation skills, which is why we should not think of them as "soft" or "mushy" factors but as qualities that hold weight and seriousness.

Now that we have the full picture, let's revisit our earlier examples of boundary setting to see how we can incorporate validation and empathy.

- "I won't let you hit your brother" as you walk between your daughter and her brother and position your body in a way so the hitting doesn't happen again. "I know you're frustrated! Having a brother who can crawl and get into all of your stuff is so hard. I'm here. I'll help you figure out how to keep your block structure safe."
- "I won't let you run with scissors" as you hold your child— gently *and* firmly—in place. "I know, you want to run run run! You can put those scissors down and run or finish your project and run around later. Which would you rather? Oh . . . you want to do both? I know, sweetie. I won't let you do anything dangerous, even when you're mad at me about it. I love you that much. You're allowed to be upset; I get it."
- "Screen time is over now. I'm going to turn off the TV." You turn off the TV and place the remote somewhere it cannot be reached by your child. "You wish you could watch another show. I know! Stopping TV time is so hard for me too. Want

to tell me the name of the one you want to watch tomorrow? I'll write it down for us so we don't forget."

Why do boundaries, validation, and empathy help a child build regulation skills? Boundaries show our kids that even the biggest emotions won't spiral out of control forever. Children need to sense a parent's boundary—our "I won't let you" and our stopping them from dangerous action—in order to feel, deep in their bodies, this message: "This feeling might *seem* as if it will take over and destroy the world, it might *seem too much*, and yet I am *sensing in my parent's boundary* that there is a way to contain it. This feeling *feels scary and overwhelming to me*, but I can see it's not scary or overwhelming to my parent." Over time, children absorb this containment and can access it on their own.

Validation and empathy, on the other hand, are how children find their goodness under their struggles. As we know, we have to feel good inside in order to change. It's common to think, "I need to change, and once I do I will feel worthy and lovable!" But the directionality is precisely the opposite. Our goodness is what grounds us and allows us to experience difficult emotions without having them take over or become our identity. And when parents get in the habit of validating a child's experience and empathizing with it, they are essentially saying to that child, "You are real. You are lovable. You are good."

Now you have your job description: keep your child safe, emotionally and physically, using boundaries, validation, and empathy. So what's your child's job in a family system? The truth is, as parents it's more important to focus on our own jobs, because this is what we can control. But it's helpful to understand the other roles within our system—this is the "know your job" principle, after all. A child's job in a family system is to explore and learn, through experiencing and expressing their emotions and wants. Kids need to learn what they are capable of, what is safe, what their role in the family is, how much autonomy they have, and what happens when they try new things. They do this by exploring—testing out boundaries, experimenting with new skills, playing with others— but also by challenging their parents, asking for what they want, and, sometimes, "acting out." When you look at the family system as a whole, you can see this elegant interplay of jobs: a child can express emotions, and a parent can validate and empathize with them. When those emotions transform into dangerous behavior, we set appropriate boundaries, while still validating and empathizing.

Once you understand the roles of a family system, you can reframe how you think about your child's difficult moments. Viewing their struggles as job fulfillment will help you remember that these are good kids doing their jobs, not bad kids doing bad things. I know that thinking about family jobs helps me evaluate the moments in my own house that feel hard. When I tell my son that I have to start work and then hear him screaming for me, I can think to myself: "The on-the-surface data would imply that things are a mess. But wait . . . did we each do our job here?"

Then I review: I said to my son in the time before separation, "Sweetie, I know it's so hard for you when Mommy has to do work. That makes sense; you love being by Mommy's side! You will be with Daddy, and I will see you for lunch. Mommy always comes back." I set *boundaries* that felt right to me, and I expressed *validation* with my words and *empathy* with my tone. My son protested. And screamed. And cried. He did his job: he experienced and expressed feelings. In response, I said, "I know it's so hard, sweetie. You're allowed to be upset. I love you," and then left. Validation, empathy, boundary. He cried. Again, experiencing and expressing feelings.

So . . . jobs well done, I suppose. Now, let me be clear: this isn't a feel-good moment for me. No "Woo-hoo, that was awesome!" celebration. But reviewing our roles is very grounding and prevents me from spiraling into self-blame ("Am I doing something wrong?") or child-blame ("What is wrong with my son that he still cries when I leave?"). For most parents I know, just getting through these moments with a little more clarity and with an absence of the "I'm a bad parent" thought cycle is a huge win. It certainly is for me.

CHAPTER 4

The Early Years Matter

*W*hy do we care about parenting? Why do we hold boundaries and tolerate tantrums and talk about feelings and look beneath the behavior for the deeper struggles? Does any of this actually matter? Especially when it comes to younger kids, will they even remember these years?

Yes. Parenting matters. And yes, kids will "remember" all of these years, including years zero to one, one to two, and two to three. They won't, of course, remember in the way we typically think about memory—they won't be able to produce a story with words that connects to an experience from their past. But even if kids can't remember with their words, they can—and do—remember with something more powerful: their *bodies*. Before they can talk, children learn, based on interactions with their parents, what feels acceptable or shameful, manageable or overwhelming. In this way, our "memories" from early childhood are in fact *more* powerful than the memories we form in our later years; **the way parents interact with kids in their early years forms the blueprint they take with them into the world.** Children digest the information they collect through these interactions and generalize about the world from there.

We've touched on this already, but it bears repeating: our earliest relationships influence what parts of us feel lovable, what parts we look to shut down, and what parts we feel ashamed of. In other words, children's experiences with their parents in their earliest years impact how they think about themselves, what they learn to expect of others, what feels safe and good, and what feels threatening and bad. If, for example, a young girl is constantly told to "not be so sensitive," she will learn early on that her feelings are "wrong" and push people away. If a father repeatedly tells his son to stop crying, that son will associate vulnerability with rejection, even if, later in life, he can't explicitly recall those memories. Furthermore, a child's early years form the foundation for emotion regulation, which, as we know, is a person's ability to manage and respond to feelings and urges that arise. Early childhood experiences dictate what feelings are manageable and permissible, versus which are "too much" or "wrong." The reason I'm so passionate about parenting is not because I'm looking to create more feel-good moments between parents and kids—though that's nice too—but because these early years form the foundation for adulthood. Feeling satisfied with oneself, tolerant of failure, firm in boundaries, capable of self-advocacy, and connected with others . . . all of these important adult dynamics come from our early wiring. The first years of life set the stage for the next hundred.

It's important to note, before we go any further, that the human brain is remarkably malleable and can rewire, unlearn, relearn, and change. If your parental guilt is running on overdrive after reading the last few paragraphs, if you're worried you "messed up" or "missed the boat" and that your kids have aged out of the most important time . . . take a breath. Say hello to the guilt, and then remind yourself that you are a good parent working on yourself and your relationships, and this is, actually, the best any of us can do. In the next chapter, we will celebrate the power of repair, because it's real and always possible (there's a reason that chapter is titled "It's Not Too Late"). In the coming pages, I lay out why the early years are critical so that we can access our motivation to do the hard work of parenting; if, at any point, it activates shame and guilt, pause. Maybe jump ahead to chapter 10, "Self-Care," and practice some of the suggested strategies before returning to this section. Then, as you read, remember we are all doing our best. If your kids are older and the "early years" are behind you, this is still true. Parenting is hard. You did, and are still doing, a great job.

In order to appreciate the impact of the early years, it helps to have a basic understanding of two psychological models that address the relationship between parent and child: attachment theory and internal family systems. Taken together, these theories provide a framework through which we can grasp the importance of early childhood and understand why even if children don't consciously remember these years, they still have a critical impact.

Attachment Theory

Babies are born with an innate drive to "attach" to caregivers. Psychologist John Bowlby, who formulated attachment theory in the 1970s, described attachment as a system of proximity: children who *figured out how to keep an attachment figure nearby*—literally, physically close to them—were more likely to receive comfort and protection, which meant they were more likely to survive, while children who *had more distance* from an attachment figure were less likely to receive comfort and protection, and thus were less likely to survive. As Bowlby explained it, attachment isn't just a "nice to have" but rather a primary evolutionary mechanism—after all, it is through a child's attachment that all of his basic needs are met: food, water, emotional security. Attachment theory suggests that children are wired to seek out and attach to individuals who provide the comfort and security they need to survive.

Children create different types of attachment based on their early experiences with caregivers. The type of attachment that is formed impacts that child's *internal working model*—the thoughts, memories, beliefs, expectations, emotions, and behaviors that influence how they interact with themselves and others, and what types of relationships they seek out in later years. Internal working models are based on what a child learns, through personal interactions, about their caregiver's responsiveness, availability, consistency, repair, and reactivity. Children filter our interactions with them based on a handful of questions: *Am I lovable and good and desirable to be around? Will I be seen and heard? What can I expect of others when I am upset? What can I expect of others when I am overwhelmed? What can I expect of others when we disagree?* They take the answers to these questions and make generalizations about who they are allowed to be and how the world works. We may think we're asking our kids to end screen time or saying no to a later bedtime, but children don't take in these specifics; they take in whether it's safe, in any given relationship, to have the desires and feelings that lead to difficult moments.

Remember, children are learning how relationships work at the same time that they're locked into a relationship with us, the parents. They're utterly dependent on us for survival and they know this, deep in their bones, so they collect data on their environment and then wire themselves accordingly to maximize attachment and keep their parents as close as possible. All of which is to say, the ways we respond to our children's needs, the range of emotions we acknowledge inside of them, how consistently we "show up" for them, whether or not we repair with them after tough moments, how grounded versus reactive we are . . . these behaviors all have ripple effects far beyond the family unit.

Here's the big takeaway: kids wire themselves to adapt to their early environment, forming expectations about the world based on the data they take in; that early wiring impacts how they think about themselves and others long after childhood. Now let's look at some examples of how early interactions teach more generalized "attachment lessons." Of course, these are generalizations, based on not one singular moment but the assumption that these moments represent a consistent pattern of interactions.

BEHAVIOR: A child is crying when his parent drops him off at school.

Parent Response #1: "Stop being such a baby!"
Attachment Lesson #1: When I feel vulnerable, I am ridiculed and unseen. Keep my vulnerability out of close relationships. It's not safe there.

Parent Response #2: "It's hard to say goodbye today. I get that. Some days are like that. I know you're safe here at school and we both know that Papa always comes back. I'll see you at pickup."
Attachment Lesson #2: I can expect others to take my feelings seriously. When I feel vulnerable and upset, I get validation and support. Vulnerability is safe within close relationships.

BEHAVIOR: A child is tantrumming about wanting ice cream for breakfast.

Parent Response #1: "I won't talk to you while you have a fit. Go to your room and come out when you're being reasonable!"
Attachment Lesson #1: When I want something, I push people away, I become bad, I am left abandoned and alone. People only want to be around me when I'm easy and compliant.

Parent Response #2: "I know, sweetie. You wish you could have ice cream for breakfast. That's not an option right now. You're allowed to be upset about it."

Attachment Lesson #2: I am allowed to want things for myself. Wanting things for myself is allowed in close relationships.

> BEHAVIOR: A child is hesitant to join a birthday party, clinging to his mom.

Parent Response #1: "You know everyone here. Come on! There's nothing to be worried about!"

Attachment Lesson #1: I can't trust my feelings because they're ridiculous and overblown. Other people know better than I do how I should feel.

Parent Response #2: "Something about this feels tricky. I believe you. Take your time. You'll know when you're ready."

Attachment Lesson #2: I can trust my feelings. I'm allowed to feel cautious. I know what I am feeling and I can expect other people to respect and support me.

From their first days of life, our kids learn what leads to closeness and what leads to distance and then adjust their behavior accordingly, all with the goal of establishing a secure attachment. From each of the first parent responses (assuming these were the general patterns of interactions), a child learns that certain feelings are *threatening to attachment.* That child will then seek to shut down these experiences, likely through the mechanism of shame or self-blame, as his survival literally depends on it. From each of the second parent responses (again, assuming these were the general patterns of interactions), the child learns that his feelings are real and valid and can be held within close relationships. Now, to be clear, these second parent responses won't lead to instant resolution. There will be no sudden end to the tears or screams. However, two things *will* happen: You will notice a short-term benefit, because your child will build regulation skills that may soon lead to an ability to manage disappointment. And you will, without a doubt, notice a longer-term gain, because you are helping your child build self-trust, acceptance, and openness with others, rather than shame, self-loathing, and defensiveness.

Now, let's fast-forward. It's decades later, and this child's internal working model and attachment system is still based on what he learned from interactions with his parent. Only now he's applying his learnings to other close relationships. He may think, "My vulnerability is not desired within intimate relationships; I have to rely only on myself." Or, "I am not allowed to ask for things unless I can be sure the other person will give them to me—this is critical to feeling safe and good in a relationship." If we want our kids to seek out relationships where they can balance dependence and independence, where they can feel close to others and still not "lose" themselves, where they can voice their vulnerabilities and get support, then we have to put in the work now, in the early years. Because the safer and more secure a child feels with his parents, and the wider the range of feelings he can feel within that relationship, the safer and more secure his adult relationships will be.

So how do we create secure attachments with our children now in order to promote their secure attachments with others later on? Generally speaking, relationships with parents that include responsiveness, warmth, predictability, and repair when things feel bad set a child up to have a *secure base*. A child who sees a parent as his *secure base* feels a sense of safety in the world, a sense of "someone will be there for me and comfort me if things go wrong." As such, he feels capable of exploring, trying new things, taking risks, suffering failures, and being vulnerable. There's a deep and critical paradox here: The more we can rely on a parent, the more curious and explorative we can be. The more we trust in our secure relationship with our parent, the more secure we are with ourselves. Said another way: dependence and independence are not necessarily opposites, but rather, each force allows for the other—two things are true! **The more children feel they can depend on a parent, the more independent they can be.** Our confidence that someone will understand us, not judge us, and support us, comfort us when things go wrong—this is what allows kids to develop into adults who are assertive, confident, and brave.

Internal Family Systems

Internal family systems (IFS) is a therapeutic model that considers different *parts* within a person, as opposed to thinking about a person in a singular manner. A basic assumption of IFS is that it's the nature of the mind to be subdivided into parts or subpersonalities. Consider yourself. Maybe you're outgoing with people you know well but reserved in new environments. Maybe you stand up for yourself when necessary but can stand back when it's time for someone else to take the lead. Maybe you're confident professionally but more reserved in social environments. You have your brave self, your anxious self, your confident self, your deferential self. You are multifaceted, not any one thing. And none of these parts are bad or worse than or superior to another—you are the sum of all of them, and the more comfortable you are when any of these parts "acts up," the more at home you'll be with yourself across a variety of situations. Our confidence and sturdiness and sense of self depend on our ability to understand this. When we feel overwhelmed and become reactive, it's almost always because one part of us has essentially taken over; we lose track of our identity and instead "become" these feelings.

The language of "parts" allows us to articulate, internally and externally, our conflicting—or at least coexisting—emotions: to feel grounded while experiencing distress, to feel centered while also being conflicted, to have angry thoughts while knowing we are a good person. Over and over in my private practice, I notice how the language of parts gives adults freedom, compassion, relief, and the ability to regulate tough experiences. And because I've seen how powerful it can be, I am passionate about using the language of parts with young children, to wire early on the idea of sensations and feelings and thoughts as parts we can *relate to*, not experiences that take over and *consume* us.

When we look at IFS and attachment theory in tandem, we start to gain a more sophisticated understanding of our children's early development. Attachment theory dictates that our children *have to* learn to attach to parents in order to survive and get their needs met. As a result, kids take in their environment through the lens of "What will maximize my survival?" When we combine this understanding with the teachings of IFS, our lens becomes more nuanced: "*Which parts of me* get connection, attention, understanding, and acceptance? I should do more of that, because it maximizes attachment and therefore maximizes survival! These parts of me are good and manageable and conducive to being close with others; they are full of connection. And *which parts of me* are met with disconnection and distance? I should put these parts of me away, since they threaten attachment and therefore threaten survival. These parts of me are bad and overwhelming and cannot be loved; they are connection-less."

Kids learn these "lessons" based on interactions with parents—not by words, of course, but rather by experiences. They take in what gets a parent's smiles and questions and hugs and presence (i.e., "You're allowed to feel that way. Tell me more about that, I'm right here, I'm listening") and what gets a parent's punishments and rejection and criticism and distancing (i.e., "Go to your room this instant! I will not be around you when you are like this!"). As psychologist Richard Schwartz, the creator of IFS, writes, "Children have a developmental tendency to translate experience into identity: I am not loved becomes I am unlovable, and a bad thing happened to me becomes I am bad." In other words, kids take experiences with their caregivers and infer larger messages about who they are. The emotions parents connect to—meaning the ones we are interested in and will stay present for—tell children that the *parts of them feeling these feelings* are manageable, lovable, and worthy; the emotions we shut down, punish, reject, or try to make into something "more pleasant," well, children learn that the *parts of them feeling these feelings* are destructive, bad, unlovable, or "too much."

This is why it's so important to distinguish *behavior* from *underlying feelings and experience*. While it's important to contain a child who is out of control and exhibiting "bad behavior," it's also crucial to recognize that under the behavior is a child (or in IFS language, a part of a child) who is in pain, has an unmet need, and is in desperate need of connection. Children interpret our interactions with them not as a reaction to the specific moment but as a message about who they should be. So when your child says, "I hate my baby brother, send him back to the hospital!" and you yell, "Don't say that about your brother, you love him!" the lesson they learn isn't that their words were inappropriate. The lesson they learn is that jealousy and anger are dangerous emotions, ones they shouldn't have at all. This is why it's so critical to separate what a child does (which may be "bad") from who a child is (good inside); of course we don't want our kids to hit (behavior), but we do want our kids to have the right to feel angry (feeling). Of course we don't want our kids to have a meltdown at a store (behavior), but we do want our kids to maintain access to desire and the right to speak up for themselves (feelings). Of course we don't want our kids to eat only cereal for dinner (behavior), but we do want our kids to believe that they have sovereignty over their bodies and can sense what feels good inside them (feelings). If we don't explicitly recognize the feelings underneath our kids' behaviors and show them that we love them even when they're acting out, they will collapse behavior and feelings into one. They will learn that attachment security depends on disavowing the *feelings* under the behaviors, leading to longer-term problematic relationship patterns.

So yes, the early years matter. They prepare our children to be confident, independent, self-aware adults with healthy interpersonal relationships . . . or not. Of course, nothing is ever quite that straightforward, and there are opportunities to nurture these qualities at all stages of life. Still, in those exhausting moments with your toddler when you wonder if all the hard work is worth it (because parenting a young child is really hard work!), take comfort in knowing that it absolutely is. The work you put in is always, always worth it.

CHAPTER 5

It's Not Too Late

There's one question I hear from parents more than any other: "Is it too late?" My answer is always no. Because it's always true.

Parents often persist: "But my child is already three and I've heard that the first three years are the most important," or "But my son is eight and I feel like he's already so old," or "My daughter is sixteen; I feel like I've lost my chance." I sometimes even hear, "I'm a grandparent now and I wish I had done all of this differently with my own kids . . . I guess it's too late, huh?" Let me say this again. NO. It is not too late to repair and reconnect with your kids and change the trajectory of their development. And it's also not too late for *you*. It's not too late for you to consider what parts of yourself are in need of repair and reconnection; as adults, we can work on rewiring ourselves and changing the trajectory of our own development. It is not too late. It's never ever ever too late.

The questions of how we consider new ideas, how we think about changing ourselves and our behavior, and how we hold on to good feelings about ourselves are at the core of my approach to parenting. How can we learn and repair and change our strategies going forward, with ourselves first and then our kids? And how can we manage the feelings of guilt and remorse that come up when we reflect on how we've handled our feelings and behavior in the past? Managing this guilt is, in many ways, the conundrum of change in any part of our lives. But given how much we love our

kids, and how committed we are to being good parents, the feelings that come up around how we raise our children are especially
intense.

Parenting is not for the faint of heart. It's incredibly demanding,
but also—and perhaps more important—it requires a huge amount
of self-reflection, learning, and evolving. I often think that parenting is really an exercise in our own development and growth; when
we have kids, we are confronted with so many truths about ourselves, our childhoods, and our relationships with our families of
origin. And while we can use this information to learn and unlearn,
break cycles, and heal, we have to do this work while also caring
for our kids, managing tantrums, getting by on limited sleep, and
feeling depleted. That's a lot. Maybe we can all take a moment, right
now, to acknowledge this incredible challenge. Place your hand on
your heart and say these words: "I am both working on myself and
working to take care of my family. I'm trying to rewire the patterns
that do not benefit me and I'm trying to wire my kids, from the
start, for resilience and feeling at home in themselves. Wow. I am
doing so much."

This is a chapter I hope you read over and over again, especially
when your self-blame kicks up ("This is all my fault"), your dooms-
day thinking gets louder ("I've messed up my child forever"), and
your hope feels lost ("Our family will never change"). It is a refer-
ence for you to revisit in order to ground yourself, and a reminder
that change and repair are possible.

The Brain's Capacity to Rewire

Two things are true: the brain wires early, and it has a remarkable
capacity to rewire. *Neuroplasticity* refers to the brain's ability to relearn and transform itself when it recognizes the need for adaption.

The brain can continue developing throughout life; our bodies are meant to protect us, so if our brain believes our old ways of being are no longer serving us, it will incorporate new patterns, new beliefs, new systems for processing and responding in the world. It's true that it gets harder as we age—the older we are, the more consistent and dedicated we must be to experience change—but at the end of the day, old dogs *can* learn new tricks.

A child's developing brain is being wired in the context of a child-parent relationship. The development of the middle prefrontal cortex—the part of the brain involved with emotion regulation, cognitive flexibility, empathy, and connectedness—is influenced by the attachment relationship with a caregiver. In other words, a child's earliest experiences have a huge influence on how her brain develops. And yet, we know from research that attachment does not have to be destiny—an individual wired for insecure attachment can rewire for secure attachment. Psychologist Louis Cozolino established therapy's role in the neuroplasticity process: a secure attachment with one's therapist, he discovered, can lead to a rewiring in the brain that results in improved emotion regulation and increased ability to manage stress. We can apply this principle to the family unit, because we know that parents can work to develop more secure attachments with their kids. When parents are willing to change, when they are willing to repair and reflect together, nondefensively, about moments in the past that felt bad to kids . . . the child's brain can rewire.

Our brains also have a remarkable capacity to learn. Decades of research have established that the brain changes in response to its environment. Neuroscientist Marian Diamond first discovered, in the early 1970s, that a neglectful environment leads a brain to shrink, while an enriched environment leads to brain growth. As the environment changes, the brain changes. One recent study confirmed this effect in the context of parenting: it examined the impact of parenting programs aimed at two-year-olds through eleven-year-olds, and found that as long as the interventions were adapted to the age of the particular child, parenting programs had equal effectiveness. They were just as impactful in building new skills for older children as they were for toddlers. It's an incredibly hopeful conclusion, and a good one to hold on to when we worry about the "damage" we've caused. With regard to the timing of parenting changes and intervention, the study's authors wrote: "It is important that our findings are never used as a reason to delay intervention, as children and families otherwise will suffer for longer. With respect to common parenting interventions for reducing behaviour problems in childhood, rather than believing 'earlier is better,' we should conclude 'it's never too early, never too late.'"

Since parents are the most significant fixture in a child's environment, perhaps it should come as no surprise that when a parent changes, so too does a child's wiring. Research has established that, oftentimes, when kids are struggling, it is not therapy for the child himself but coaching or therapy for the parent that leads to the most significant changes in the child. This is powerful research, because it suggests that a child's behavior—which is an expression of a child's emotion regulation patterns—develops in relation to a parent's emotional maturity. There are two ways to interpret this data. The first is, "Oh no, I'm messing up my kid because *I'm* messed up. I'm the worst!" But there's another, more optimistic and encouraging interpretation: "Wow, this is amazing. If I can work on some of my own emotion regulation abilities—which will feel good for me anyway!—my child will change in response. How empowering!"

Here's what I always tell parents: It's not your fault that your child is struggling. But it *is* your responsibility, as the adults in the family system, to change the environment so that your child can learn and grow and thrive. Our kids' brains wire in response to our interactions with them. We know this by now. If we continue to do the same thing over and over, then yes, we will reinforce whatever patterns have already developed. However, if we reflect and grow and try new things, if we grow ourselves and shift the way we approach our kids, then we are helping our kids develop new circuits at the same time as we are helping ourselves. This is why you're here. You're someone who is brave enough to reflect and grow and try new things. This is why I'm here too. I don't have it all figured out. I have plenty of my own anxieties and points of reactivity, and I consider myself a member of this amazing community of cycle-breakers and forever learners.

The Power of Repair

There is no such thing as a perfect parent. All parents have moments that feel "off" with their kids: where they lose their cool, where they yell words they wish they could take back, where they shoot "dart eyes" and a judgmental look at their well-meaning son or daughter. Deep breath. I've been there, your friends have been there . . . we've all been there. And this is okay! The key is what happens next. Our parenting doesn't have to be defined by our moments of struggle. It should be defined by whether or not we connect with our kids after the struggle, and whether we explore how those moments felt to them and work to repair the rupture in the relationship.

When we, as parents, wonder, "Is it too late?" we're assuming that the story of our relationship with our child already has an ending. In doing so, we miss something critical: that we can always layer on a new experience, and that new experience will change the ending to that chapter. Let's say you've had a rough day, your child is protesting your no-snacks-right-now decision, and you end up yelling, "You make everything difficult! You're an ungrateful spoiled child and I don't even know what to do with you!" In response, your child runs to his room screaming, "I hate you, I hate you, I hate you!" Okay, first things first—deep breath. If you're thinking, "Yes, I've said things like that," or "Wow, was she in my house last night?" or even "*That's* Dr Becky's example? I lose my cool *way* worse than that," or "My losing it looks totally different"—no matter what, let me tell you this: I still think you're a good parent inside. I know you're here to work on doing even better. So please, stay with me for this next important part.

Now your child is alone in his room. What's going on for him? Mostly, intense distress. Your child is dysregulated, which means he's feeling overwhelmed by the sensations in his body and he's in a state of physiological threat ("This feeling is too much, I don't feel safe"). His body has to figure out how to feel safe and secure again . . . but he's alone without a trusted adult to help. Children who are left alone with intense distress often rely on one of two coping mechanisms: self-doubt and self-blame. With self-doubt, kids invalidate their own experience in an attempt to feel safe in their environment again. They might tell themselves, "Wait . . . my mom didn't actually say those awful words to me, that couldn't have happened, no way . . . Yeah, no, I must have remembered that wrong. After all, my mom hasn't apologized yet or even said anything to me about it, she definitely would say she's sorry if she said those words." Kids use self-doubt to protect themselves from the overwhelming feelings that would arise if they accepted the reality of what really just happened. They do this because being alone in their feelings seems like "too much," and self-doubt offers a way to escape and self-preserve. And yet, a child is wiring herself to believe, "I don't perceive things accurately. I overreact. I cannot trust how things feel to me. Other people have a better idea of my reality than I do." This is a scary circuit to build, because it leads to teens and adults who don't trust themselves and cannot locate intuition. Instead, they use other people's treatment of them to define who they are and what they deserve.

Self-blame is another common coping mechanism for kids whose parents don't attempt reconnection after tough moments. Self-blame allows a child to feel in control, because as long as he convinces himself that he's a bad kid doing bad things, and that if he was better he would feel more secure . . . well, then he has a viable option to change. Psychiatrist Ronald Fairbairn may have said it best when he wrote, regarding children and child development, "It is better to be a sinner in a world ruled by God than to live in a world ruled by the Devil."* If children couldn't rely on an adult to come help them, to be there, to repair and reconnect in difficult moments . . . well, then, the world would feel pretty unsafe. It's more comforting for a child to internalize badness ("I am bad inside"), because at least then he can hold on to the idea that the world around him is safe and good.

And yet . . . this is how we got to the point where we wonder if we're too late, right? We layer self-blame ("I am such a bad parent") onto tough moments, and because we are consumed by our not-good-enough-ness, we find ourselves unable to make productive change. Let's wire our kids differently, and rewire ourselves at the same time.

All of this is why "repair" is one of my favorite words in parenting. Sure, we can work on our own "stuff" and try to improve our regulation and learn parenting tricks and scripts and strategies . . . but still, the goal is never to get it right all the time. That's not a thing. I often tell parents that the worthiest goal might be to get

---

* W. R. Fairbairn, *Psychoanalytic Studies of the Personality* (Routledge & Kegan Paul, 1952).

really good at repair, which acknowledges the reality that parents will continue to act in ways that don't always feel great, and there will continue to be hard, misaligned moments. But if we develop the skill of *going back*, *nondefensively*, to our kids and showing them that we care about the discomfort they experienced in those "rupture moments," then we're tackling the most important parenting work of all.

What Does Repair Look Like?

There's no one right way to repair. The key element is connection after disconnection—a parent's calm and compassionate presence after a moment marked by dysregulated reactivity. When we return to a moment that felt bad and add connection and emotional safety, we actually change the memory in the body. The memory no longer has such overwhelming "I'm alone and bad inside" labels. It's now more nuanced, as we layer on support after criticism, softness after yelling, understanding after misunderstanding. The ability to transform the body's memory is pretty amazing, and it's what always motivates me to repair with my own kids.

I will revisit the details of repair, including lengthier scripts for handling these tricky moments, in the next part of this book. But for now, I want to offer some baseline to-dos: Say you're sorry, share your reflections with your child—restating your memory of what happened, so your kid knows it wasn't all in his head—and then say what you wish you had done differently and what you plan to do differently now and in the future. It's important to take ownership over your role ("Mommy was having big feelings that came out in a yelling voice. Those were my feelings and it's my job to work on managing them better. It's never your fault when I yell and it's not your job to figure out how I can stay calmer. I love you") instead of insinuating that your child "made you" react in a certain way. And remember: as a parent, you are your child's role model. When your child sees you as a work in progress, he learns that he, too, can learn from his struggles and take responsibility when he acts in a way he isn't proud of.

Repair can happen ten minutes after a blowup, ten days later, or ten years later. Never ever doubt the power of repair—every time you go back to your child, you allow him to rewire, to rewrite the ending of the story so it concludes in connection and understanding, rather than aloneness and fear. This limits your child's tendency to self-blame and sets him up for a stronger relationship with you and also healthier adult relationships. Because, as we all know, solid relationships aren't solid because they lack conflict, they're solid because the people in them possess the ability to reconnect after disagreements and to feel understood again after feeling misunderstood. Before you move on to the next chapter, maybe push yourself, right now, to repair a moment with your child. Or challenge yourself to do this when you see your kid in the morning or after school. And hold yourself accountable. Remind yourself, right now: "Good parents don't get it right all the time. Good parents repair."

I love the stories of repair I hear from parents in my community on social media—stories that span all ages, from newborn to adult children. A parent recently DMed me: "Now I even repair with my 9-month old . . . he may not understand every word but you've taught me that he will feel my intentions and my reconnection. I recently said to him, 'You were crying and we didn't know why. I'm sorry I yelled. I know that felt scary. I'm here and I love you.'" And this, from another mom: "I feel guilty for all those years I punished my daughter and gave time-outs. I always thought, 'It's too late, I've messed up my kids forever.' But today I told my 8-year-old that I've learned more about what kids need and that I wish I hadn't given her so many time-outs in the moments she needed me most. I saw her body soften. I really did. We hugged. It felt really important." And this is one I'll remember forever, from a grandparent: "A few months ago, my daughter asked me to follow you so I could understand how she is parenting her kids. Wow, has this been an education for me. I called my daughter this morning and told her that I wish I could rewind and parent her in this way and that I see now that it must have felt so bad to her when I yelled or saw the worst in her, not the best. She cried. I guess she really needed to hear this. We talked about it for a while. It was one of the most important moments of our relationship."

Whether you're repairing something big or small, your children will feel that repair in their bodies, and this moment of connection and explanation will soften the initial memory of aloneness and confusion. The big repairs, the small repairs—they all matter. Every little bit counts.

CHAPTER 6

Resilience > Happiness

M*y kids should be happier than they are," a mother tells me.* "They have everything they could ever need and still, all this small stuff bothers them."

"My daughter worries so much about such big things—homelessness, death, inequity around her . . . and she's only seven!" a father says in my office. "I always tell her, 'Stop worrying! Let's think about all the good things in your life!' but still, she's up at night, unable to fall asleep."

"I was a pretty lonely, depressed child," a mother admits to me. "I want to be a different parent to my kids than my parents were for me. My partner gets annoyed with me, because he says I'm always rescuing our kids and making their lives too easy. Is that so bad? Don't you want your kids to be happy, Dr Becky?"

Do I want my kids to be happy? Sure! Of course! And yet, I don't think happiness is what these parents are really talking about. I think there's something much deeper going on. Consider this: What actually leads to happiness? Does eradicating our kids' worry and loneliness and ensuring they feel good at all times enable them to cultivate happiness on their own? What do we really mean when we say, "I just want my kids to be happy"? What are we talking about when we say, "Cheer up!" or "You have so much to be happy about!" or "Why can't you just be happy?" I, for one, don't think we're talking about *cultivating happiness* as much as we're talking about *avoiding fear and distress*. Because when we focus on happiness, we ignore all the other emotions that will inevitably come up throughout our kids' lives, which means we aren't teaching them how to cope with those emotions. And, again, how we teach our kids—through our interactions with them—to relate to pain or hardship will impact how they think about themselves and their troubles for decades to come.

I don't know a single parent who doesn't want the best for their kids. Count me in: I want the best for my kids! And yet, I'm not sure that "the best" for them is to "just be happy." For me, happiness is much less compelling than resilience. After all, **cultivating happiness is dependent on regulating distress.** We have to feel *safe* before we can feel *happy*. Why do we have to learn to regulate the tough stuff first? Why can't happiness just "win" and "beat" all other emotions? That certainly would be easier! Unfortunately, in parenting, just like in life, the things that matter most take hard work and time; helping your child build resilience certainly isn't easy, but I promise it's worth it.

Picture your body as a large jar. Floating around are all the different emotions you could possibly feel. For simplicity's sake, let's say there are two major categories of emotions: ones that feel upsetting and ones that feel "happier." In our emotion jar, we have every single feeling under the sun. The size of each emotion—and therefore the space it takes up in the jar at any given moment—is constantly changing. Now, remember: our bodies have an innate alarm system and are constantly scanning for *danger* before anything else. When we aren't able to cope with emotions like disappointment, frustration, envy, and sadness—when they take up all the space in the emotion jar—our bodies initiate a stress response.

And it's not just the difficult feelings themselves that prompt our bodies to feel unsafe. We also feel *distress over having distress*, or experience *fear of fear*. In other words (assuming there's no actual physical threat, but simply the "threat" of uncomfortable, overwhelming emotions), as we start thinking, "Ah! I need to make this feeling go away right now," the distress grows and grows, not as a reaction to the original experience, but because we believe these negative emotions are wrong, bad, scary, or too much. Ultimately, this is how anxiety takes hold within a person. Anxiety is the intolerance of discomfort. It's the experience of not wanting to be in your body, the idea that you should be feeling differently in that specific moment. And this isn't a product of "being a downer" or "seeing the glass as half-empty"; it's a product of evolution. Our bodies will not allow us to "relax" if we believe the feelings inside us are overpowering and frightening. So, where's the happiness here? Well, it's crowded out. It cannot surface.

Of course, it doesn't have to be this way. The wider the range of feelings we can regulate—if we can manage the frustration, disappointment, envy, and sadness—the more space we have to cultivate happiness. Regulating our emotions essentially develops a cushion around those feelings, softening them and preventing them from consuming the entire jar. **Regulation first, happiness second.** And this translates into our parenting: the wider the range of feelings *we* can name and tolerate in our kids (again, this doesn't mean behaviors), the wider the range of feelings *they* will be able to manage safely, affording them an increased ability to feel at home with themselves.

Do I want my kids to experience happiness? Without a doubt, yes. I want them to feel happiness as kids and as adults; this is why I'm so focused on building resilience. Resilience, in many ways, is our ability to experience a wide range of emotions and still feel like ourselves. Resilience helps us bounce back from the stress, failure, mistakes, and adversity in our lives. Resilience allows for the emergence of happiness.

The Power of Resilience

Developing resilience doesn't mean we become immune to stress or struggle—these are, of course, unavoidable facts of life—but our resilience determines how we *relate to* those difficult moments as well as how we experience them. People who are resilient are better able to cope when stressful moments arise. Here's a helpful (though slightly oversimplified) equation: *stress + coping = internal experience.* The good news? Resilience is not a static character trait that children possess or lack; it's a skill that can be cultivated, and one that, hopefully, parents help instill in their kids from a young age. Because we can't always change the stressors around us, but we can always work on our ability to access resilience.

You might be surprised how often the need for resilience shows up in childhood. Building a block tower back up after it falls, sticking with a puzzle that's tricky, learning to read, handling social exclusion—all of this requires resilience. In each of these situations, kids who can access their resilience are able to take a deep breath, say something kind to themselves, and continue engaging in the task even though it's challenging and they won't necessarily succeed. Adults often think of resilience as the ability to succeed in the face of challenge—to finish the block tower, complete the tricky puzzle, read the hard chapter, or say "No big deal" after being left out. But in reality, resilience has nothing to do with successful outcomes. If we all knew we'd be successful, there'd be no need to flex our "Come on, I can stick with it!" muscles. Building resilience is about developing the capacity to *tolerate distress*, to stay *in and with* a tough, challenging moment, to find our footing and our goodness even when we *don't have confirmation of achievement or pending success.* Resilience building happens in the space *before* a "win" arrives, which is why it can feel so hard to access. But that's also why it's so worthwhile. The longer we learn to tolerate the challenges of learning, the more we maximize the likelihood of reaching our goals.

So how do we develop resilience in our kids? Psychologists Robert Brooks and Sam Goldstein, authors of *The Handbook of Resilience in Children*, found that the qualities children most need from their parents in order to develop resilience include: empathy, listening, accepting them for who they are, providing a safe and consistent presence, identifying their strengths, allowing for mistakes, helping them develop responsibility, and building problem-solving skills. This book, I hope, will give you the tools to do all of this important work. The ideas and interventions in these pages are designed to help wire children for resilience over the course of their lifetime, including the strategies and scripts to help your kids stay in a moment of struggle, find their coping skills, and watch themselves get through tough times instead of avoiding them. But for me, more powerful than knowing exactly what to say to my kids in a difficult moment is coming back to a general goal or principle. So if our general goal is to support and not solve, or tolerate and not escape, then to build resilience in our kids, we should be guided by one question: am I helping my kid tolerate and work through this distress, or am I encouraging my child to avoid and beeline out of the distress? We want the first, not the second.

At the heart of any practical strategy I offer is the desire to help kids build resilience. As a parent, I challenge myself to sit *with* my child in his feeling of distress so he knows he isn't alone, as opposed to pulling my child *out of* this moment, which leaves him alone the next time he finds himself there. For example, when my child says, "Ugh, the block tower keeps falling! Help me!," instead of saying, "Here, let me build you a sturdy base," in order to help him out of the hard moment, I might say, "Ugh, how annoying!" Then I'll take a few audible deep breaths and say, "Hmm . . . I wonder what we could do to make it sturdier . . . ," and model a look of curiosity. All of this is designed to connect to my child within the distress. When my child says, "Everyone in my class lost a tooth, I'm the only one who didn't!" I don't say, "Sweetie, you will soon, and you're one of the kids who can read chapter books!" in order to distract him from his disappointment. Instead, I might say, "Everyone else lost one already, huh? You wish you lost a tooth, I get that. I remember feeling something really similar in kindergarten . . ." The goal here is to help my child feel less alone in her distress. Reminding ourselves, "Connect! Connect!" encourages us to first be present *in* our child's experience instead of leading our child *out* of his own experience.

Happiness vs. Resilience

Let's return to the beginning of this chapter, when a mom asked me this question: "Don't you want your kids to be happy, Dr Becky?" Here's my answer: Happiness is not my ultimate goal for my own kids. *Un*happiness certainly isn't my goal for them, but here's a deep irony in parenting: **the more we emphasize our children's happiness and "feeling better," the more we set up them up for an adulthood of anxiety**. Setting happiness as the goal compels us to solve our kids' problems rather than equip them to solve their own. We live in a goal-oriented society, so in order to make our kids happy and encourage their "success," we often minimize or eliminate their disappointments in favor of providing immediate wins. We take them out of struggle and place them into triumph, out of an uncomfortable feeling and into a more pleasant one.

It's an understandable impulse, but one that is shortsighted. As we learned in chapter 4, the way we interact with our kids today impacts them not only in the moment but for decades to come, because we are building their circuits for processing emotions, managing feelings, and self-talking in difficult circumstances. When we tell ourselves that we just want our kids to be happy, we take on the job of happiness police, eager to help our kids *avoid* discomfort instead of teaching our kids how to *cope with* discomfort. This wires a child for a circuit that says, "Discomfort is bad, wrong, and a sign I need immediate ease. I need to look for that 'better' feeling because I never learned how to tolerate distress." This is very different from the circuit built by nurturing resilience: "Discomfort happens, discomfort is where I learn. I am not scared of discomfort because I learned to tolerate it in my childhood—because my parent tolerated it in me."

When we tell our kids, "I just want you to be happy," we are telling them they need to get out of distress and into comfort. When our daughter says, "All the other kids run faster than me," we remind her that she is excellent at math; when our son seems sad and says, "I wasn't invited to Anuj's birthday party," we convince him that the party had to be small and that Anuj does, in fact, really like him. We think we are helping, but what our child hears is, "I should not feel upset. When I feel uncomfortable, my job is to make my way into comfort as soon as possible."

These same ideas are true for large life stressors: deaths in the family, divorce, moves, the pandemic. When we tell kids, "You're going to be fine," or "You're so young, you don't need to worry about this," our kids learn that they *shouldn't* be feeling the way they do. Many parents tell me they want to "protect" their kids from tough feelings; this well-intentioned intervention often backfires, because most efforts at "protection" actually leave a child alone with the feelings they're already having, which is scarier than the feelings themselves. Parents don't so much need to *protect* kids from having tough feelings as much as we need to *prepare* our kids to have those feelings. And the best way to prepare our kids is through honesty and loving presence. This means instead of telling your child, "Grandma just . . . went away. She's in a better place," saying, "I want to tell you something that you may have big feelings about. Grandma died yesterday. That means her body stopped working," and then pausing as you sit next to your child and waiting to see what happens next. Maybe later you add on, "It's okay to be really sad," or "What great questions you're asking—I'm so glad we're talking about it." The larger lesson we are teaching our kids is that distress is a part of life and when upsetting things happen, we can talk about them and get through them with the people we love.

This lesson is not just important for childhood. Adults, of course, cannot successfully avoid distress. I don't know one adult who has ever said, "Wow, my parents really got all those uncomfortable feelings out of me! The disappointment and frustration and envy . . . they convinced me out of all of them! They successfully distracted me so much that now, as an adult, I never feel these things! I am happy all the time!" And yet . . . I do know adults—so many adults—whose internal alarm bells go off whenever they feel disappointment, frustration, or jealousy that they cannot "make go away" relatively quickly. Adults whose childhoods were focused mainly on happiness are not only unprepared for tough moments, they experience *more* discomfort in those tough moments because, deep down, they think they're doing something wrong if they can't "find the happy" and get themselves to a "better place." When it comes to resilience, what matters by adulthood is that we can manage distress, because we had someone in our childhood who validated it and allowed us to experience it. If we learned that we can only be at home with ourselves when life is going our way and we are "happy," we will be in for a rude awakening.

Imagine how amazing it will be if today's parents become the generation that reframes their dreams for their kids, focusing on healthy emotional development above all else. It would be pretty wonderful if parenting was driven by this one goal: "I want my child to be able to cope with whatever the world throws her way. I want her to feel supported in distress when she's younger so she can support herself when she's older."

You are the architect of your child's resilience, and that is the ultimate gift you can give them. After all, successfully managing life's many challenges is a person's most reliable path to happiness.

CHAPTER 7

Behavior Is a Window

*P*icture this: *It's five thirty p.m., that dreaded time when nothing ever seems to go smoothly in your household.* You're in the kitchen, about to prepare dinner, when you overhear your kids fighting about whose turn it is to play with their favorite toy. An email pops up on your phone—it's from your boss, explaining that she's not happy with your latest project. Then, just as you're about to start cooking, you realize the chicken you thought was in your fridge is long gone, so you grab a box of Cheerios from the pantry and decide tonight will be a cereal-for-dinner kind of night. Then your partner walks in and says, "We're out of toilet paper—why didn't you get it at the store?"

You throw the cereal box to the ground, Cheerios spilling every-where, and yell, "Can you do one thing—just one thing!—for this family? I can't take it anymore!" You turn around and storm off.

Let's unpack this. What's really going on here? What was hap-pening when you reacted harshly, when you yelled and threw the cereal box? On the surface, you behaved in a way that was out of control and dysregulated. But under the surface, I think we can all see a person who is in emotional pain, who is feeling not good enough, not seen or supported, and frustrated.

Isn't that interesting? On the surface we see a *behavior* and underneath we see a *person*. Throwing the cereal box wasn't the main event. It was a window *into* the main event. Behavior, in all its forms, is a window: into the feelings, thoughts, urges, sensations, perceptions, and unmet needs of a person. Behavior is never "the story," but rather it's a *clue* to the bigger story begging to be addressed.

So now, put yourself back in that kitchen. What would you, the thrower of the cereal box, need from your partner in that moment? If it were me, I'm pretty sure I would already know that it's not okay to throw a cereal box; my throwing and yelling was a sign that I was overwhelmed with an emotion, not a sign that I don't know right from wrong. I wouldn't need my partner to teach me or lecture me or punish me or shame me in any way. What I would need is to feel safe and good inside again. Then, when I'd cooled down a bit, I would need to reflect on the larger story of how I got to that moment. What made my distressing feelings build up so much that they came exploding out of me in such a big way? And how could I strengthen my ability to cope with frustration and not-good-enough feelings so that I could regulate these tough emotions the next time they came up?

The only way I'd be able to change and show up more grounded and less reactive in the future would be to embrace *curiosity* about what was happening for me *underneath* the behavior. It may sound counterintuitive, but when we focus too much on judging and changing a specific behavior, we get in the way of that behavior actually changing, because we miss the core struggle that motivated it in the first place.

Now consider these two reactions from your partner:

Partner reaction #1: Becky is so unreasonable. How she could do something like that? Does she not respect me? This isn't okay! She is so dramatic and has such intense reactions! I cannot let Becky think this is appropriate behavior. I'm going to tell her, "Becky, it's not okay to throw a cereal box! You know better!

How disrespectful! You cannot watch TV for the next three nights."
Partner's feelings: Angry, distant, indignant, judgmental.

Partner reaction #2: Wow, Becky had a big reaction there. I didn't like it. I wonder what was going on for her in that moment. It's not okay to throw a cereal box—she probably knows that—so something powerful must have been happening for her. She's a good person, so she must be really struggling. I've struggled before too, and in those moments, I wasn't at my best. I'll go to her and say, "Hey, that was a lot. And yet, you must have had something big happening for you, because I know you don't like reacting that way. So let's talk about it—I care more about what was going on for you than I do about the specific reaction. I'm here. Let's figure it out together."
Partner's feelings: Curious, empathic, a bit hesitant, connected.

I think we would all prefer to be granted the generosity of the second reaction—the behavior-as-a-window approach—rather than the first reaction, which takes what I call a behavior-first approach.

Let's move now from ourselves to our kids. For years, most parents have been fed a model of parenting that is very behavior-first. Sticker charts, rewards, praise, ignoring, time-outs . . . these are all behavior modification methods that focus on the question "How do we change behavior?" And, listen, I'm a pragmatist, so I know we want to change behavior sometimes. I want that with my own kids! But it's all about the *how* of our approach. When we focus on what's *under the surface*, when we give children what they need to be less combustible inside, their behavior will appear less explosive on the outside. By understanding what *motivates behavior*, we can help kids build resilience and regulate emotions, which will inevitably lead to behavioral changes. There will be some lag time, of course, but when the change takes hold, it will be in a way that is lasting, meaningful, and generalizes to a wide range of situations.

Say your son keeps grabbing toys from his new baby sister. When we focus on the behavior first, we see a kid who is selfish and can't share. But when we look at his behavior as a *window* into his feelings about having a new sibling, suddenly we see his insecurity in his world and his fear that the important things in his life may suddenly be taken from him. When this happens, we intervene differently. We may still remove the toy from our child and return it to the baby, but then we'll connect with this child, saying something like, "Ugh, it's so hard to have a new baby in the family!" And now that we understand what's going on beneath the surface, we can give our child more one-on-one time or explore these themes in pretend play. ("Dump Truck wants to go grab that toy from his new sister Bulldozer! Hmm . . . I wonder what we can do here . . . Let's help Dump make a better decision.") After all, this was never about the toy at all—it was about your son's massive world shift and his need for his parents to affirm his safety. And once he feels in control again, he'll end up changing his behavior on his own. Because the behavior is really just a symptom—once the core problem is addressed, the symptom will, eventually, go away.

I also feel compelled to point out that in my family, when my older child grabbed a toy from a baby sibling, the baby usually didn't care. And because I was less attached to the behavior itself and more interested in what the behavior was telling me, I would often . . . do nothing. I'd pause and wait. I wouldn't make my child give it back. And these were some of the most amazing moments: I saw my kid as good inside, I wasn't scared the behavior would continue forever, and so I didn't react. I knew the underlying issue had nothing to do with the toy and everything to do with his feelings, and, no joke, more times than not my child would return the toy on his own.

Prioritizing Relationships

When we use methods of behavior modification, we can—temporarily—change behavior. I won't deny that. I also won't deny that it can take time to do the deeper work, which is a privilege we don't always have. There are some situations where we need to correct a child's behavior and do it quickly, and others where we simply can't dedicate our limited resources to doing the additional work—where we're already stretched too thin between work and family and the many demands of being a parent and a person in the world. But without attending to what's under the surface, we cannot change the dynamics that *motivate* a child's behavior. It's like putting duct tape on a leak in the ceiling instead of wondering about the source of the leak. When we address the behavior first, we miss the opportunity to help our children build skills, and beyond this, we miss the opportunity to see our kids as people rather than a collection of behaviors.

If I see toy-grabbing only as an undesirable behavior, I will become obsessed with changing it; I may give my child a sticker chart with a gold star for every day he doesn't grab. I may tell my child, "If you keep grabbing, you will lose your screen time!" Or, when my child grabs, I may say, "You have a time-out!" and send him away to his room. These approaches fail in many ways: they leave your child alone instead of connected, they reflect back to your child that you think he's a "bad" kid who needs to be controlled in order to behave well (remember, our kids are always absorbing the versions of themselves we reflect back), and most powerfully, they miss *what is actually going on inside the child*, whatever distress and overwhelming feeling led to the behavior in the first place.

If you have a people-pleasing child, behavior modification methods might appear especially successful, because these children are oriented to becoming the versions of themselves that their parents want. However, while reinforcing our kid's people-pleasing ten-dencies can be "convenient" in childhood, it can lead to major problems—a reluctance to say no, an inability to assert or even lo-cate one's own needs, a prioritization of other people's wellness to the detriment of one's own—later on. And for non-people-pleasing kids? Well, these methods often intensify challenging behavior, not help it. Because when we are not heard or seen on the inside, we escalate our *expressions* on the outside, in hopes of being taken se-riously and getting our needs met. In short: when we see behavior as "the main event" instead of as a window into *an unmet need*, we may "successfully" shut down the behavior, but the *underlying need remains*, and it will pop up again, Whack-a-Mole style. When we don't attend to the source of the leak, the water flow remains unchanged.

The other problem with behavioral control methods is right there in the label: control. Prioritizing control over relationship building is a dangerous trade-off. If all you want is to change your child's behavior, then sure, sticker charts and time-outs may be "successful" when your kids are young. But as they get older and the gold stars lose their power, the result can be downright scary. I once sat down with a mother and father who came to me to discuss their sixteen-year-old son. He was, they said, out of control—he was nasty to his siblings, going out late at night and coming back long after curfew, and now refusing to go to school. It was this latest development—the school skipping—that led these parents to my office.

This was a family in which early childhood was defined by be-havior modification approaches: punishments, rewards, sticker charts, time-outs, and other forms of control. The parents shared with me that their son had always been a "difficult kid," and they had consulted many professionals who encouraged various sched-ules of rewards, punishment, and consequences. These methods would appear successful, they said, until a new problematic behavior popped up. Then they'd rely on one of these methods, again, to address the new problem, which would seemingly go away . . . and then another would appear in its place. This cycle lasted for over a decade, they said.

As I listened to their story, something struck me: these parents missed out on sixteen years of building a *relationship* with their child. When they first came to my office, there was, simply, nothing there. When we approach our kids with charts and reinforcement and stickers and time-outs, we essentially tell them that their behavioral compliance is what matters most. We display an indifference to their distress and their personhood (an interest in which is critical to forming human relationships), and our kids can feel that. Now, sixteen years later, this couple's son was essentially saying: "I don't care about your sticker charts and your punishments. I'm bigger now, and you can't throw me in a time-out. I'm no longer scared of you, and you have no leverage because there is nothing *connecting* us." When our kids get older and bigger, methods of behavior control stop working. Children simply aren't motivated anymore by our rewards, and they're too physically big for us to enforce punishments and consequences. When we sacrifice relationship building in favor of control tactics, our children may age, but in many ways, they *developmentally* remain toddlers, because they miss out on years of building the emotion regulation, coping skills, intrinsic motivation, and inhibition of desires that are necessary for life success. When we are busy exerting *extrinsic control* over our children's *external behavior*, we sacrifice teaching these critical internal skills.

And here's another reason we want to focus on connection over behavior modification: if we don't build a sturdy foundation with our kids—one based in trust, understanding, and curiosity—then we have nothing keeping them attached to us. I think about the term "connection capital" a lot. It refers to the reserve of positive feelings we hopefully build up with our children, which we can pull from in times of struggle or when the relationship between us gets strained. If we don't build this up during our children's earlier years, well, we have nothing to draw on when our kids are adolescents and young adults—years when the behavior modification methods we may have once relied on are no longer at our disposal because our kids are physically bigger, are more independent, and can rebel against our sticker charts, rewards, and punishments.

Is it too late for this family? Is it too late for *your* family? No, of course not. It's never too late. We know this. But it *is* hard work. Change is possible *and* challenging. I, along with some other professionals, worked with this family for a long time, and we saw some major changes. The work was intense, full of ups and downs, and by the time we stopped working together, there was major progress and also major work left to do. I still connect with these parents, who have been amazingly open and reflective, about their continued work to repair with their now twenty-year-old son, and also about how they're parenting their younger children differently. "I wish I had thought of all this earlier," the father told me about a year into our work together. "So many professionals advised us to use the system of time-outs and punishments and rewards, and it all seemed so logical. And they quoted impressive data, like a ninety percent reduction in difficult behavior. Who wouldn't want that? But I didn't see the bigger picture. We don't want to 'craft our child's behavior' . . . we want to help our son develop into a good person. We want to understand him, to help him with the things that feel bad to him. It never occurred to me that our earlier approach was actually making our problems worse. This is so important for parents to know."

I agree. This is why we are here.

Evidence-Based Approaches to Parenting

I love science. I love evidence. And there is a ton of scientific litera-
ture out there—very real studies in credible journals—that provides
evidence for behavior modification methods. Parents often ask me:
"How can you be against a parenting approach that has data showing it changes kids' behavior? How can that be bad?" Well, it's not
necessarily bad. But here's my issue with it: the evidence around
behavior change can make us lose sight of what *actually matters*
in favor of what is *immediately observable*. And there's something
a little absurd about it too. One of my favorite supervisors once
said to me: "I could run a study that shows a one hundred percent
reduction in difficult behavior if I wanted! If, every time a young
child did something 'undesirable,' a parent hit the child or made
him sleep on the street for a night . . . I am pretty sure my study
would show that a child would appear more compliant after a few
weeks." My supervisor was certainly not endorsing abuse; his point
was that data needs to be consumed thoughtfully, and that behavior
change through methods of fear and coercion is not data to brag
about. Evidence-based parenting guidance often measures success
by whether or not a behavior changed—it follows a behavior-first
framework. But, if you ask me, that alone isn't enough to make
something a success. If your child has stopped snatching toys but
still worries that his baby sister is going to upend his whole world,
you haven't really helped him, you've only helped yourself—and
only temporarily, until the feelings that motivated the behavior,
now larger because they haven't been seen or helped, pop up somewhere else. Focusing too much on behavior change can cause us to
lose touch with our humanity; we end up looking at ourselves and
our children only for what we produce on the surface, without any
regard to the elements that make us whole—our feelings, our fears,

our needs, our compassion. I suppose my main point here is that two things are true: I appreciate data and I think it's important to reconsider what evidence base we care about. Data that shows behavioral change through control, coercion, and abandonment fears is data that needs to be digested with skepticism; it's certainly not data that feels especially convincing to me.

Another reason why behavior-first methods can feel appealing is that they're tangible and clear. It is, quite frankly, easy to understand how to reward a good behavior with a sticker. But it's not so easy to figure out how to get to the root of why your child was avoiding that good behavior in the first place. The directions for saying "Time out!" may seem more actionable than asking the tough questions. But when we choose the "harder" option, we are taking an important step. In his landmark education book *Beyond Discipline: From Compliance to Community*, author Alfie Kohn writes that any time parents or professionals "frame the issue in terms of the need to change a child's behavior, they are unwittingly buying into a larger theory, one that excludes what many of us would argue are the things that really matter: the child's thoughts and feelings, needs and perspectives, motives and values—the things, in short, that result in certain behaviors. The behavior is only what's on the surface; what matters is the *person who does the behaving* . . . and why she does so." Traditional discipline, he explains, can temporarily "change behavior, but [it] cannot help people to grow." Instead, Kohn urges adults to develop "the ability to look 'through' a given action in order that we can understand the motives that gave rise to it as well as figuring out how to have some effect on those motives."

So how do we do this? How do we look through the action to see the deeper behavior? It certainly sounds like a good idea, but it's not so easy to execute when our son is talking back to us, or our daughter is throwing food, or both kids are jumping on the furniture. It begins, as I mentioned earlier, with being curious. Here are some questions to get you started, to ask yourself after any tough moment:

- What is my most generous interpretation (MGI) of my child's behavior?
- What was going on for my child in that moment?
- What was my child *feeling* right before that behavior emerged?
- What urge did my child have a hard time regulating?
- What is a parallel situation in my life? And if I did something similar, what might I have been struggling with in that moment?
- What does my child feel I don't understand about them?
- If I remember that my child is a good kid having a hard time . . . what are they having a hard time with?
- What deeper themes are being displayed underneath this behavior?

Once we've asked ourselves these questions—and assuming we've been honest with ourselves about the answers—the natural next step is to attend to whatever it is we've uncovered and give relationship-building attention to the very child who has just behaved in an undesirable way. Let's walk through this with an example, to bring it to life. You've just told your four-year-old son that you need him to be quiet while you finish a work call. But instead of being quiet, he's throwing items from your desk and screaming. When your work call ends, instead of reprimanding your son, you remind yourself that his behavior is a window and come up with your MGI: your child really wanted your attention, felt unseen, and couldn't manage these feelings in his young body. You reflect on a time you wanted your partner's attention when he was scrolling on his phone, and how annoyed you felt and how you ended up screaming at him—not entirely different from what happened between you and your child! After coming to this realization, you say to your son, "It was really hard to stay quiet while I was on my call. I know it feels bad when we're playing and suddenly I have to get on the phone. I understand that. In a little bit, let's practice this moment again, and maybe we can come up with a secret handshake for when I have to pick up a call so you know I'm still paying attention to you."

For many parents, a non-punishing approach like this seems worrisome, or at least counterintuitive. They fear that giving "positive attention" to a "misbehaving" child will only encourage that child to keep engaging in the problematic behavior. As one parent recently told me: "I'm no longer punishing my child, but now we're in a cycle where she does something bad and as a result she gets special time with me. I don't want her to learn that this is how she gets my attention, but right now it *is* how she's getting it! Help!"

I understand both of these concerns. But rather than responding by reducing the connection after these behaviors, I'd think about *increasing the connection outside of these behaviors*. Behavioral issues are often a call for attention or connection—if those needs are met, that cry for help is no longer necessary. This is why a bad behavior is rarely "fixed" in that behavior's immediate aftermath. It takes ongoing connection to really move the needle, and kids in difficult behavioral cycles need more proactive attention, more one-on-one time, more assurance that they are seen and valued and have an identity outside of their acting out. Increased connection might mean scheduling ten minutes of distraction-free time every day (I call this Play No Phone, or PNP, Time—more on that in a bit) or a "Hey, want to grab some ice cream? We could use a special treat!" When you carve out time with your child, especially one who has a history of acting out, you're telling them, "I see you as more than a bad kid." And for the times they do engage in troublesome behavior? Take a deep breath, remind yourself that progress isn't linear, and remember that when we connect with our kids after they act out, we don't have to throw a party for them. You might say, "Sweetie, I know you're having a hard time, and we will work on ways of telling your brother you're mad while keeping your body safe. Now, I need to finish folding laundry. You can sit with me if you want. Let's make sure you and I get some time together, just the two of us, later, okay? I love you."

Adjusting to the outlook that behavior is a *window*, and actually learning to look through that window to see what's going on underneath, is hard. If you struggle with it . . . that's okay! There's nothing wrong with you. In fact, it's likely that no one ever looked at *your* early behaviors as part of a larger story, either. Seeing behavior as a clue will take practice, and I encourage you to treat yourself with the same understanding you'd give yourself if you wanted stronger biceps; it takes consistent hard work, repetition, and tolerance of moments that don't feel good or natural. But once you start to notice the change . . . well, there's no prouder feeling than watching all of your efforts, which actually *feel right* and *feel good*, pay off.

CHAPTER 8

Reduce Shame, Increase Connection

Although parents who come to my office express a huge variety of concerns and offer a wide range of examples to illustrate their child's "bad" behavior, there's often a common theme at the root of each story. Take these three examples:

"My daughter won't say 'I'm sorry.' Yesterday she hid her sister's favorite lovie. Her sister was crying and crying. When she refused to own up and say sorry, I just lost it. It was so mean. Does she have no empathy at all?"

"My son is so stubborn. He is really struggling at math and I'm carving out time to help him, yet he tunes out when I teach him things and then he just explodes. It's infuriating, I don't understand why he won't let me help him!"

"My daughter keeps lying. Usually it's about small things like eating candy that I said she couldn't have, but recently she lied about something big: she didn't tell me that she got cut from her soccer team. I remind her that she has to tell me the truth and that lying is wrong but nothing changes."

What's happening here? Is there a common underlying struggle for each of these kids? It may not seem immediately obvious, but in each of these scenarios—the refusal to apologize, the stubbornness, the lying—I see a child who is shutting down. These children are struggling to live in their painful realities—the reality of having stolen a sister's lovie, the reality of struggling at math, the reality of wanting something for herself and not getting it. In each scenario, the parent described a child who felt guilty or humiliated or bad about something and then reacted in a dysregulated way in an attempt to avoid dealing with the guilt or bad feeling. This is the essence of shame—the experience of "I can't be me right now, I can't be feeling this way."

The Danger of Shame

Everyone experiences shame differently, so first things first, let's get on the same page with a working definition. I define shame as the feeling that "this part of me is not connectable—no one wants to know or be with this part." It's a powerful feeling that tells us we should not want to be seen as we are in the moment. Shame encourages us to avoid contact with others—to hide, to distance ourselves, to move *away* rather than *toward* others. And shame activates the ultimate fear for a child, the idea "I am bad inside, I am unworthy, I am unlovable, I am unattachable . . . I will be all alone." Given that children's survival is *dependent on attachment*, their bodies read shame as: "Ultimate danger! Ultimate danger!" There is nothing as dysregulating to a child as a set of emotions or sensations or actions that leads to the threat of abandonment; it truly is an existential danger to survival.

But here's what's critical to understand about shame: it is an evolutionarily adaptive feeling. Being *alone* as a child is synonymous with being *in danger*, so shame works, within the attachment system, as a signal to a child to *hide the part of them that does not successfully gain attachment*. Shame feels so awful because it awakens our body to a painful but important piece of information: You will not get your needs met if you keep on being who you are right now. Instead, you will be met with rejection—often in the form of judgment, invalidation, ignoring, punishment, scolding, or time-outs—that feels like abandonment. Shame says: you must change course so you can feel safe and secure.

Understood in that context, you can see why shame is actually a helpful emotion within a child's (or adult's) threat-detection system. Shame "freezes" a child in place as a protection mechanism, and that "freeze" might look like an inability to apologize, a reluctance to accept help, or an unwillingness to tell the truth. The problem, though, is that a numb, glazed-over child tends to infuriate a parent, because we think our child is ignoring us, or we misinterpret their behavior as rudeness or apathy. As a result, rather than recognize or address the shame, we yell or get into a power struggle with our kid or send him away to his room—all approaches that escalate the shame and continue the cycle. But once we see shame pop up and label it for what it is, we have the ability to intervene differently.

Shame Detection and Reduction

Shame detection is a critical skill to have in any parent's toolbox. The ability to identify shame in all its forms is something of a parental superpower, because once we can see it, we can modify our behavior accordingly—not to be permissive but instead to be effective. So many of our kids' most difficult moments include shame as a common factor, and **shame makes any situation more combustible**. The next time you're in a power struggle with your child, or you're thinking, "I know parenting is hard, but does it have to be *this* explosive?" pay attention: shame is often what adds fuel to the fire.

Our goal as parents should be to notice when shame arises in our child, understand what situations bring it up, and see how it presents behaviorally. After that, we want to develop shame reduction, which enables us to help our children feel safe and secure again. Detect first, reduce second.

So how do we do that? Let's revisit the situation with the child who hid her sister's lovie and refused to own up to it or apologize despite her sister's obvious distress. Refusal to apologize is a classic example of shame: it presents as *cold* and *unempathic* when, in fact, in these moments, a child is overwhelmed with "badness" and freezes up. She cannot apologize because to do so she'd have to "see" herself as the person who just did something awful, and she'd have to face the unwanted feeling of being unlovable to others. ("No one would want to love or take care of a kid who is so awful.") She cannot confront the fear of abandonment that would inevitably come up if she did apologize, so instead she freezes to avoid further distress. Yes, this is all happening in a simple refusal to say "sorry." Shame may also appear as indifference, numbness, or ignoring a parent. Whenever your child seems "stuck," consider that she might be in a moment of shame, and when you see that shame pop up, when you *detect* it, the key is to take pause. When a child is overwhelmed with shame, we must be willing to put our original "goal"—to elicit an apology, to inspire gratitude, to prompt an honest answer—to the side and instead focus solely on reducing the shame.

Here's an intervention that doesn't help to reduce shame: "Irha, you *have* to say sorry. It's a simple word! You're making the situation worse! How could you care so little about your sister? COME ON!" Here, Irha is put in the "bad kid" role and spirals further into her badness, and further into her frozen shame state.

Here's an intervention that's aimed at shame detection and reduction: "Hmm . . . it's hard to find your 'I'm sorry' voice. I have times like that too. I'll use it for you before you find it again." Then *you, the parent*, go to your other child and say, "I'm sorry I took your lovie. I know that was upsetting. Is there anything I can do to make it better?" And then—and this is key—no dart eyes, no lecture, no "See, that was easy!" Just trust—yes, TRUST—that this sank in and move on. Maybe later in the day, when you see that *shame is no longer present* (you'll notice because your child is back to her playful self), you can say something like, "Apologizing is hard. It's even hard for me and I'm an adult!" Or you can use stuffed animals to act out a situation that didn't feel good to one of the animals and model a struggle around apologizing. Then pause and see what your daughter says. But note that none of this reflection or learning or growth is possible when shame is present. We have to be willing to pause our agenda, to pause what feels "fair," when a child is overwhelmed with shame. We have to shift from a goal of correcting behavior to a goal of helping our child feel good inside, showing our child her lovability and worth, affirming our connection. This helps a kid "unstick." You cannot bypass this step; our bodies simply won't allow it.

Does this apology example seem too "soft" for you? Too "touchy-feely," or too easily letting your kid off the hook? I've felt this way before. I've worried that by letting my kid forgo the "I'm sorry," and by delivering it myself, I'm condoning my child's non-apology. And when that concern creeps in, plenty of parents go on to think, "I can't have a fifteen-year-old who thinks her mom will just model an apology for her, that's ridiculous! She has to get over herself and learn to do it on her own!" But children feel shame at any age, whether five or fifteen. So take a look at what's in front of you: if your teenager is lying about the soccer team, she too might be "stuck," though this time in a lie rather than a refusal to apologize. So while I might use different words—maybe "I understand it's hard to talk about things we wish weren't true" instead of "It's hard to find your 'I'm sorry' voice"—I'd intervene based on the same principles.

Now, let's pause and take a deep breath and come back to our child's (and our own) inherent *goodness*: remember, our kids are good inside. We don't have to train them to be kind. We have to help them manage some of the barriers to kindness that can look, on the surface, like harsh behavior but that, in reality, emerge to protect a child. Working to reduce shame and, in this situation, modeling (and definitely not forcing) an apology isn't an intervention I recommend because it "feels better" to a child; it's an intervention I recommend because it gives a child the highest likelihood of eventually reflecting on wrongdoing and producing an apology *on her own.*

Of course, some of the shame our kids experience can be brought on by external factors—not because a child did anything "wrong," but because we live in a world, unfortunately, where kids are judged on attributes or circumstances that are out of their control. Body shame, for example, or shame brought on by economic differences from their classmates—it can be hard to be a kid today. But the good news is that the more you work to reduce shame and increase connection *where you can*, the more your child will be equipped to handle those shaming moments that are outside your sphere of influence. Because no matter the source of a child's shame, the best way to lessen it is always the same: knowing they are good inside, knowing they are lovable, and knowing they have worth.

When Shame Goes Unchecked

When we're not able to detect and reduce shame, when we let it fester in our children, there are likely to be long-term effects. Plenty of modern parents know these effects firsthand, because our parents' generation was—and this is a generalization—less focused than we are on pinpointing the feelings underneath the behavior. For many of us, shame is wired into our bodies. It essentially attached itself to the parts of ourselves that were not embraced by our parents. Then, when it was suddenly safer (and even encouraged!) to behave in ways that may have been discouraged when we were young—expressing our controversial opinions or delivering a firm NO or sharing our emotions so we can allow other people to connect with us—the shame feeling remained, leading us to feel like we were stuck at age three or eight or whatever age these behaviors developed in the first place. Now, instead of adapting those behaviors in a mature way, we avoid them or feel anxious about them.

Let's say you grew up in a home that assigned a lot of value to being "strong," which you now know really just meant suppressing your emotions. Maybe you remember your parents saying things like "You're such a crybaby," "You're such a downer," or "No one wants to be around you when you're in such a mood." The family ethos was "Pull yourself up by your bootstraps, put on a smile." So what happened to the part of you that sometimes feels vulnerable . . . or sad . . . or worried? Well, that part learned that it must not surface. It was essentially told: "You're bad! You're dangerous! Safety means connection with others and you threaten this closeness! Keep yourself far away, for my sake!" This. Is. Shame. Of course, the idea that this part of you threatens attachment and leads to aloneness *isn't actually true in the greater world*—you can have emotions and still make strong connections. But it was true in your *family* in the time you were *wiring your body for survival.* These old habits die hard.

Fast-forward a few decades. You're married now and you're stressed at your job; your boss is constantly berating you, you're worried about being fired, you're always on edge. There's a part of you that . . . well, wants to cry, wants to open up to your partner, wants to share your awful experiences so you can get support. And yet, this lesson from childhood lurks beneath the surface, subconsciously dictating your actions: "Support? You think you'll get support for having your vulnerability and anxiety surface? These are the things that threaten relationships, not strengthen them! Push these feelings away away away—for your own protection!" And so you don't go to your partner. You don't go to a friend. Instead, the feelings build up until they emerge as increased reactivity, frustration, and anger. Or maybe they lead you to withdraw and shut down. Perhaps you turn to alcohol to turn these feelings off and push them away. You may even have a partner who says, "I can tell something doesn't feel good . . . talk to me, let me in!" But still your body sends the message: "Ha! I won't fall for *that*! I know better! 'Let me in'? These experiences will shut me out!"

Just like with our children, shame for adults is an obstacle to positive change and growth. Our shame impacts how we form and maintain intimate relationships, how we parent, and how we react to difficult moments with our kids. So as you work on developing your ability to detect and reduce shame in your kids, take a moment to turn that reflection onto yourself. What parts of you did you have to learn to "put away"? How does this impact you now? How does your child trigger this shutdown response in you? What parts of you, still to this day, need recognition, compassion, and permission to exist?

Connection First

After many months of work together, one of my clients told me she created a mantra for herself: "Connection first." She said she keeps this phrase in mind at the beginning of every day and even has it written on a note on her refrigerator. She explained it to me this way: "It seems that the underlying theme of everything you talk about is connection. Connection first, everything else second. My son says, 'I hate you!'—I can still connect first to what's happening inside. My daughter isn't listening to me—I can connect with her having a hard time listening instead of trying to force her to comply, which of course never works anyway. Even my husband, when he is mad at me about something, I can connect to what he's saying before defending myself. And with myself! No matter what I'm feeling or thinking, it never becomes bad or overwhelming if I can add my own connection or connection with others to it. 'Connection first' has helped me in every area of my family life."

This stuck with me: connection first. Connection is the opposite of shame. It is the antidote to shame. Shame is a warning sign of aloneness, danger, and badness; connection is a sign of presence, safety, and goodness. Now, to be clear, connection does not mean approval. Approval is usually about a specific behavior; connection is about our relationship with the person underneath the behavior. And that's another reason why connection with our children in their difficult moments does not "reinforce" bad behavior: shame has never been a motivator of positive behavior change at any time, in any place, for any type of person. Shame is sticky; it stagnates us. Connection is opening; it allows for movement. Connection is when we show our kids, "It's okay to be you right now. Even when you're struggling, it's okay to be you. I am here with you, as you are."

CHAPTER 9

Tell the Truth

This might sound like a silly principle, an obvious one—perhaps my most straightforward idea in this book—and yet, telling the truth is surprisingly tricky to put into practice. Speaking to your kids honestly, without vagaries or avoidance, requires sitting with a lot of *your own* feelings, even the unpleasant ones, for the benefit of your children. And that's something that's hard for most of us.

If you're reading this book, you probably condone honesty. You don't consider yourself someone who tells falsehoods, and you probably teach as much to your kids. But when it comes to addressing complicated, nuanced issues, naming what is true is often uncomfortable. Reassuring your kid after she overhears an argument between you and your spouse brings up doubts or sadness or frustrations about your partnership and your reactivity. Admitting that it stinks that your child didn't make the soccer team—and acknowledging the fact that sadness sometimes stays around for a while—reminds us how hard it is to sit in our own feelings of rejection. Confronting and explaining racism can put us in touch with rage or fear or guilt, or some combination of those feelings and more. Explaining how babies are made—like actually getting into the physiological details that kids want to understand—leads to all types of complicated feelings around how sex and sexuality were addressed in our own childhood homes.

Our ability to talk with our kids about important, vulnerable, hard truths is dependent on our ability to tolerate the emotions that come up for us during these moments. Which is only one more reason why working on ourselves, as parents, is more critical than any single parenting intervention; the more we get to know our own circuitry, learn to tolerate and explore our own distress, and build coping skills for hard feelings, the more present we can be for our children. Our parenting is dependent on our willingness to confront our own truths, and from there, we can better connect with our kids.

Parents often fear that telling their kids the truth will be too scary or overwhelming, but we tend to have it all wrong when it comes to what scares children. It's not information so much as feeling *confused and alone in the absence of information* that terrifies them. Children are wired to notice changes in their environment ("Why is everyone suddenly saying 'earthquake'?" "Why do my parents look worried?" "What did that conversation I overheard about Grandma mean?"), and they register fear when they don't understand those changes. They perceive a threat until an adult helps neutralize that threat and determines they are safe. Blame it on evolution: for our species to survive, a child has to assume a rumbling in the forest is a bear until an adult confirms it is actually a squirrel. Or maybe the adult sees that it is, in fact, a bear. Either way, the child registers fear until an adult is present. Then, even if the parent confirms "the worst," a child will feel safer knowing an adult is protecting them. Our supportive, honest, caring presence is what feels safe to our children—when kids have this, even difficult truthful information is manageable.

And if an adult isn't present? If a child is left alone with the perception of change and the feeling of fear without an explanation of what's going on? Well, there's a fancy term for this: "unformulated experience."* It's basically the feeling that something's not right, without a clear explanation of what's happening. Unformulated experience is terrifying to a child, because that "something's not right" feeling free-floats around the body without an anchor of safety. Plus, when kids are left to make sense of a scary change on their own, they usually rely on the methods that give them control: self-blame ("I must have done something to cause this. I'm bad, I'm too much") and self-doubt ("I must have misunderstood the tension around me. I am not such a good feeler of things. If something really was different, my parents would explain it to me").

What's an alternative to leaving a child feeling alone? Clear, direct, honest information shared while connected to you, your child's loving, trusted adult. This is what helps kids feel safe and build resilience. Now, please note: I am not a proponent of unnecessarily *scaring* children. Quite the opposite. I'm a proponent of empowering children, and empowerment often comes from learning how to cope with stress. This requires having a parent who is willing to *approach* rather than *avoid* the truth. The path to *regulation* starts with understanding. In other words, watching a parent confront hard truths will help a child learn to regulate his feelings.

Telling the truth will look different in different situations. It doesn't always mean giving your child the full, unfiltered information they are asking for—sometimes you may not even have that information. Let's walk through four different ways you might tell the truth: confirming your child's perceptions, honoring your child's questions, labeling what you don't know, and focusing on the *how* instead of the exact *what*.

---

* D. B. Stern, "Unformulated Experience: From Familiar Chaos to Creative Disorder," *Contemporary Psychoanalysis* 19(1), 1983, 71–99.

Confirming Perceptions

When I find myself in a "tell the truth" situation with my own kids, I often start with these words: "_____ happened. You were right to notice that." This is critical. Our children are deep sensors and perceivers of their environment. They simply haven't amassed enough life experience to differentiate what is dangerous from what is merely annoying from what is safe. In fact, research has found that children notice *more* details in their environment than adults. We often tell ourselves stories such as "My child is too young to have noticed that," or "There's no way he picked up on that," but . . . no. If you've noticed something in your environment, your child has too. Children are, generally, helpless—they are keen observers because noticing changes (i.e., potential threats) is what allows them to seek safety.

Let's say you and your three-year-old daughter are building with blocks and your partner starts vacuuming in the hallway. A vacuum doesn't terrify most adults—we have life experience such that the vacuum noise is accompanied by a story we reflexively tell ourselves: this sound is a cleaning appliance, and we are safe. A young child, on the other hand, receives this as an unexpected change; she might cry or cling to a parent or jump in the opposite direction. In order to confirm your child's perception, you might say something like: "We were playing with blocks and then Daddy turned the vacuum on. That was loud . . . and you didn't expect that to happen . . . Loud things we don't expect can feel scary, I know. That was a vacuum and vacuums make loud noises! I'm right here with you. You're safe."

Your child isn't giving you a hard time or "making a big deal out of nothing" here. Remember, it's not the vacuum itself that scares the child, but the sudden loud noise she doesn't understand. The goal in this scenario isn't to have your child not notice the sound—

it's to have her develop a story about the sound. Once children learn to associate a vacuum sound with a narrative, and they feel a parent's supportive presence, the sound starts to become less scary.

This approach is equally important in situations a child might *not* visibly react to. Imagine you and your partner are arguing in the kitchen while your child is eating lunch. Things escalate to the point of loud voices, nasty words, and visibly angry facial expressions. Naming what's true might sound like, "Papa and I just used very loud voices. You were right to notice that." Would I say this even if my child kept eating his lunch, looking as if he didn't *need* an explanation? I absolutely would. I know that children are wired to notice and perceive, so I would assume that even if my child *appeared* calm, feelings of fear would be living inside his body and I wouldn't want him to be alone with them. Keep in mind, the beginning of my "loud voices" explanation was quite simple—I mentioned the voices and I validated my child's perceptions. This is really important. Telling the truth often involves delivering the simplest, most straightforward version of events. I often have to remind myself: "Only say what happened. Name what's true, and nothing more complicated." This allows me to give my child what he needs in the moment: my presence + a story to understand. From there, depending on the situation, I might do more. I might assure my child that he wasn't at fault (especially powerful when kids notice your big emotions or an argument between adults) or brainstorm a mantra to speak to my child's worry (this might be useful in the vacuum example: "That is loud, I am safe. That is loud, I am safe"). But all of this comes second to confirming a child's perceptions as accurate.

One reason why it's so necessary to confirm our children's perceptions is that when we *don't* name what's true, when we assume, "That wasn't a big deal," or "He's so young, I'm sure he didn't even notice," our children learn to *doubt* their perceptions. They might think, "Huh, I guess there wasn't anything that changed in my environment, I guess I was wrong," and, over time, that message sticks. It's as if we're training our kids to tune out what's happening around them, and that training will stick with them into adolescence and adulthood. Want your son to stand up to his friends and resist peer pressure? In order to say, "Hey, guys, this doesn't feel right. I'm not doing this," a child needs to believe in his perceptions of his environment and in his own feelings. Want your daughter to stand up for herself when she's uncomfortable in a hookup or dating scenario? If, when she was a child, her parents validated her perceptions and wired her for self-trust, she'll be more inclined to say, "No, I'm not comfortable with that," or "Stop. I don't like that."

Confirming our children's perceptions sets them up to recognize when things don't feel right later, and it will empower them to trust themselves enough to speak up. This ability doesn't develop on its own in adolescence or adulthood—it is wired into our bodies in our earliest years. And for those of you thinking, "Oh no! My child is a teenager and I totally didn't do this; I've missed the window!"—let's come back to the all-important principle of "it's not too late." We can always rewire. Talk to your adolescent about your parenting, about what you've realized, about how you want to do things differently. Try phrases like "You're allowed to feel that way" and "You're the only one in your body, so you're the only one who can know how you feel and what you want." You've got this.

Honoring Your Child's Questions

Next, let's think about questions—what are we to do when our kids ask questions that makes *us* feel uncomfortable, that feel too "mature" for their age? Questions like, "Are you going to die one day?" and "Okay, but how does the baby get *into* the belly? Like actually get *in* there?"

If you're like most parents, you have the urge to skirt around the truth or think, "My child isn't ready for this information!" Here's how I see it: when kids start asking these questions, they are ready for answers. Or at least the start of the answer, with real words and real truths, at which point you can pause and see if more explanation is needed. Despite how it may seem, asking a question doesn't entirely indicate ignorance—it also indicates awareness and readiness to learn. In order to ask a question, we have to have baseline knowledge and curiosity. Let's say I had a friend who was a physicist, and she said to me, "Becky, I'm doing a study on molecular photodissociation. I'm so excited! Ask me all the questions you have!" I would be pretty lost. I know nothing about molecular photodissociation, and I couldn't ask much besides "What is molecular photodissociation?" If I were able to produce a more complex question, I would be demonstrating an already complex knowledge about the topic. Kids who ask about death are already thinking about death. Kids who ask about the anatomical details of conception have already considered how it all happens. Kids who ask questions need answers so they aren't left alone with the feelings, thoughts, and images that *already* live inside them. So try to catch your "My kid isn't ready for this!" reflex and remind yourself, "Ready or not, the foundation is already there."

Labeling What You Don't Know

Sometimes, parents simply can't answer their kids' questions truthfully—not because they don't want to, but because they don't have the answers. Talking honestly with our children about *what we don't know* is an important iteration of the "tell the truth" principle. In the early days of the coronavirus pandemic, for example, parents would tell me, "I don't know what's going to happen, so

I can't reassure my child this will all end soon!" They'd use their lack of knowledge as an excuse for not talking to their kids about the virus and the changes in their lives. The thing is, kids don't need reassurance about the future. They need to feel supported in the current moment. They don't need answers, they need to not feel alone in their feelings. It's what adults need, too, and what we want to wire into our kids' bodies as early as possible: you won't always have answers, but you can always work on feeling safe and competent in the present moment.

When I don't have clear answers, I often use a "Here's what I don't know and here's what I do know" formula. "What I do know," in these cases, essentially just confirms my presence and my ability to be there for my child. That's all we ever *really* know, anyway. This might sound like, "You're worried about getting your blood drawn today. Exactly how long it will take and how much it will hurt, I don't know. What I do know is that it will hurt, and then it will stop hurting at some point. I will be with you the whole time, and we'll get through it together."

Let's take something bigger. Maybe you tell your child that his grandmother has cancer. He asks, "But is she going to be okay? Is she going to get all better?" Telling the truth about "I don't know" would sound like this: "What a great question. I hope she gets better, sweetie. And the truth is that . . . we don't know. We don't know if she will get better. What I do know is that I will tell you the truth, even if it feels uncomfortable, and that I am here for you with all the feelings you have about this."

Focusing on the How

Parents often get hung up on the *what* of communicating with honesty: "What should I say to my child to break the news that his grandfather died?" "What phrases should I use to explain home-lessness?" "What's the best way to tell my kid that the reason we don't see my brother anymore is that he's toxic and won't change?" Pause here. There are no perfect words to explain imperfect sit-uations. In fact, the *how* of our talking—the pace, the tone, the pausing, the checking in with our child, the rub on the back, the "What an important question" or "I'm so glad we are talking about this"—these factors are more impactful than any specific words. Even if there were some "perfect phrase," words delivered in a cold or distant manner, or that don't inquire about your child's experi-ence, will lead to his feeling confused, alone, and overwhelmed. It's your loving presence and attention to your child's experience that his body will remember the most.

When it's time to talk about hard truths, start by preparing your child for what's to come. I often say something like: "I want to talk about something that we'll all have big feelings about." Say this slowly and with eye contact. Afterward, take a deep breath—this will ground your body and also give your child an opportunity to "borrow" this regulation from you in a tough moment. Next, use real words, not euphemisms, to describe what's happening. This means saying, "Grandpa died today. Dying means the body stops working," rather than "Grandpa isn't here anymore," or "Grandpa went to sleep for a long time." After you've delivered a hard truth, pause. Before giving more information, check in with your child. You might ask, "How does it feel to talk about this?" or say, "It's okay to be sad about this. I feel sad too." Maybe you just look at your child with a supportive glance, placing your hand on his back.

If your child shares a feeling—with words ("I feel sad") or an ex-pression (crying, angry look on his face)—respond with acknowl-edgment, validation, and permission to feel. And if your child asks a question that you know has a tough answer, maybe start your response by saying, "That's such an important question. I am going to tell you the answer. It might feel hard to hear, but as we talk, I'm right here with you." In those moments, you might want to collect yourself before answering. "That's a great question and I want to give you a great answer. I need some time to get back to you—but I absolutely will because answering your questions is so important." The key here is to go back to your child with a response when you're ready, even if your child doesn't bring it up again. If you don't, your child will be left with *more* fear, because he'll be alone with the feelings and knowledge that inspired him to ask the question in the first place. Finally, remember: it's okay to cry. Label your feelings as your own and remind your child that you're still their strong parent who is here for them, even when your own feelings are pretty big. Because none of us is immune to emotion. Showing our children that we feel the tough stuff, that we struggle with it and still get through, is truly the best lesson you can give them.

CHAPTER 10

Self-Care

Here are some things I don't want my children to say about me when they're older: "My mom? She did everything for me," or "My mom always put me first," or "My mom never took care of herself, she was too busy caring for us." I hope they never say any version of, "My mom ran herself into the ground while she parented me."

What do I want my kids to say instead? How about: "My mom? She knew when she needed time for herself and balanced that with meeting my needs," or "My mom was an awesome model for self-care. She taught me the importance of taking care of myself, and how to do that while still being connected to someone else." Or maybe even, "My mom showed me that parenthood doesn't mean losing yourself. Parenthood means helping your child develop and grow while you yourself are developing and growing at the same time."

In today's world of intensive parenting, there's a common misconception that having kids means sacrificing your own identity — that once you're charged with taking care of young children, you are no longer entitled to take care of yourself. In reality, however, selfless parenting doesn't help anyone — it doesn't help the parents, who become depleted and resentful when they give so much of themselves without filling their own cups, and it doesn't help kids, who absolutely notice their parents' depletion and resentment and might feel guilty, anxious, or insecure in response.

There are plenty of reasons why parents struggle with self-care. They worry they're being "selfish," they feel pressure to dedicate every free moment to "bettering" their children or setting them up for "success," or they simply don't have the time and energy to do anything for themselves at the end of a long day. And for parents who work multiple jobs or long hours or who don't have reliable childcare, the concept of self-care may seem out of reach.

When parents are able to prioritize themselves, they often experience guilt—guilt that is only made worse when their children protest. For example, if you choose not to host a playdate (a small act of self-care!), your kid might be incredulous: "I can't have friends over today because you don't want anyone else in the house??" Or if you decide to take a walk to clear your head, you might hear: "You're going on a walk alone? Don't you want to be with me?" And on a night when you decide to socialize with your own friends, you may be faced with a kid-sized guilt trip: "You're going out to dinner tonight instead of putting me to bed?!?"

But despite all these indications to the contrary, kids actually feel comforted when parents set firm boundaries around self-care. Parents, after all, are the leaders of the family, and children want a sense of sturdiness and self-assurance in their leaders. Selfless parenting is parenting by a leader *without a self*, and that idea is terrifying to a child. Kids don't want to feel that their leader is someone who cannot be located, who is easily overrun by others, who is . . . lost.

No one is naturally wired to suppress their own needs in favor of meeting the needs of others. If you tend to sacrifice yourself in service of your family system, these values were likely transmitted to you at an early age, while your body's circuits were developing. So, if you have trouble prioritizing self-care, start with self-compassion. Remind yourself of this truth: "Over the course of my earlier years, it must have been *adaptive* to be *vigilant about the needs of others*, and this vigilance overpowered my attunement to my own needs." We must give our patterns respect and validation before we can take on the bold challenge of changing or trying something new. We have to understand our struggles in order to access our good-inside-ness, which is a necessary component of change. After we show ourselves this kindness, we can shift our self-talk and start to say: "I am working on a new pattern. I am trying to locate my own wants and needs and remind them they are worthy. Whenever I try something new, my body will feel uncomfortable; this discomfort is a sign that I'm wiring a new circuit, one that wasn't practiced in my earliest years. My discomfort is evidence of change . . . not evidence that I'm doing something wrong."

Self-care can also feel overwhelming if we frame our attempts at it as another item on the to-do list. "What? I have to change all this stuff in myself before I can change things with my kids?" But a simple reframe can transform self-care into something empowering and hopeful: "I have an opportunity. I can heal things within myself at the same time as I parent my kids in a way I feel proud of. I can do both at the same time."

I could write a whole book about parental self-care. In fact, I'd like to at some point, once I engage in the self-care I'll need after finishing *this* book—likely some rest and time away from writing in order to replenish and honor my body's need for stillness and recovery. In the meantime, I want to share with you some of my favorite self-care strategies, ones you can use right away, even if you have few resources to devote. Remember, we cannot pour energy into our kids if we have no energy to give. We cannot exude patience if we don't show ourselves patience. We cannot change externally until we have rewired internally. The quality of our relationships with others is only as good as the quality of the relationship we have with ourselves.

Self-Care Strategies

1. Breathing

I know, I know. Everyone talks about deep breathing and how important it is . . . blah blah blah. I get it. And yet, I can't skip this topic and I'd urge you not to as well. Here's why: every self-care strategy I offer relies on our ability to temporarily ground ourselves so that we have access to the parts of our brains that house these strategies. And there's nothing more grounding than a deep breath. So think of deep breathing as the key that unlocks the room where all your coping strategies live.

Deep breathing is effective because it regulates a number of important bodily processes, including those involved with lowering stress levels and reducing blood pressure. Diaphragmatic breathing, also known as "belly breathing," stimulates your *vagus nerve*, which is the longest and most complex cranial nerve in the body. The vagus nerve is a main component of your *parasympathetic nervous system*, or your "rest and restore" system (the opposite of your sympathetic or "fight or flight" system), and helps your body access feelings of safety and regulation. That's just a fancy way of saying that deep belly breathing activates the circuits in our bodies that start the calming-down process. When we're feeling upset, angry, frustrated, anxious, or out of control, the simple act of deep belly breathing will turn on the part of the brain that sends the message "You are safe . . . all will be okay . . . you'll weather this storm." Once our bodies start to *regulate*, we can make good decisions and interact with ourselves and others in ways that feel good.

How to Do It

I use something called "hot cocoa breaths." This is also what I teach my kids, so feel free to practice this one together.

- Sit comfortably on a chair with your legs uncrossed, your feet on the ground, and your back upright.
- Close your eyes or focus softly on a spot on the ground.
- Place one hand on your belly and the other on your chest.
- Imagine a cup of hot cocoa in front of you. Breathe in slowly to smell your hot chocolate. Breathe out so slowly that you don't blow off any marshmallows. You might imagine that you're holding a straw between your upper and lower lip; this helps us slow down the out-breath. **Long out-breaths are key to calming down.** Repeat five to ten times.
- It's normal for your thoughts to distract you. Label the thoughts as they come—say to yourself, "Hi, thought," or "Hi, worry," or "Hi, planning"—and then return to your next in-breath.

2. Acknowledge, Validate, Permit (AVP)

Avoiding your feelings never ends the way you want it to. In fact, the more you avoid distress or will it to go away, the worse it becomes. Our bodies interpret *avoidance* as confirmation of danger, and it triggers our internal alert system. The more energy we use to push emotions like anxiety or anger or sadness away, the more powerfully those emotions spring back up. Rather than avoiding emotions we'd rather not face, we need to make a shift. We need to say to ourselves, "[Anxiety/anger/sadness] is not my enemy. My [anxiety/anger/sadness] is allowed to be here. I can tolerate my discomfort." This tactic is useful for addressing any uncomfortable feeling. The next time you find yourself drowning in an emotion you'd rather avoid, remind yourself to *acknowledge, validate, permit*. If there's a secret recipe for self-regulation, that's it.

How to Do It

- **Acknowledge:** Label your feelings. For example: "This moment feels hard!" or "Today was *rough*!" or "I'm noticing anxiety right now," or "My chest feels tight and my heart is racing."

- **Validate:** Respect your feelings enough to assume they aren't lying to you. Now tell yourself a story about *why your feelings make sense*. This might sound like: "I'm exhausted. Caring for two kids and cooking dinner while they argue with each other . . . it makes sense that this feels hard." Or, "My boss yelled at me and then my friend canceled on dinner plans; it makes sense this day feels rough." Or, "I have so much going on, so much to do, and my brain is overloaded with tasks. It makes sense my body feels anxious and uptight." Reminding ourselves that our sensations and experiences "make sense" helps us feel more at home in our own bodies, so try using this phrase in your self-talk.

- **Permit:** Give yourself permission to have your feeling in whatever way it's showing up. I know this sounds silly, but it's so powerful. Tell yourself, out loud or internally, "I have full permission to feel like life is hard," or "I'm allowed to feel exactly as I do," or "It's okay to feel like parenting is totally unenjoyable right now." Now, remember: we can permit our anger and still remind ourselves to use a calm voice; we can permit our frustration and still remind ourselves to gaze kindly at our kids.

3. Getting Your Needs Met *and* Tolerating Distress

Time for an experiment! I want you to say the following sentence aloud, preferably in front of a mirror, and then observe how your body responds: "I am allowed to have things for myself even if they inconvenience others." Now pause. Does your body want to accept or reject what you just said? What's your natural reaction to that statement? Do any memories or images come to mind? The only goal here is to learn about yourself. One reaction isn't better than another; all data is good data.

Now, what did you notice? Were you uncomfortable? Did you feel an immediate need to correct yourself? Were you able to say it with conviction? Or was it hard to believe the words coming out of your mouth? Many of us have trouble asserting ourselves *and* tolerating someone else's being inconvenienced by those assertions, whether we're asking for help, taking time for ourselves, or even relegating childcare to our partner. We find it so difficult that we often end up undoing our request, saying, "Never mind, I can just do it myself," or "I guess I can walk with my friend at a different time," or "Okay, fine, I'll get up in the morning with the kids." These comments often come up at the end of a pattern. First, you want something for yourself. Next, you suggest or ask for it. Then, a partner or friend seems inconvenienced. Finally, you take back your request and don't get your need met.

It's time to change this pattern—but we can only do that when we accept that we cannot avoid someone else's inconvenience or distress; it's not our job to make sure someone else is happy, and it's not someone else's job to cheerlead us as we assert ourselves. We need *cooperation* from others, but not *approval*.

I regularly remind myself that in order to get what I need, someone else might have to be inconvenienced or annoyed, and this is okay. Someone else's distress shouldn't be a reason why I can't meet my own needs. Understanding and accepting this allows me to, say, go for a walk on my own without guilt. If my partner seems annoyed, I try to greet that feeling with an "Ugh, I know, it's hard to be with the kids on your own, I hear that," and still walk out the door. It allows me to remember that I can choose where the family is ordering dinner from, even if one of my kids complains. If I really want sushi and not pizza, I have to be willing to tolerate my son's pushback. Many of us were raised to take in another person's distress as our responsibility, so when we see our partners or friends or kids get upset when we assert ourselves or say no, we backtrack. Taking a breath and remembering that **often the only way we get our needs met is by simultaneously tolerating others' distress** helps prevent us from losing ourselves.

How to Do It

- Tell yourself, "Someone else is allowed to be upset when I assert myself; this doesn't make them a bad person and it doesn't make me unable to uphold my decision."
- Visualize yourself on one side of a tennis court and someone else on the other side. Remind yourself, "I am over here . . . I have my need and my decision on my side. He is over THERE, on his own side. His feelings about my decisions . . . those are on HIS side of the court, not mine. I can see them, I can even empathize with them . . . but I didn't cause them and I don't need to make them go away."

4. One Thing for Myself

If self-care is especially hard for you, start with one thing you can do for yourself. The key here is not to start too big—don't immediately try for a thirty-minute workout class or a strict nine P.M. bedtime. Begin with something that makes you think, "I'm pretty sure I can do that." Self-care involves making and keeping promises to ourselves, even in the midst of lives that are filled with caring for others. If you haven't done much of that, you'll need to practice building your muscle for self-prioritization and self-worth.

Here's a list of small self-care activities to get you started:

- Drink one glass of water in the morning
- Meditate for two minutes
- Drink your coffee while it's hot
- Cook yourself a legitimate breakfast
- Listen to calming music
- Read a few pages of a book
- Have a good cry
- Take five hot cocoa breaths while seated
- Rest in child's pose
- Color
- Talk to a friend
- Brush your hair
- Journal

Doing one thing for ourselves often depends on our ability to say no to others who are, at that exact moment, asking us for something. Below are some scripts for saying no that will make your "one thing for myself" time more successful:

- "Ah . . . no, that doesn't work for me."
- "No, I can't."
- "I appreciate your asking me. No, I'm not free."
- "I am doing something for myself right now, so you have to wait a few moments."
- "No, I cannot come right now. I know waiting is hard and I know you can figure out something to do before I get there."

5. Repair—with Yourself

I know one thing about every parent reading this book: you want to be there for your kids, you want to parent in a way that makes sense and feels right, and you want to raise children who feel good about themselves and put goodness out into the world. You're spending time reading this book, which means that you are willing to spend the most precious commodity of all—your attention—on reflecting, learning, growing, and experimenting.

I also know that many of you are cycle-breakers. You are the pivot point in your family, you're the one saying, "Toxic relationship patterns stop with *me*. I will be passing on something different, something better, to my kids." Being a cycle-breaker is an epic role. You are amazing.

And here's something else I know: You're going to mess up. You're going to yell. You're going to say something and think, "Ugh, why did I say that? I didn't want to say that!" But that's okay. You are not defined by your reactivity or your moments of depletion or your latest behavior. You are a parent who is good inside, and you are working on yourself at the same time as you are giving to your kids.

Self-care involves getting really good at repair. We have to be generous with ourselves when we make mistakes or behave in ways we don't feel good about. This book talks a lot about repairing with our kids, but to repair well with others, we must start by repairing ourselves.

How to Do It

- Place a hand on your heart and tell yourself: "It's okay to struggle. It's okay to make mistakes. It's okay to not know. It's okay to not have it all together. Even as I am having a hard time on the outside . . . I remain good inside. I am good inside."

- When parenting moments, specifically, have you feeling mad at yourself or disappointed in your own reactions, tell yourself: "I am not my latest behavior. I am not my latest behavior."

PART II

BUILDING CONNECTION
AND
ADDRESSING BEHAVIORS

CHAPTER 11

Building Connection Capital

During a recent consult, the parents of two young children opened our conversation with a plea. "Dr Becky, we don't know where to start," they said. "Our house is a mess. There's so much yelling, and we're always making empty threats because we don't know what else to do. Our kids don't listen to us, and it feels like we're in an endless cycle of tantrums with our four-year-old and rudeness with our seven-year-old. Heston, our oldest, is suddenly saying he's stupid and has no friends, and whenever we try to talk to him about it he says we don't understand and slams his bedroom door. Izzy, our four-year-old, is hysterical every morning when we drop her at preschool. It's so draining and such an awful way to start the day. PLEASE HELP!"

I took a breath. "First of all, I'm so glad you're here," I said. "Second of all, I am going to solve *all* of that. Every single thing."

They laughed. I smiled. I started again. "Okay, that's not true. We aren't going to solve any of it, at least not today. Here's the thing: we can't change behavior until we build connection, so our first interventions need to focus on that. The real problem here isn't any of the specific issues you named—it's not the tantrums or the back talk or the door slamming or drop-off crying. The real problem, it seems, is that your family system is out of balance. No one feels secure or safe."

At this point, these parents seemed to breathe easier. Just hearing someone identify an issue—one that truly resonated with their experience—and sound confident in a path forward was a relief. So instead of discussing yelling or empty threats, we began our conversation with connection. I presented these parents with a handful of what I call "bang-for-your-buck connection-builders." These are the tried-and-true strategies I return to time and again—in my own home and with my clients—when families need to reconnect and get back in balance. Some of these tools, and their more practical applications, might seem like "ideal world" strategies—but I believe there is something here for everyone. It doesn't matter if the imbalance in your family is manifesting as rudeness, lying, sibling rivalry, tantrums, or any of the other specific behavioral issues I'll address in the chapters that follow—these strategies ignite positive change regardless of the surface issue, because they help parents reorient their efforts toward building connection and closeness with their kids, rather than correcting a behavior. Because, as we know by now, behavior is never the problem; it's only the symptom. Bang-for-your-buck strategies get to the root issues and, as a result, build more peaceful homes.

As I explained to my clients, when parents struggle with their kids, it almost always boils down to one of two problems: children don't feel as connected to their parents as they want to, or children have some struggle or unmet need they feel alone with. Imagine your child has an emotional bank account. The currency in this bank account is connection, and their behavior at any moment reflects the status of their account, how full or depleted it is. I mentioned earlier the idea of this "connection capital"—when we really connect with a child, see their experience, allow for their feelings, and make an effort to understand what's going on for them, we build our capital. Having a healthy amount of connection capital leads kids to feel confident, capable, safe, and worthy. And these positive feelings on the inside lead to "good" behavior on the outside—behavior like cooperation, flexibility, and regulation. So in order to create positive change, we have to first build connection, which will lead kids to *feel* better, which will then lead them to *behave* better. But note, behavior comes last. We cannot start there. We must start with connection.

It's also important to keep in mind that connection capital flows two ways. Like a bank account, we draw from our connection capital regularly. Parents spend connection capital when we ask kids to clean their rooms, when we tell them we need a few minutes for an unexpected work call, when we say, "Time to leave, sweetie," or "Screen time is over." Parents are big connection capital spenders, because we often have to ask kids to do things they don't want to do and to respect our rules when they'd rather not. **This means that parents need to be even bigger connection-builders.** We need a strong reserve to draw from so that we don't run out of funds.

Here's the kicker when it comes to connection-building: we get the biggest bang for our buck when we're calm. Trying to connect in the heat of the moment is not especially effective, because our bodies don't learn well when they're in fight-or-flight mode. During calmer moments, we can slow down, connect with our kids, see their goodness, and develop stronger relationships. The following interventions are meant to be used in calmer moments, prime time for improving your relationship with your child, building new skills, and developing pathways for change. When things feel off in my own family, I begin with these strategies, which essentially result in connection capital deposits.

Play No Phone (PNP) Time

Play No Phone (PNP) Time is the parenting strategy I recommend most often. When it comes to bang for your buck, nothing else even comes close.

PNP Time is exactly what it sounds like: phone-free playtime. I came up with PNP Time after realizing how distracting it is to have my phone anywhere near me as I try to engage with my child. With my phone in the room, I always feel pulled to check it: to respond to that text message, place an Amazon order, or do the million other things that come up in a day. I can promise myself I won't go near it, that instead I'll play that game of Quirkle or build with blocks . . . but the pull is just too strong.

Our kids want our full attention more than anything else. Our attention communicates that they are safe, important, valuable, loved. And yet, our devices are powerful magnets for our attention, and our kids feel that distraction. To be clear, I'm not arguing against technology or using devices. I'm suggesting that we create *boundaries around devices*—not only for our kids but for ourselves. We need boundaries around our device use so that we can *help ourselves* to give our kids our full attention. Not all the time. But definitely some of the time.

Spending time with your child when you are fully present is the most powerful way to build connection capital. Have a child who struggles to listen? PNP Time to the rescue. Have a child who is angry and rude? PNP Time will help. Have two kids arguing all day? Start a PNP Time routine for each. I could go on, but you get the point.

PNP Time only needs to last 10–15 minutes. The goal is to enter your child's world—which is very different from the rest of a child's day in which we, over and over, ask them to enter our world. During PNP Time, allow your child to direct the play and take time to witness and notice but not direct—your presence in their world is what matters most.

And here's one of the best parts of PNP Time: Play becomes more enjoyable to *parents*. Without a phone in the room, we can more easily focus on play. During PNP Time, I tell myself, "Becky, there's nothing more important than doing exactly what you're doing right now," or "I don't need to be doing anything else. Playing with my son is enough. I am enough"—and without my phone in the room seemingly calling on me to "do more," I can actually settle into play.

Ok, let's get practical and talk about how to implement PNP Time in your home:

1. Give it a name to indicate that this time is special. I use the term PNP Time because I happen to love a good acronym and, also, there's something a bit silly about the term that my kids really like. Feel free to name it something else, like Daddy-Marco Time or Mommy-Daughter time.
2. Limit time to ten to fifteen minutes.
3. No phones, no screens, no siblings, no distractions.
4. Let your child pick the play. This is key.
5. Allow your child to be in the spotlight; your job is only to notice, imitate, reflect, and describe what they're doing.

It's important to actively state that you are putting your phone away. This shows your child that you're aware of how distracting a phone can be and ensures that they feel seen and special.

Here are scripts for introducing PNP Time:

- *For younger kids:* "Let's have some PNP Time! I'm going to put my phone in another room so I can really focus on being with you. It'll be just us, and you can choose what we do!"

- *For older kids:* "Hey, sweetie. You know what? I need PNP Time with you—just you and me, with my phone far away—because I know it's annoying when it makes noise and distracts me. How about later today we get some time just us? It will last for ten to fifteen minutes, and you can pick what we do."

Remember, PNP Time is focused on your child's world. Try to avoid asking questions; instead, join in your child's ideas. If this feels unnatural, that's okay! Most parents are unused to engaging in this way. Try these approaches:

- *Describe:* "You're building a tower," or "You're coloring with a red crayon."
- *Mimic:* If your child is drawing a flower, grab your own piece of paper, sit near her, and draw your own flower. No need for any words. When you mirror, you show your child that you're paying full attention and they are valuable and interesting to you.
- *Reflective listening:* When your child says, "I want to play trucks!" respond with, "You want to play trucks!" If your child says, "The pig wants to come into the barn," say back, "That pig wants to go into the barn, huh?"

If these ideas feel awkward, remember that the goal is simply to spend uninterrupted, distraction-free quality time with your child. And if fifteen minutes isn't possible? Try ten or five or two. PNP Time makes kids feel important and loved, and once those feelings are in place, improved behavior will eventually follow.

The Fill-Up Game

I invented this game when my eldest child was having a hard time adjusting to my youngest's birth, and I've used it ever since. My son was being obstinate, rude, quick to anger . . . all the stuff that made me want to spend *less* time around him. But I soon realized that he was really struggling. Underneath his anger were questions: "Will I still be noticed?" "Will I get my needs met?" "Will I get enough of Mommy and Daddy?" He was in so much distress over the transition to becoming a family of five that his emotional bank account felt nearly empty. He needed an influx of connection capital at the very moment that his behaviors were pushing me away.

And so I created the Fill-Up Game. Every time my son was difficult, instead of reacting, I'd take a deep breath and say, slowly and warmly, "I think you're trying to tell me that you're not filled up with Mommy." My softening led to his softening, and he'd often reply by saying something like, "Yeah . . . I'm only up to here," and point somewhere on his legs. Then I'd give him giant hugs and squeezes, over and over, until the "Mommy level" moved all the way up to the top of his head, at which point I would give him one more big squeeze so he had "a bit extra Mommy" to get him through the next little while. And did his behavior improve? No. Not right away. This "game" didn't change things on a dime, but it was absolutely a turning point. It was the first step, because it made concrete exactly what my kid needed: *more of his parent*.

The next time your child's behavior is making you want to run in the opposite direction, try introducing the Fill-Up Game. Offer the idea that your child's defiant behavior is the result of not being filled up with Mommy (or Daddy), and so it must be time to get a big dose. Add silliness and laughter.

Once you see how beneficial the Fill-Up Game really is—you'll likely see "evidence" in your child's softening and in your own softening as well—you might want to start doing fill-ups proactively, before your child's tank gets so low that she has to let you know with her rude tone or dysregulated behavior. Maybe you fill up before your kids start playing Legos together or before you tell them to start their nighttime routine. Ask them, "Can I fill everyone up with Mommy before we start?" and then play the Fill-Up Game with each child.

Script for Introducing the Fill-Up Game

1. Tell your child, "I don't think you are filled up with Mommy/Daddy right now. I think Mommy is only up to your ankles! Let's fill you up!"
2. Give your child a long tight squeeze.
3. "How about now? Whaaaat? Only to your knees? Okay, round two . . ."
4. Squeeze your child again; maybe grimace, as if you're using all your might.
5. "What? Only to your belly? I thought I got higher with that squeeze! Okay, more Mommy coming, round three . . ."
6. Once you or your child feels filled up, give one more squeeze, saying: "Okay, well let me give you some extra, just in case. There are so many changes these days, it's probably good to have some extra Mommy stored up in there."

When to play the Fill-Up Game:

- When your kids wake up in the morning, as a way to start the day.
- Before any separation. The Fill-Up Game makes concrete the idea that your child can *internalize* a parent before saying goodbye.
- Before you start your workday. The Fill-Up Game allows your child to hold on to you.

- Before a moment you know will be tricky (for example, before you ask your son to share his toys with his younger sister; before he comes into the kitchen, where his younger sister is using his favorite plate; before your child starts doing a puzzle that you know will be challenging).
- In response to difficult behavior. Interpreting a child's behavior through a lens of goodness and connection capital is a real gift. "Filling them up" with you builds their emotion regulation capacity by making them feel good and safe inside.

Emotional Vaccination

Emotional vaccination works just like a vaccination for an illness: we strengthen our bodies today so we're more prepared to cope with hardship in the future. As we know, humans cope with difficult moments not by changing or avoiding their feelings but by learning to regulate their feelings. If your child struggles to end screen time, they won't one day be happy to give up the screen or have sudden "perspective" that allows for an easy iPad handoff; instead, they will (hopefully) be able to acknowledge, validate, and allow their emotions, which will lead to a smoother transition from iPad to no iPad. If your child struggles with being a gracious loser in board games or sports, they won't suddenly have a less competitive spirit or an "it's just a game" attitude that allows for good sportsmanship; instead, they will acknowledge, validate, and permit their emotions, which will lead to a deep breath and a more gracious ending.

So if the goal is regulating our emotions rather than fixing, changing, or erasing them, how can we help our children with their recurring difficult moments? Here's one powerful strategy: we prepare for the emotional struggles ahead. With emotional vaccination, we connect with our children *before* a big-feelings

moment, thereby strengthening regulation skills before our child
needs to use them. We connect with our kids, discuss and validate
the challenge they might soon face, and verbalize or even rehearse
how we might handle it—all before it happens. By connecting,
validating, and anticipating, we build up our child's "emotion
regulation antibodies" before the full-force emotion arises. In
this way, we are *pre-regulating* a feeling, and when the challenging moment comes, our child is more equipped to handle it. That
doesn't mean she will suddenly be a good sport when she loses at
Sorry!, but as we all know, practice is key to progress.

Remember, kids' most dysregulated moments occur when they feel
emotions intensely and *in a state of aloneness*; emotional vaccination
also gives us an opportunity to infuse connection into these moments
before they even occur. This helps to interrupt the meltdown cycle.

And here's another powerful takeaway: while our children can
benefit from emotional vaccination, so can we. Visualize a situation that might be tough for you today. Now, direct inward caring,
understanding, and allowing in advance: "I am allowed to feel this
way. I am going to take a deep breath now, in anticipation . . . and
maybe I'll find that deep-breath-and-compassion circuit when the
moment itself comes." You'd be surprised how powerful it can be.

Scripts for Emotional Vaccination

**Emotional Vaccination = Connection + Validation + A Story to
Understand**, all carried out before the "main event." Here are two
examples of how it might sound:

Emotional Vaccination to Prepare for the End of Screen Time

> PARENT: *"Before we begin screen time, let's think about how
> it's going to feel when we end. It's hard to stop things we love,
> right? For me too."*

CHILD: *"Can you just turn the show on now?"*
PARENT: *"We will, soon. I'm going to take a deep breath now and get my body ready for when we stop watching screens."* Model this pause. *"Also . . . I'm wondering if we can get out some of those end-of-screen-time protests now, to get our bodies ready."* Find a lighthearted, but not mocking, tone as you protest: *"Five more minutes! My friends get so much more! I was just about to . . . please please . . . you never let me do anything I want to do!"*

- **What are you doing here?** You're infusing connection and silliness into a difficult transition *before* it happens. This doesn't mean that at the end of the show, your child will say, "Here's the iPad, Mom, easy-breezy!"; it does mean that you're building the skill of managing tough emotions, and there will be a moment soon that your child looks at you and says, "Aw, I wish I could watch another episode!" instead of screaming and throwing a remote control.

Emotional Vaccination for Challenging Academic Work

PARENT: *"I'm thinking about your homework and how it might feel hard when you sit down to do your writing. I totally get that. I always found writing really hard, and annoying too."*
CHILD: *"Yeah."*
PARENT: *"I'm wondering if we can take a deep breath together, now. I read that if we anticipate difficulty and talk to ourselves in advance, the moment feels a little easier."* It's okay if your child doesn't engage. Still: place a hand on your heart and look toward the floor or close your eyes and say, *"When writing begins, I may get frustrated. That's okay! I'm going to take a deep breath now,*

in advance, and remind myself that it's okay that writing feels hard and also remind myself that I can do hard things!"

- **What are you doing here?** Loading up on connection and validation before a challenging moment arrives.

The Feeling Bench

One thing we know about feelings is that they are only scary if we are alone with them. If someone says to us, "Hey! You're feeling [sad/scared/angry/left out]. That's okay. I'm here. Tell me more," the feelings immediately start to subside. We no longer feel so over-whelmed. We feel safer.

When kids are upset, it's as if they are plopped down on the bench of that feeling. It may be an Angry Bench or Disappointed Bench or even a Nobody-Likes-Me Bench. And what kids (and also adults) want when they're on a bench, especially the dark uncomfortable ones, is someone to sit with them. Once someone sits with us, the bench doesn't feel so dark and cold. Now we have a "bench warmer."

When your son tells you, "I wish I didn't have a younger brother, he's always messing up my stuff!," imagine that he's on the It's-Hard-to-Share-My-Life Bench. Sit with him. You might also need to set a boundary, but you can still sit: "Ah, you're thinking about how hard it is to share. I get that, honey. I won't let you hit; you can still feel all that anger. I'm here with you."

When your daughter is processing her best friend's move to a different town and yells at you, "Why can't our family move so I can still be with Liv? I hate living here and I hate all of you!," first, take a deep breath. Under this attack is a feeling, and she is asking for validation and support. She's on the Loss Bench. Sit with her: "I hear you. This totally sucks."

And . . . try sitting with yourself on *your* bench. Find the part of you that is comforting (she's there! Always!) and ask her to sit with the part of you that's scared or sad or self-critical. Say to the part of you that's feeling overwhelmed: "I'm here, overwhelmed feeling. I see you. I'll listen to you. You're a part of me, not all of me. I'll sit with you."

Scripts for Sitting on Your Child's Feeling Bench

The next time your child tells you about a difficult feeling, remind yourself: "Sit with him. Sit down on this bench without making any attempt to pull him off. This is how I am building connection with him and resilience inside of him." Show your child you are right there with him, rather than asking him to feel another way.

Words

- "That sounds really hard."
- "That stinks. It really does."
- "I'm so glad you're talking to me about this."
- "I believe you."
- "Being a kid right now . . . ugh, it feels so so hard. I get that."
- "You're really sad about that. You're allowed to be, sweetie."
- "I'm right here with you. I'm so glad we're together talking about this."
- "Sometimes we don't have a way to feel better right away. Sometimes when things feel tough, the best we can do is talk nicely to ourselves and talk to people who understand."
- "I love you. I love you the same no matter how you're feeling and no matter what is happening in your life."

Actions

- Sit on the couch or the bed with your child as they talk to you.
- Say very little as they talk. Nod. Look sympathetic.
- Offer your child a hug while they're upset.
- Breathe deeply together.

Playfulness

Parenting can feel really serious. There are so many logistics ("You have school, then I'll pick you up and take you to the dentist, then drop you at soccer, then homework, dinner, and early to bed, okay?"), and it's easy to get locked into a relationship with your child that feels exasperating, frustrating, and just plain unenjoyable. In my practice, I find that an element missing in lots of families is playfulness. Silliness. Ridiculousness. FUN.

Fun is important. Really important. Silliness and playfulness are amazing connection capital builders. Laughter reduces stress hormones like cortisol and adrenaline and increases antibodies and immune cells—which means laughter is actually pretty serious business, since our bodies become healthier every time we giggle or let loose. Plus, silly dance parties and made-up songs and tag games make kids feel important, safe, and loved. Since one of our main jobs as parents is to help our children feel safe, playfulness is one of the most important aspects of parenting; we can't laugh when we sense danger or threats, so laughing with our kids sends the message "This is your secure family home. You are protected here. You can be yourself here."

Playfulness comes easier for some parents than others. If it comes naturally for you, you can skip to the next paragraph. But if acting silly with your kids feels awkward or unnatural—if you consider yourself more of a serious parent—then take a moment to remind yourself that self-awareness is the first step. Every parent struggles with some aspect of parenting, whether it's setting boundaries, dealing with conflict, playfulness, or something else entirely. And if playfulness is hard for you, it's likely that it was never *modeled* for you. Oftentimes, parents who struggle to be playful with their kids grew up in households that, early on, shut down a child's silliness with shame ("You are embarrassing me, stop that right now!"), ignoring (a parent who disengaged when a child wanted to play a game or act goofy), or even punishment ("There's no place for potty language here. Go to your room!"). If this was the case in your house, you likely learned to distance yourself from your playfulness, because we disconnect from the parts of ourselves that receive negative attention early on. It might help to revisit the last chapter, on self-care, for some ideas on reconnecting with your playful side. That part of you is in there, it's just quiet and understandably timid to emerge.

I've listed a few ideas for playful activities below, but please know there are a million ways to be silly. If the kids are laughing, there's a levity in the air, and you're not focused on any deliverable or outcome, you're doing it right.

Suggestions for playfulness:

- Silly dance parties.
- "Talent Show"—everyone in the family gets called to the "stage," one at a time, to do some silly movement. Everyone else watches with amazement and then claps wildly as the person takes a bow. If you have a child who wants to watch and not participate, that's perfectly fine; no pushing or shaming. (I

have to give a shout-out to my kids' amazing babysitter Jordan for creating this!)

- Making up songs or rhymes.
- Family karaoke.
- Playing dress-up, playing house, or other fantasy play.
- Building a fort.
- Use playfulness as a first response to missed manners, not listening, or whining. Examples: "Oh no, the thank-yous are missing again! Okay, okay, where can they be . . . oh wait, wait, I found them! Under the couch! Let me get them back into you. Okay! Got it. Whew!"
- Ask yourself: "What did I like to play when I was a kid? What did I always want someone to do with me?" I once worked with a family in which the father really struggled to play with his kids; he lit up as he remembered playing the game Crossfire as a child, then ordered it online to play with his own children. This was the first step down the pathway of connecting through playfulness.

"Did I Ever Tell You About the Time . . . ?"

The trickiest relationship moments between parents and kids usually arise when we're stuck in a difficult behavioral cycle—our kid acts out, we react and yell something like, "How are you doing that *again*?," and then our kid shuts down, won't talk to us, and we feel at a total loss. When we get into these cycles, the problem becomes too "hot" to handle directly. There's too much shame (in kids) and reactivity (in parents), and almost always, our attempts to work through the issue get met with rejection ("You don't understand me, get out of my room!") or continued escalation (you try to talk to your child about the issue only to get into an even larger struggle around it). As a result, we have to find a strategy that allows us not to tackle the problem head-on, but to meander around it—to go in the back door rather than trying to barge in through the front.

Enter, "Did I ever tell you about the time . . . ?" This approach— which involves the parent's relating to the child's struggle from a personal perspective—builds connection, acknowledges a child's good-inside-ness, and teaches problem-solving skills, all without talking about the problem directly, which can feel too intense for a kid in the moment.

Script for "Did I Ever Tell You About the Time . . . ?"

1. Identify the essence of your child's struggle. (Is it hard for her to feel happy for other people's accomplishments? Hard to stay engaged when math feels hard and frustrating?)
2. Take on the problem as your own: remember a moment, in the recent past or when you were a child, when you struggled with something similar.
3. Talk to your child *not* in the heat of the moment but when things are calm, starting with, "Did I ever tell you about the time . . . ?," and share a story about yourself having a similar struggle.
4. Engage your child in this story, ideally one where you didn't come up with a quick fix but struggled and just kind of got through it.
5. Do not end your story by directly relating it to your child. There's no need to spell out, "Isn't that just like when you . . . ?" Allow the story and moment to stand on their own, trusting that it will reach the part of your child that needed connection.

Why is this strategy so effective? Why does it give so much bang for your buck? First, when you share a story of struggling in the same way as your child, you're essentially saying, "You're good inside. You're lovable. You're worthy. You're a good kid having a hard time. I see that goodness under your behavior, *because I am good and I had the same struggle.*" You can't say that to your child directly in this moment, because it would feel too intense and they'd reject it, but by telling this story about yourself, all these themes come through.

Second, you're connecting deeply, because you're showing your child your vulnerabilities. We forget that our children tend to see us as infallible. After all, we can so easily do all the things they struggle with—from simple things like putting on a jacket and tying shoes to more complex things like math problems or driving a car. The gap between a child's world of struggle and a parent's world of capability is intimidating for kids, and it can be (unintentionally) shame inducing. Any of us would have trouble learning and trying new things if we were surrounded only by experts all the time. Imagine trying to learn to cook with a famous chef watching over your shoulder or learning to play tennis with Roger Federer by your side. It's much easier to learn to cook with someone who knows more than you but still burns garlic sometimes, or to learn to play tennis with an instructor who was a college player but still sometimes double-faults. These people know a lot but not too much. When they model their struggles, they essentially say to us, without ever using these words: "Mistakes are a part of learning. Goodness isn't the absence of struggling. Two things can be true: you can be good and you can struggle . . . just like me." Ah . . . relief. This is what we want to give to our kids.

But the most powerful part of this strategy? As you tell a story describing yourself struggling with a problem that mimics your child's, something amazing happens: your child can access her own inner problem-solver. This is much harder when she's considering the problem as her own and her problem-solving self is overwhelmed. When she hears your story, she'll probably brainstorm or offer ideas, and as she does this for you, she'll be strengthening her own problem-solving circuit, and it will become more accessible to her when she needs it. This happens for adults too, right? Sometimes it's the act of talking about other people's problems that activates a light bulb inside of us, igniting a thought or urge to change that we didn't have when the discussion was focused on us directly. It often takes externalizing a struggle to reduce the shame and self-blame inside of us, which frees up the space for our more compassionate, problem-solving voices to emerge.

Change the Ending

We all mess up. You do. I do. The "perfect parent" on Instagram does. We yell, we react, we take out our own stuff on our kids, we blame, we label . . . we do all this not because we are bad parents but because we are normal humans. So when we have moments with our kids that feel awful, what should we do next? Repair. As we discussed in chapter 5, repair offers us the opportunity to *change the ending to the story*; instead of a child's encoding a memory where she felt scared and alone (and remember, even if a child doesn't bring it up, the memory is stored in the body), she now has a memory of a parent returning and helping her feel safe again. This is everything.

I often think that healthy relationships are defined not by a lack of rupture but by how well we repair. All relationships have rough patches, and yet, these moments can be the greatest sources of deepening connection. A rupture moment occurs because both people are in their own experience, and they are unable to temporarily put that experience to the side to understand and connect to the other person. Even if we're working on understanding our triggers, or trying to become more self-aware so that we recognize our experiences without letting them take over, we still can't avoid rupture moments in our close relationships—not with our friends or spouses and certainly not with our kids. So we need to get better at repair.

And yes, there is a difference between repairing and apologizing. Oftentimes, apologies attempt to shut down a conversation ("I'm sorry I yelled. Okay, can we move on?"), but a good repair opens one up. A repair goes further than an apology, because it looks to reestablish a close connection after a moment when someone feels hurt, misunderstood, or alone. The words "I'm sorry" might be *part* of a repair, but they are rarely the entirety of the experience.

Script for Changing the Ending

1. Share that you've been *reflecting*.
2. *Acknowledge* the other person's experience.
3. State what you would *do differently* next time.
4. Connect through *curiosity* now that things feel safer.

Here's an example of a repair with all four components: "I keep thinking about earlier today [*reflection*], when I came into the playroom after you knocked over your sister's tower. I'm sure you were upset about something to have knocked it down [*acknowledgment*]. I'm sorry I yelled. I wish I had asked more about what was going on for you instead [*what to do differently*]. Can I have a redo? Can you tell me what was happening before you knocked it down? It's important. I'd love to listen and understand [*curiosity*]."

When someone reflects with you ("I've been thinking about...") and acknowledges your feelings ("You must have been upset to have..." or "That must have felt scary when I...."), they make it clear they they're considering your state of mind instead of just your surface-level behavior. As we already know, looking at the feelings underneath the behavior is how we help our kids start to build emotional awareness and emotion regulation. So when we change the ending, we're not only strengthening our relationship with our child but we are helping them build regulation skills. Talk about . . . well, bang for your buck!

Next, when we share what we wish we had done differently, we let someone know that we take our actions seriously; we are not only taking responsibility for what we did, but we're holding ourselves accountable for making a change. And when we're brave enough to express curiosity about someone else's experience during our tough moments, we forge closeness, because in acknowledging that our apology doesn't undo their pain, we are signaling that we care more about their feelings and their reality than our pride or comfort. We also learn more about the other person, thereby deepening our relationship because we are willing to hear their truth.

Now, let me be clear: I don't always go through all four components with my own kids. Sometimes I say, "I'm sorry for yelling" (*reflecting*) or "I reacted harshly to your question and I am guessing that felt really bad to you . . . I see that and I'm sorry and I love you" (*reflecting* and *acknowledging*). Or I say, "I was in a bad mood yesterday—I was stressed about work and it wasn't your fault when I got annoyed that you didn't like dinner. That was a me thing, not a you thing, and I wish I hadn't taken it out on you," (*reflecting, acknowledging, saying what I'd do differently*). So, of course, feel free to repair in a way that feels right to you. Some repairs will be shorter and others lengthier. Overall, the key is to take ownership and tell your kids that *they aren't responsible for causing your feelings or fixing your reactions*. When kids are alone with tough feelings, they turn to self-blame ("I'm a bad kid") and self-doubt ("Maybe I overreacted? Maybe that wasn't a yell? Maybe this is how I should just expect to be treated by others?"); when we repair, we ensure that kids don't default to these explanations, which helps to preserve their confidence and sense of safety in the world. And remember: nothing feels as awful to kids as the painful feelings they are *left alone with*; repair replaces this aloneness with connection, and this should be the ultimate trade-up for all of us.

CHAPTER 12

Not Listening

> Sonia, a mother of two young children, arrived in my office in a state of exasperation. "My son Felix ignores everything I say and doesn't do anything I ask him to do," she tells me. "He has no respect, so of course I end up yelling. What else can I do? Help me, Dr Becky!"

When we say "*My kid doesn't listen,*" we're not really talking about listening. I've never heard a parent complain their child doesn't listen when they say, "Ice-cream sundaes are on the kitchen table!" or "You can start an extra TV show now!" What we're really talking about in situations like Sonia's is cooperation. We *say* "My kid won't listen," but what we *mean* is "My kid won't cooperate when I want him to do something he doesn't want to do."

How do *we*, as adults, behave when someone asks us to do something we don't want to do? Well, that usually depends on how close we feel, in the moment, to the person making the request. If I'm feeling really good about my marriage and my husband asks me to grab him something on my way home from work, I'll probably say yes. But if I've recently been feeling unappreciated or misunderstood, I'm more likely to tell him I don't have time.

The more connected we feel to someone, the more we want to comply with their requests. Listening is essentially a barometer for the strength of a relationship in any given moment. So when our kids aren't listening to us, it's critical to frame the struggle not as a child problem but as a relationship problem. If your child ignores you or rarely cooperates with your requests, he's trying to tell you that your relationship needs some TLC. Now, to be clear, this is not a referendum on your parenting . . . you are not a bad parent, you don't have a bad kid, and your relationship with your child isn't in the gutter. All **parent-child relationships need extra love and attention sometimes.** In my house, with my three kids, I am constantly receiving feedback (in the form of a kid not listening) that I need to slow down, think about each child's unique needs, and do some relationship strengthening. When this happens, I try to set aside time to consider what's going on for that child, what must feel hard or frustrating, and why my child might be feeling "unseen" or pushed to the side. That doesn't mean I'm taking on blame, but I *am* taking responsibility for thinking through why my child might feel distant and what parts of our relationship need attention. I remind myself that connection always increases cooperation, because we all like to help the people we feel close to.

There's a second element to the not-listening problem too. My oldest son made this point once: "Parents are always asking kids to stop doing something fun to do something less fun. That's why kids don't listen." I think he's right. Maybe our child is playing with blocks and we want her to transition to the bath, or she's eating chocolate chip pancakes and we want her to put on her shoes to leave the house, or she's watching TV and we want her to turn it off. We ask our kids to do something they "have to do" but don't want to do—something that is a priority for us but not for them. It's reasonable to struggle with cooperation in these scenarios. Adults probably would too. Let's say you were having lunch with a friend and another friend came by and said, "Hey, can you call off your lunch and help me clean my toilet?" I'm pretty sure you'd both say no and continue on with your meal. Parents often do just this with their kids: ask them to stop something they enjoy to do something they don't enjoy. That doesn't mean we should avoid making requests—we'll always have to ask our kids to do things they don't want to do. But it's about the process and the way we deliver our requests. Yelling, for example, is not an effective way to inspire co-operation. In fact, it's counterproductive. When we yell, our kids' bodies enter into threat mode—they perceive danger from a parent's aggressive tone, volume, and body language, and they cannot even process what the parent is saying because their energy is focused only on surviving the moment. If you've ever been so frustrated with your child's lack of cooperation that you yell, "ARE YOU EVEN LISTENING TO WHAT I AM SAYING?"—well, the answer is no, kids are *not* "listening" in these moments. And that's not a sign of disrespect or disobedience but rather the body entering into an animal defensive freeze state. But we don't want our kids to be scared of us, and we don't want them to freeze in the very moments we are trying to get them to work with us (reminder: you're still a good parent if you do yell, and after yelling, you can repair). When we infuse connection, respect, playfulness, and trust into our asks, exchanges that once felt antagonistic start to be met with cooperation.

Strategies

Connect Before You Ask

The single most important strategy in regard to listening is to connect to your child in *their* world before you ask them to do something in *your world*. A child has to feel seen before they're able to switch out of something that feels good to them (drawing or playing with clay, for example) and fulfill a request that's a priority for you (like cleaning up the art supplies). Feeling seen is a powerful bonding tool, and feeling close to someone motivates us to want to co-operate with them. When we verbally acknowledge what our child is doing in the moment, it's as if we're saying, "I see you: you are a real person with real wants and thoughts and feelings." We send the message that we are *listening to our child* in this moment, which allows them to return the favor and listen to us.

Examples:

- "Wow, you've been working so hard on that tower. I know it's going to be tricky to pause and take a bath. If we do a quick bath now, you will have time to build more before bed."
- "I know it's so hard to end playdates, because you've been having so much fun! We have to leave now, but Matias's mom and I can set up your next playdate really soon."

Give Your Child a Choice

This strategy works really well when paired with "connect before you ask." If you can give your child the agency to make a choice, they'll be more likely to cooperate. No one likes feeling dictated to, especially children, who already feel controlled so much of the time. This is a strategy that you can use for kids of all ages; even your two-year-old will be more likely to cooperate for toothbrushing if you give the option of racing to the bathroom or zooming there like a rocket ship. Only offer your child options that you are okay with, and then let them know that you trust them to follow through on that choice.

Examples:

- "We can leave Abby's house now or you can play one more card game together. I'll leave it up to you . . . After one more game? Okay. I know you'll follow through with that choice, so that's fine with me."
- "You can clear your dishes now or come back to do it after your shower . . . After your shower? Okay, I trust that you'll do that. Sounds good."

Humor

Humor allows for a change in perspective, which is what we're looking for when we ask things of our kids. When we infuse playfulness instead of frustration, we join our children in the world they always prefer—one filled with silliness, lightheartedness, and laughter. Frankly, it's a world we want to be a part of as well. When we bring laughter into the equation, our kids feel more connected to us and are more likely to cooperate.

Examples:

- "Oh no . . . your listening ears are lost! Okay, wait, I think I found them. Oh my goodness, can you believe this . . . I found them in this plant! How did they get there? Let's get them back on your body before they sprout into a flower!"
- "I know . . . listening to your parents is such a bummer! What if I talked while I was dancing around in circles, would that make it more enticing?"

Close Your Eyes Hack

I'm not usually a fan of parenting "hacks" or "tricks" because they tend to prioritize short-term compliance over long-term connection and skill building. But that's not the case with one of my all-time favorite strategies, the Close Your Eyes Hack. This trick gives our kids the core elements they need in order to want to listen to us—it infuses respect, trust, independence, control, and playfulness all at once. Here's what it looks like: "I am going to close my eyes"—then place your hands over your eyes—"and all I'm saying is that if there is a child with his shoes on when I open my eyes . . . oh my goodness, if there is a child all Velcroed up . . . I just don't know what I am going to do! I am going to be so confused! I may even—oh no oh no—have to do a silly jumpy dance and wiggle all around and I may even fall on the floor!" Then pause. Wait.

The chances of your child's running to put his shoes on just sky-rocketed. Why? Because now your child is in charge. He feels in control rather than like he's being controlled. Your child feels you trust him because you're not watching (even though you may be peering through your fingers), and you're adding in silliness and the promise of doing something absurd—what kid doesn't love to watch a parent dance and fall down and look ridiculous?

This strategy can be applied to older kids as well; so many parents of seven- and eight-year-olds tell me they are consistently shocked that their kids not only "fall for" but *ask* for the Close Your Eyes Hack. If you're convinced this will fall flat with your older child, then try using the foundational ideas from this strategy and adapt it for your tween or teen. Try saying, "I see you didn't clean your room yet . . . hmm, all right, I'm going to get dinner started and I trust you to keep your promise to put your clothes away before you come downstairs." This operates on the same principle of trust. And if you want to add that element of playfulness? As you walk away, add: "All I'm saying is that if that room ends up getting clean, I just may break out in song!"

If you're wondering why this strategy actually works, imagine how you'd feel if your boss wanted you to redo a report and then stood over you at your desk versus walking away with a message of trust and encouragement. I'd definitely do better work in the second scenario. We all like to feel trusted rather than controlled. And if my boss promised to do something silly once I edited the report? Well, I'd get straight to work. That would just be too good to pass up.

Role-Reversal Game

There's plenty we can do outside of the moments we need cooperation to increase the odds of compliance when it's needed. The more we help a child, in general, feel seen, independent, trustworthy, and in control, the more willing they will be to listen to our requests. Understanding this can feel really encouraging, because there are innumerable opportunities throughout the day to build connection capital and, in a way, listening capital.

One great way to do that is by playing what I call the "I have to listen to you now" game. Introduce this by saying, "I know being a kid is tough. There are so many things that parents ask of you! So let's play a game. For the next five minutes, you're the adult and I'm the kid. I have to do what you say, assuming it's safe." Explain to your child that the game does not involve food or gifts (your child cannot tell you to go buy them a hundred new Pokémon packs or give them thirty bags of Skittles)—it's really about the routine of your day. But the details here aren't important. What's important is to reverse roles, allow your child to experiment with the position of powerful adult, and express empathy for the difficulties of being a child. While you play the game, exaggerate how hard it is to listen to your "parent"; voice things like, "Ughhhhhh, really? I have to clean up the Magna-Tiles? I don't waaaaaaant to," and "Ughhhhh, I wish I didn't have to take a shower *right now*!" I find this game useful for myself as well—it reminds me how hard it can be to take orders when you don't want to do something.

How Does This Play Out for Sonia and Felix?

The next time Felix doesn't listen, Sonia notes her frustration: "Ah . . . hello, frustration. Yes, it is so hard to be a parent when your child is in a not-listening stage." Then she reminds herself, "Listening is really cooperation, and cooperation comes from connection." She takes a deep breath, and later that day she plays the role-reversal game with Felix. He tells Sonia to jump up and down on one foot, put the crayons away, and do silly dances over and over. Felix, unsurprisingly, loves this game, and Sonia finds herself enjoying it more than she expected.

Later that night, when Sonia asks Felix to clean his room, she remembers to make him feel seen and says to Felix, "Aw, buddy . . . time to stop playing blocks soon. I know, playing is so fun! We'll have to say good night to them and clean up your clothes from the floor and start brushing your teeth soon. Do you want to clean up right now or in two minutes?" She's pleasantly surprised to see less resistance when she approaches Felix by connecting and giving him a choice.

CHAPTER 13

Emotional Tantrums

Three-year-old Ezra comes into the kitchen and asks his mom, Orly, for ice cream for breakfast. Orly says kindly, "Ice cream? No, sweetie, that's not an option. How about a waffle?" Ezra demands: "ICE CREAM NOW! Only ice cream, I need it nowwwwww!" Then he drops to the floor, crying and screaming, seemingly endlessly, for ice cream.

antrums are normal. In fact, they're not only normal . . . tantrums are healthy. Of course, that doesn't mean they're fun or enjoyable or particularly convenient. They are none of these things. Tantrums are challenging and exhausting for everyone involved. And yet, they're a part of healthy child development. Tantrums—those moments when children seem to "lose it"—are a sign of one thing and one thing only: that a child cannot manage the *emotional demands* of a situation. In the moment of a tantrum, a child is experiencing a feeling, urge, or sensation that overwhelms his capacity to *regulate* that feeling, urge, or sensation. That's an important thing to remember: tantrums are biological states of *dysregulation*, not willful acts of disobedience.

Tantrums often begin when a child wants one thing (like ice cream), and something else (or some*one* else, like a parent) gets in the way of them getting that thing. Having a desire thwarted is one of the most difficult human experiences—for kids, but also for adults. Tantrums are a child's way of saying, "I still know what I want, even when you say no. My whole body is showing you that I know this desire and I am frustrated in not having it realized." Do we want to limit dangerous behaviors midtantrum? Absolutely. Do we want to stay calm ourselves? For sure. Is our goal to stop a tantrum in its tracks or stop them from happening entirely? No, it's not. Here's why: **We want our kids to want for themselves.**

As parents, we want our kids to be able to recognize and assert their desires, to be able to hold on to the idea "I know what I want, even when people around me tell me no." **But we cannot encourage subservience and compliance in our kids when they're young and expect confidence and assertiveness when they're older.** It just doesn't work that way. Imagine your child is twenty-five years old. Do you want your child to be able to say, "No, that's not okay with me," when someone asks her an inappropriate question? Do you want her to be able to ask for a raise? To be able to tell her partner, "I need you to talk to me more respectfully"? If we want our kids to be able to *recognize their wants and needs* as adults, then we need to start seeing tantrums as an essential part of their development.

If tantrums are set off by wanting and not having, what exactly is released with all that "losing it"? Well, below the surface of any tantrum is a child who has been *building up feelings* of distress—some combination of frustration, disappointment, jealousy, sadness, and anger. I sometimes visualize tantrums as feelings exploding out of the body, as if my child's "distressing feelings jar" was completely full and whatever event immediately preceded the tantrum led the entire jar to overflow. This helps me recognize my child's tantrum not as an annoyance or ridiculous overreaction but as a human expressing feeling overwhelmed or in pain. It can be helpful for adults to remind ourselves that we too have meltdowns. We too get filled up with distress and, sometimes, have a big release when one small thing goes wrong. Imagine a day in which you lost your wallet, got yelled at during a work meeting, and heard that your friends had a dinner date without you; now you get home and want to put on your favorite cozy sweatshirt, only to see that it shrank in the wash and no longer fits. I'll speak for myself here: I could imagine falling into a puddle of tears. Maybe I'd even release a really loud "NOOOOOOO!!! NO NO NO!" And if my partner said to me, "Becky, it's no big deal, just pick a different shirt!" . . . well, let's just say my reaction wouldn't be pretty. But if he saw my release as a sign that I must be going through a hard time, that there must be more to the story than he witnessed on the surface . . . then I would start to feel calmer, because I would feel seen, understood, safe, and good inside. The shrunken sweatshirt was the trigger event, but the buildup of disappointment, frustration, and sadness below the surface laid the foundation. Helping our kids through tantrums relies on our ability to see through the event that set off the "meltdown" and recognize the real, painful feelings underneath. Learning to recognize a tantrum for what it is on the inside rather than reacting to what is happening on the outside is a vital parenting skill.

The strategies I'm about to offer will help you with this recognition, and they can be applied when a child is having a pure *emotional meltdown without any physical aggression like hitting, spitting, biting, kicking, or throwing.* Tantrums that involve physical aggression and boundary violations require some different approaches, which I detail in the next chapter. These strategies all have the same goal: help a child build emotion regulation skills. They are not intended to end a tantrum. When our intention is simply to stop the yelling or crying, kids feel it and learn only one lesson: "The feelings that overwhelm me also overwhelm my parent. My parent is trying to end this, which means my emotions truly are as bad as they feel." Our kids cannot learn to regulate a feeling that we, the adults, try to avoid or shut down. Our goal during a tantrum should be to keep ourselves calm and keep our children safe. After that, we want to infuse our presence so that children can absorb *our regulation in the face of their dysregulation*. The strategies below are all aimed at connecting to your child, showing them you understand, and helping them hold on to their internal goodness.

Strategies

Remind Yourself of Your Own Goodness

Parents struggle to stay calm in the face of tantrums because our children's dysregulation brings up *our own* self-blame feelings. External blame is always paired with internal blame—if we wonder, "What's wrong with my kid?" then we are also wondering, "What's wrong with me?" We might even be thinking, "I'm not doing this parenting thing right." That's a painful thought, so much so that we often seek to shut down a child's tantrum in an attempt to shut off our own distress. So the next time your child starts "losing it," before you do anything else, tell yourself: "Nothing is wrong with me. Nothing is wrong with my child. I can cope with this." Maybe hang that mantra somewhere private, like on your bathroom mirror or your nightstand. See if you can practice incorporating this thought into your daily routine. It'll probably do more to help you stay calm during a tantrum than any other parenting strategy.

Two Things Are True

I want you to memorize these words: "Two things are true: I'm in charge of this decision and my answer is no. You're in charge of your feelings and you're allowed to be upset." The words themselves actually matter less than the idea and the tone. The idea is that we are allowed to make decisions and our kids are allowed to have their own feelings. As for the tone? We don't want to deliver these words with coldness or aloofness, as if to say, "You're allowed to be upset and I don't care." We want to convey true permission and empathy, maybe even saying, "I get why you feel this way," or "It feels *so* bad, I know!" or "Being a kid can be so hard." The key to managing meltdowns is to remember three things: we are not in charge of our children's feelings, our kids don't need to say "Sure, no problem!" when we make decisions, and communicating that we are okay with our children's feelings will teach them to be okay with having big feelings, which is critical to developing emotion regulation.

Name the Wish

One of my favorite tantrum strategies is to name the wish underneath a child's meltdown—literally say out loud what your child is wishing for that they aren't getting. There's always an unmet wish to be found, whether it's something tangible, like ice cream for breakfast, or something more internal, like wanting more independence or to feel heard. When we name the wish, we immediately see beneath the surface and identify what feels so hard—wanting and not having. Naming the wish connects you with your child, brings out your empathy, and makes your child feel seen, which helps them feel safe and good inside, and also helps them calm down. Naming a wish can be small and concrete or large and more thematic. It might be as simple as "You wish you could have ice cream for breakfast. I know," or "You wish you had a later bedtime," or more big-picture, like "You wish you got to make all your own decisions," or "You wish that didn't happen."

Validate the Magnitude

Parents are often told to "name the feeling" when our children are upset ("You are so mad!" or "You're feeling sad, I know"). This can be useful when we are trying to connect with our kids in "regular" moments, but in moments of big tantrums, I find that validating the *magnitude* of the feeling is much more effective. When we validate the intensity of their feelings, we help to reframe a confusing mass of emotion into something concrete and easier to understand. Maybe your child is struggling to wait her turn for the crayons her sister is using. You might say: "You want those crayons . . . You want them SO big . . . as big as this room! Or no . . . as big as this whole house! What? Oh wow. As big as this whole neighborhood!" Or let's say you have to leave the park and your child is really mad about it. To validate the magnitude, you say, "You're not 'usual' upset about this . . . you're as upset as this whole car! No, bigger—your upset is as big as this whole street!" Hopefully your child will run with it, saying, "No, I'm as upset as the whole WORLD!" This is a good thing—it means a child feels seen in how *big* the feeling feels and they are able to express the seriousness of how the moment feels. Once you've validated the magnitude, pause. Look at your child lovingly. Maybe add, "I'm so glad I know how big it is. It's so important. I'm here with you."

How Does This Play Out for Orly and Ezra?

Orly watches Ezra fall to the floor and reminds herself of her job during a child's tantrum: "My job is to keep my body calm and my child safe . . . not to end the tantrum." This allows her to take a deep breath and see Ezra as *having* a hard time, not *giving her* a hard time. She remembers that this meltdown is likely a sign that multiple emotionally taxing moments have been building up in

Ezra, moments that didn't feel good and required him to hold it together. And now, in this ice-cream-for-breakfast moment, it's all spilling out. Orly tells herself, "Nothing is wrong with me, nothing is wrong with my child, I can cope with this." Then she tells Ezra: "Two things are true . . . Ice cream is not an option for breakfast and you're allowed to be upset about it. I get it. I love ice cream too. When you're ready we can find something else yummy for breakfast." Ezra seems to pause a moment when he hears this but then goes back to crying and screaming for ice cream. Orly sits on the floor next to him and says, "You really wish you could have ice cream. I know. You want it as big as this whole kitchen . . . as big as this house! It's so hard to want something that much and not have it." She waits out the tantrum, and eventually it ends. Orly is exhausted, and Ezra is too, but Orly reminds herself she did her job and did it well.

CHAPTER 14

Aggressive Tantrums (Hitting, Biting, Throwing)

> Four-year-old Liam watches his six-year-old sister, Charlotte, grab a blue water bottle in the kitchen. Liam yells, "No, I want that one! Blue is my favorite color." Their mom, Allison, holds a boundary, saying, "Charlotte already has that one. Ugh, I know. You can use the red one or the green one today." Liam explodes. He walks to the water-bottle drawer and, before Allison can get there, reaches in and starts throwing bottles across the room. Allison gets near him and he starts hitting and pinching her, screaming, "I hate you! I hate you!!!!"

Even these tantrums are normal. Even these tantrums are healthy. I promise. These types of tantrums—ones that involve *boundary violations* (contacting someone else's body and aggressive behavior)—are a signal that a child's frontal lobe, the part of the brain responsible for executive functioning, including controlling impulses, is totally offline and that he is physiologically flooded and in a "threat" state. Hitting, kicking, pinching, spitting, biting . . . these behaviors show us that a child's body believes it is in danger and he is unable to regulate it in the moment, so he's reacting the way any of us would in a dangerous situation: fierce self-protection.

The prefrontal cortex of the human brain, which is responsible for the development of language, logic, forward thinking, and perspective (all factors that help us regulate and stay grounded), is extremely underdeveloped in young children. This is why they have such intense emotional explosions. Kids come into the world fully able to feel and experience, and yet not at all able to regulate the intensity of their feelings and experiences. They don't understand the feelings of anxiety and discomfort in their body the way adults do, so when they are having a hard time, it can feel scary rather than just uncomfortable. In the water-bottle situation above, Liam not only has to contend with feeling frustrated that he cannot have the blue water bottle, but also with the sense of feeling hijacked and surprised at the surge of his frustration. He is feeling frustrated, but also scared of the sensations of frustration. And what does this mean biologically? His cortisol, the body's stress hormone, increases, as do his blood pressure and breathing rate, and, as a result, his unclear thinking. He is in fight-or-flight mode, caused by the "threat" of overwhelming and confusing feelings inside his own body. Since kids interpret changes as threats until caregivers show them otherwise, emotionally explosive outbursts are a child's way of saying, "I'm scared of the feelings in my body. I don't understand what's happening to me. I'm being attacked by these awful sensations and yet I cannot get away from them because they are inside me. Help me, help me, help me!"

Learning to stay grounded and help your child in truly explosive tantrums is really hard, and that's partly because of our children's behavior, but also because of what's required of *us* in these moments. Stopping their spiral requires parents to *embody their authority*. And while this sounds empowering, it's at the core of what's challenging for so many adults, especially women, in their adult lives: to assert themselves and take up space. And because this is so hard, many parents unconsciously ask kids to be responsible for remedying difficult moments instead of saying, "I am the adult here, I am in charge, I know what to do." The other difficult thing is, when we embody our authority in this way, we have to tolerate our kids' not being happy with us. We must get ready for our child to scream, "No, don't pick me up!" as we carry them away flailing or to look at us with anger as we step in to separate them from a friend. It forces us to ask ourselves tough questions, such as: "What is it like for me to make a decision that may be met with pushback?"; "What is it like for me to assert my authority?"; "When I think about someone I love being angry with me, how do I feel? What do I have the urge to do?" These questions are critical in the journey to embody our authority, so that we can provide love through boundaries when our kids are out of control.

Once you've confronted your own struggles with asserting authority, you still face the challenge of dealing with a child who is exhibiting out-of-control behaviors. It's important to remember, first, that these explosive moments happen because a child is *terrified of the sensations, urges, and feelings coursing inside their body*. When you think of your child as *terrified* rather than *bad* or *aggressive*, you'll be more able to give them what they need. Then, remind yourself that your job during these tantrums is the same as your job in less-explosive tantrums: keep your own body calm and keep your child safe. Keeping a child safe in this case means focusing on *containment*, because a child who is out of control needs a parent to step in firmly, put a stop to the dangerous behavior, and create a safer, more boundaried environment where the child cannot continue to do damage.

Don't try to teach or lecture or build new skills with your kid in these explosive moments; containment is the only goal. I sometimes say over and over in my head, "Contain, contain, contain. I'm doing all I can do. I'm doing enough. Contain, contain, contain."

Strategies

"I Won't Let You"

Say this aloud: "You can't throw water bottles!" and "Please stop throwing! Please!" Then pause. Take a breath. Now try this one: "I won't let you throw water bottles." These four words—"I won't let you"—are critical for every parent's toolbox. "I won't let you" communicates that a parent is in charge, that a parent will stop a child from continuing to act in a way that is dysregulated and ultimately feels awful. Because we often forget, kids don't feel good when they are out of control. They don't enjoy experiencing their body as unable to make good and safe decisions, just as adults don't enjoy watching ourselves behave in awful ways. And yet, in these tantrum moments, kids are developmentally incapable of stopping themselves. If they could stop throwing they would; if they could stop hitting they would; if they could stop biting they would. A dysregulated child needs an adult to step in and provide the containment that *they cannot provide for themselves*. Stepping in with "I won't let you" and following up to make the "I won't let you" happen—this is an act of love and protection.

What do I mean by "following up"? Well, "I won't let you kick your sister" often requires a parent to physically separate two children; "I won't let you hit me" often means getting your hands ready so you can block a hit before it connects; "I won't let you jump up and down on the counter" often means physically picking your child up and removing her.

It's important to note that "I won't let you" isn't a go-to strategy for day-to-day occurrences; I'm not recommending you dictate what your kids do all the time and assert your dominance. "I won't let you" is for moments when your child can no longer make good decisions—when he is being unsafe or behaving in a way that begs for sturdy leadership. In these situations, if you use "please stop" or "you can't" language, a child becomes terrified that he is in the driver's seat. This will only make him further dysregulated, because he will *feel* you avoiding authority and essentially think, "Why is my parent putting me in charge? My parent clearly sees me struggling and won't step in to help! The feelings that have overwhelmed and taken over my body have now overwhelmed and taken over my parent . . . and that is scarier than anything else." It's no wonder our kids can't "calm down" this way.

Differentiate Urge from Action

Having the urge to bite is okay; biting a person is not okay. Having the urge to hit is okay; hitting a person is not okay. Finding safe ways to redirect our children's urges can be much more successful than trying to shut down the urges themselves. For example, a child who has been biting can be given a chew necklace. When you notice them getting upset, offer the chew necklace in order to interrupt the cycle of discharging the urge on another child. A child who is kicking can be put in a room where they can move their legs and flail and kick, but do it safely, not in a way that connects with another child. After all, we can only learn to regulate feelings *and urges* that we allow ourselves to have; parents often have the goal of getting rid of the urge ("Why would you want to hit someone else? What's wrong with you?"), but humanizing the urge and then shifting where we allow a child to discharge it allows the child to gain regulation and, over time, make better decisions.

Contain the Fire

Picture your child's dysregulated feelings as a fire—this shouldn't be too hard, since these moments generally feel hot and explosive. There is no fire extinguisher for the fire of emotional dysregulation (after all, our emotions are core to who we are—we wouldn't want to extinguish them), so our goal must be simply to contain the fire. How would you do that with an actual fire? Well, you'd want to make the room with the fire as small possible; if you could, you'd "move" the fire from an expansive area to a more confined one, close the door, and safely wait it out.

If a child is still raging after you've said "I won't let you" and you've stepped in to stop the out-of-control behavior, then your child is essentially pleading for containment. A firm boundary—stopping a child from doing something that is dangerous—is sometimes the highest form of love and protection. It signals to a child that their emotional fire will not take over the entire house or yard or birthday party. This can be broken down into steps:

1. Recognize when a child is past the point of no return. Tell yourself, "My child's emotional fire needs containment. I can do this." Your child will try to reject your help because their body is interpreting everything through the lens of *threat*, but they're really saying to you, *"Please be strong. Do the thing that's best for me even when I scream and protest."*

2. Pick your child up and carry them into a room that is relatively "safe" (meaning there aren't dangerous items that will get swept into the emotional storm) and small. A small room shows a child—through body communication, not words— that their emotional fire cannot burn down the entire house. Tell them: *"My number one job is to keep you safe, and right now safety means carrying you to your room and sitting with you there. You're not in trouble. I love you. I'm here."* In

many ways, these words are more for you, to hear your own authority and remember your job, than for your child. Stay the course even as your child flails; remember, they're not in a state of defiance, they're in a state of terror. You are the only one who knows what they need right now: your loving presence and containment.

3. Get into the room, shut the door, sit at the door so your child cannot get out. Will they try? Probably, yes. Luckily, you're bigger than them. Sit there.

4. Prevent any physical aggression. To feel safe and to regulate, children need proof that parents can stop them from making bad decisions and that their feelings do not endanger themselves or others. Get your hands ready so you can block a hit or a kick and say to your child, "I won't let you hit me," or "I won't let you throw books."

5. Focus on your own deep breaths. Make them a bit exaggerated and audible, both for yourself and for your child. If you do nothing but sit at the door and take deep "hot cocoa" breaths, you're ahead of the game. Kids pick up on their parents' emotional state; if they can feel *your* regulation, even in *their* state of such major dysregulation, you are helping them calm down.

6. Tell yourself, over and over, "Nothing is wrong with me, nothing is wrong with my child. I can cope with this." If it feels odd to be sitting with your child in this way, tell yourself, "This feels weird, which is a sign that it's really new for me. That's a good sign, a sign of change."

7. Don't try to reason, don't lecture, don't punish, don't say too much at all. Your child is in a threat state; they cannot process any words and is likely to interpret anything you say as additional danger. But they may be able to respond to nonverbal communication such as our body language, tone of voice, and

pace. It can be useful to imagine your child speaking a different language in these moments, as if they can "understand" your intention and your movements but not the words themselves. As a result, your deep-breathing, calm presence is what they need. Wait it out. It may take five minutes; it may take thirty.

8. Before you talk to your child, find your slow pace and soft tone. **Loud, chaotic tantrums need calm, steady voices.** Tell your child *some* of the following, more slowly and quietly than feels natural, while looking off to the side or to the ground, because when a child (or adult) is in fight-or-flight mode, direct eye contact can be interpreted as a threat. *"You're a good kid having a hard time. I'm here. I love you. Do your thing. You're allowed to feel this way."* Or try to sing a simple song over and over, very slowly. Something like, *"Blake, Blake, it's okay . . . Blake, Blake, it's okay . . . Blake, Blake, it's okay . . . let's take a deep breath,"* and then take an audible slow diaphragmatic breath.

All of this containment work sends a message to a child: "Your feelings can come out, but I will stop them from destroying the world around you. Getting the feelings out will help you, but acting out in fury will make you feel worse. So I will allow the first and prevent the second."

Personify the Feelings

In the heat of the moment, kids can say some nasty things: "I hate you!" or "Leave me alone!" or "I hope you die!" Let's pause and reframe how we look at these words. Your child isn't talking to you. Yes, your child is saying these words aloud and seems to be throwing them in your direction, but consider this: your child is actually talking to the overwhelming, terrifying, threatening feelings *inside his body*. It's as if your child is saying to his dysregulation: "I hate you!" and "Leave me alone!" and "I hope you die!" as a way of protecting himself or even as a plea for relief. When you reframe kids' words in this way, you'll find it much easier to stay present and grounded. You'll see that your child feels terrified and under attack and clearly needs you there.

Telling the Story

Most of us survive a tantrum and think, "Whew, glad that's done, let's move on!" But we can get a big bang for our buck if, once everyone is calm, we connect with our child and review the dysregulated moment. By returning to the scene of the emotional fire and layering on connection, empathy, and understanding, you add key elements of *regulation* on top of the moment of *dysregulation*. Then, the next time your child has a hard time, these elements will be easier to access.

Telling the story is essentially reviewing a chaotic meltdown moment in order to build coherence. This is a sometimes strategy; you don't have to review every single meltdown, but it can be helpful to pull out of your toolbox every now and then. Let's say your child had an aggressive tantrum when his brother said he couldn't join his playdate. Hours, or even a day, later, you might say: "Let me see if I got this right . . . you wanted to play with Dante and Kaito . . . and Dante said no . . . and you said, 'Please please,' and Dante said no again . . . that felt so bad, so hard, and then you were kicking and screaming . . . Daddy picked you up and brought you to your room and sat with you . . . and then we waited together and your body calmed down . . ."

This is when many parents ask, "*And then what?* What do I

do next? Do I tell them how to handle it differently next time?" Nope! The simple act of adding your presence, coherence, and a narrative will change how the experience is stored in a child's body; remember, the pathway that ends in regulation (i.e., fewer tantrums!) starts with understanding and connection, and telling the story does exactly this. Now, you might sense a softening or an opening to say, "Hmm, it feels so bad to not be included. I wonder what you could do if that happens again when Dante has a friend over . . ." This is fine, it will do no harm. But remember that the key element is the connection and storytelling, not the solution.

How Does This Play Out for Liam and Allison?

Allison walks over to Liam and pulls him away from the water-bottle drawer, saying, "I won't let you throw!" Allison knows that Liam is in a complete threat state and doesn't take the bait of his "I hate you"—she recognizes that the real issue is Liam's dysregulated, scary feelings, not his words or behavior on the surface. Allison sees that her son is feeling out of control and carries him to his room, blocking an attempted hit by holding his wrist. She says only, "My number one job is to keep you safe, and right now safety means carrying you to your room and sitting with you there. You're not in trouble. I love you. I'm here." She closes the door, places him down, and sits next to him. Liam flails and screams and yells, "Get out! I hate you!" Allison visualizes this as if Liam is actually speaking to his feelings, not to her, which helps her acknowledge her role as the sturdy leader weathering this storm. As Liam continues, Allison feels her heart start to race and notices her frustration build. She tells Liam: "I need a moment—I'm stepping right outside to take a few breaths and then I'll be right back. I love you. You're a good kid." She steps out of the room, takes a few deep breaths, and reminds herself that she is safe and she can handle this. She then steps back in, stops Liam when he tries to kick her, and says only a few words here and there: "I'm here," and "Let it out," and "It's okay, you're a good kid having a hard time." Liam eventually calms down and asks for a hug. Allison doesn't punish or hold a grudge—she gives him a hug and says, "I know . . . I know . . . I love you."

CHAPTER 15

Sibling Rivalry

Hari, age six, and Annika, age four, are playing with blocks while their father, Ray, is preparing lunch. Ray hears a scream, then a cry, then a cacophony of noises. He runs into the playroom to discover Hari hoarding the blocks, preventing his sister from having any of them. Annika runs to her father, saying, "He pushed me! He made me fall down!" Hari is screaming, "Not true! She took the blocks I was using! She's always getting me in trouble!"

Why do siblings argue so much? Well, let's start with a brilliant analogy from Elaine Mazlish and Adele Faber, authors of one of my favorite parenting books, *Siblings Without Rivalry.* They remind us that when a child gets a sibling, it feels to them similar to how it would feel for you if your partner got a second spouse. Imagine your partner comes home and says, "Amazing news! We're getting a second wife! You're going to be a big wife and now we'll have a little wife and we're going to be one big happy family!" If you're like me, you'd look around the room thinking, "WHAT? Am I in an alternative universe? Why is this good for *me*?" All of your relatives and neighbors ask you if you're *so* excited about this new wife, then nine months later everyone showers her with gifts and hugs, and forever after, you're expected to love this woman and get along swimmingly. Imagine one day you take one of her items—something that used to be yours—out of her hand and everyone yells at YOU about it, saying, "You can't do things like this! You can't take a toy from a little wife! Look how small and helpless and innocent she is!" By this point, I think we'd be *beyond* confused . . . we'd be filled with the rage that comes from feeling unseen. This. Is. Siblinghood.

For an older child, the addition of a sibling activates *attachment needs* and *abandonment fears*. Kids, when viewed through the lens of attachment, are *always trying to figure out if they are safe*. They're asking, "Will my needs be met? Do I feel seen and appreciated for who I am, for my unique set of traits and interests and passions and ways of being? Am I seen as a kid who is *good inside* in my family?" When kids are going at it with each other, they're "telling" their parents that they feel unsettled, that their sibling feels like a threat to their essential need to feel secure in the family. Let's go back to the metaphor of what might be going on for *us* and what *we* would need from a partner if we were struggling with a second spouse: assuming we couldn't convince our partner to "get rid" of this other spouse, we would at least need our partner to really hear us, see our experience, give us some special time and attention, and tolerate the range of feelings we would have about this new spouse. The more we felt secure in our relationship with our partner, the less of a threat the new spouse would be. Of course, it would still be difficult and conflictual, because having to share the attention of someone you love with another person is a constant challenge, but there are some factors that would make this worse and some that would make it more manageable.

In the "more manageable" category: parents need to accept that their kids have a *range of feelings* about their siblings. Many parents hold on to a common but unrealistic narrative: "Siblings should be best friends!" or "My kids should always be nice to each other!" or "I gave my child the gift of a sibling, they should be so happy!" Am I suggesting that having more than one kid is a bad idea, that siblings are usually enemies, that siblings should be awful to each other? No, not at all. Those ideas are just as extreme as the first set. I'm saying that sibling relationships are complex, and the more we appreciate this complexity, the better we can prepare our kids to tolerate all the feelings that arise, so they're better able to regulate them. When that happens, their feelings won't come out as often in behavior, and *this* is our goal. Remember: it's not our feelings that are the problem, it's the regulation of the feelings. And kids' ability to regulate feelings depends on our willingness to acknowledge, validate, and permit those feelings (and put up boundaries when the feelings spill into dangerous actions). The more we connect with our kids about how they feel—in this case maybe jealous or angry toward a sibling—the less likely they are to explode in the form of behavior: insults, hitting, mockery, put-downs.

Here's another important consideration when it comes to understanding sibling rivalry: birth order. Birth order deserves its own book, but let me say a few things about it here. First kids get accustomed to being alone; they are *wired* with their parents' full attention, so having a new sibling completely rocks the foundation of their world. These kids can adjust, of course, but we have to appreciate the magnitude of the change, considering the fact that all their expectations of the world were built upon seeing themselves as the only child in the family. First children often appear self-centered when a new sibling comes into the family, but underneath the "I don't like her, send her back to the hospital!" or the pleas of

"Watch me! Watch me!" is a child whose circuitry is going through a massive shift. Second and third (and fourth, etc.) kids have the opposite wiring: their circuitry is shaped by the presence of someone else *constantly* in their space, *constantly* able to do things they cannot (yet) do, *constantly* competing for time and attention. It's frustrating to be a second kid. You can't build a block tower without seeing an older sibling do it more easily, you can't run in the backyard without seeing a sibling run faster, you can't work on early reading without seeing your older sibling read effortlessly. There's no problem to fix here, just a dynamic to understand. Of course, sibling dynamics aren't all the same. Some families watch their younger child do things more easily than an older sibling— the younger child is reading while the older child is struggling, the younger child is a star athlete in a sport where the older one is mediocre; these subtleties have their own challenges. But keeping birth order dynamics in mind is critical as you think through what's really going on for your kids, how they're feeling, what insecurities get evoked, and what unmet needs your kids are showing through their behaviors.

Strategies

PNP Time

There is no strategy as important for healthy sibling relationships as PNP Time, or dedicated alone time for each child to spend with a parent. The more secure a child feels with their parents, the more they can view a sibling as a playmate and not a rival. When my own kids are in a particularly challenging sibling stage, I remind myself: "They feel untethered and insecure. They each need more connection with *me* to feel anchored in this family. Okay, let's schedule some PNP!" PNP Time is foundational to change in a number of areas—check out pages 122–124 for details on how to make it happen.

"We Don't Do Fair, We Do Individual Needs"

I see so many families set a goal of being "fair" as a method of attempting to decrease conflict, but in fact, making things *fair* is one of the biggest propellants of conflict. The more we work for fairness, the more we create opportunities for *competition*. When we make things fair, we increase a child's hypervigilance; we essentially say, "Continue to watch your sibling like a hawk. Make sure you keep track of everything your sibling has, because that's how you can figure out what you need in this family." And there's a longer-term reason why we don't want to aim for "fairness" in our families: we want to help our kids orient *inward* to figure out their needs, not orient *outward*. When my kids are adults, I don't want them to think, "What do my friends have? What are their jobs, their homes, their cars? I need what they have." Talk about a life of anxiety and emptiness. It leads to a life with no *interiority*—no sense of who you are on the inside, only a sense of how you stack up to other people on the outside.

Here's how to move away from fair: When your kid screams, "Not fair!," work to shift his gaze *inward*. Don't force this; model it. Instead of making things equal ("You'll get new shoes soon!"), label what's happening inside your child: "It's so hard to see your brother get new shoes. Can you get new ones? Not right now, sweetie. In this family, every kid gets what they need—and your shoes are still in great shape. You're allowed to be upset. I get it."

Or what if your child screams, "No fair, you took Mara to get ice cream when I was at soccer practice! You need to take me to get ice cream tomorrow, all alone—you need to!" A "fairness orientation" would lead you to say, "I will take you to get ice cream tomorrow, it's okay," which would teach your child that he should look to others (in this case, his sibling) to determine what he needs. Here's a script for a response based on an "individual needs" orientation:

> PARENT: *"You wish you got ice cream with me, huh?"*
> CHILD: *"Yes, you need to take me!"*
> PARENT: *"Okay, so when you think about our PNP Time tomorrow, the way you'd like to spend it is by going to get ice cream?"*
> CHILD: *"Um . . . maybe. Or we had said we could go to the park together. Hmm. Maybe that. Can I let you know?"*
> PARENT: *"Sure. Think about it, then tell me what feels best to you."*

In this scenario, a child learns to look inward, toward himself, to determine what he needs.

Allow Venting (but Only to You)

When your children know they can talk to *you* honestly about their feelings toward their sibling(s), they become much less likely to take out their feelings on their brother or sister. So make it a point to say to your kids, "Having a sister can feel hard, huh?" or "It's okay to have so many feelings about your new brother— happy excited feelings and sad or angry ones. All of those feelings are okay and we can talk about them." As your kids get older, they may benefit from something even more direct: "We're going to your sister's gymnastics competition later . . . I know it can feel tricky to watch a sibling do something and get so much attention. You're still a good kid if you feel that way. We can talk about it." Remember: our feelings are forces; the feelings we don't permit ourselves to have are more likely to catapult out of our bodies as behavior. The more you allow your kids to feel jealousy, the more you can problem-solve around the moments the feeling comes up; the less you allow jealousy ("Don't say that about your sister!"), and the fewer skills a child develops for dealing with it when it arises, the more likely it is that jealousy will come out as insults ("Maxie is the worst gymnast here, she sucks!") or behavior (making loud noises while spectators are supposed to be quiet, running away from you and screaming loudly).

Here's the catch about venting: I have a zero-tolerance policy for siblings' insulting each other or calling each other names. In my mind, this is bullying, and it's something I encourage families to take a hard line about. Name-calling is not innocent teasing; it's one way a kid can chip away at another kid's confidence, especially when parents don't step in to stop it. And this is why I encourage parents to establish with each child that it's okay to talk to *them*, alone, about their angry or jealous sibling feelings—this way, there's a dedicated space to air those feelings. You can even spell this out with your child when you're alone: "I know having a sibling is tricky. And I know you have a ton to say about your sister. You can talk to me about this when we are together, just the two of us, and I won't try to convince you otherwise or tell you not to feel this way. I'll try to understand and help you out. And . . . here's the other important thing: I absolutely will not allow you to speak with harsh words or insults or teasing toward your sister. My number one job is to keep everyone in this family safe, and safety includes the words we use with each other."

Step In When There's Danger, Slow Down and Narrate When There's Not

We want to teach our kids to problem-solve with each other, not rely on us to judge who is right and who is wrong, who goes first and who goes second. To do this, we have to teach our kids to *slow down* when they're activated; once kids regulate, they tend to be natural problem-solvers. The exception? When there's danger, and that means not only hitting, throwing, physical altercations, and threats, but also verbal escalations that are cruel, involve name-calling, or involve emotional bullying. In these situations, we must step in to protect *both* kids: the kid who is being threatened and the kid who is out of control. Both kids need our help.

Step In (Dangerous Situations)

When our kids are out of control, they need us to assert that we are in control. This is, again, where you might use the "I won't let you" that we covered in the previous chapter: "I won't let you hit your sister. Something upsetting must have happened. You're allowed to be mad, and I can help you find another way to express that." This "I won't let you" might need to be combined with a physical action to enforce these words, such as stepping between your kids or pulling one child away from the other. After you've stepped in, assess whether your kids are calming down or if they need to be further separated—not because anyone is bad or in trouble but because you need more space to keep everyone safe. If that's the case, use these words: "I need both of you to go to your rooms, right now. You're not in trouble. My number one job is to keep everyone safe, and right now safety means two kids apart so we can calm our bodies. I'll check on both of you soon. I love you." It might also mean carrying one dysregulated child to her room while you say to the other, "I know this felt bad to you. Hitting is never okay. Your sister needs my help calming down her body. I'll be back to check on you too, I know you also need me. I love you."

Dangerous "I won't let you" situations may also include nasty words or taunting or teasing; this is another reason why a parent might step in and separate their kids, to protect one child from bullying and to protect the other from continuing to take on the role of bully. Both kids need our help.

Slow Down and Narrate (Not Dangerous Situations)

When our kids are arguing or escalating but there's no boundary violation with bodies (hitting, kicking) or words (threats, name-calling), our role is to *slow things down* but *not solve*. Model regulating *yourself* without forcing regulation on them ("I know I need a deep breath!" rather than "Take a deep breath!"), reminding your kids that you're not the arbiter of truth, and helping each of them narrate their perspective without taking sides or making someone the "bad kid" or the "good kid." Here's an example: Your kids are trying to figure out who gets to play with their favorite fire truck toy. They're both screaming and upset. Solving would sound like, "Just let Jessie use it first, she's two years old, geez!" or "Micah, you get it now and then, Jessie, you get it after." But slowing down would sound like, "Let me take that fire truck for a second—okay, I have it. Now, I know *I* need a deep breath." Take a few deep breaths to allow your children to "borrow" your regulation. "Hmm, two kids, one truck! That is so tricky. I wonder what we can do? I wonder if I have any problem-solvers here . . ." Then pause. Remind yourself, your job is to slow down the situation so your kids can regulate their bodies and have access to their own problem-solving skills; your job isn't to solve this as quickly as possible. Here, you're helping your children learn the process that leads to problem-solving; when we fix things for our kids, we just lock them into needing us to problem-solve, and this becomes frustrating to everyone.

How Does This Play Out for Hari, Annika, and Ray?

Ray remembers, "Slow down, don't solve," and starts by modeling regulation *himself*: "Wow, lots going on in here! I know *I* need a deep breath!" He places his hand on his heart and takes a few audible breaths; this is so different from what Hari and Annika usually see in a parent that it's enough to make them pause themselves. Ray continues, "I see two upset kids . . . I know both of you don't like how things are going. I also know I am not going to be the person who decides what was right or wrong or what did or didn't happen. Annika . . . seems you wanted to play with the blocks too . . . and Hari, seems you had a building plan and wanted to keep them for yourself. Oh, that is so tricky. Two kids, both wanting blocks, both full of creative ideas . . . I bet if we really think . . . we can find a solution here. Hmm . . ." Then he pauses. Eventually, Hari says, "Here, take these," and Annika seems satisfied. Ray is exhausted from this, but he reminds himself that his kids are learning how to problem-solve, and this process was hugely helpful toward that goal. He also stores data for later, noting that Annika and Hari might each be finding siblinghood tough, so he decides to schedule in some PNP Time for each.

CHAPTER 16

Rudeness and Defiance

Eight-year-old Farrah asks her mom, Heather, if she can go to her friend's house on Saturday night. "You know we're seeing Grandma on Saturday, so that can't work," Heather says.

"I hate this family," Farrah mutters under her breath.

"What did you just say?" Heather asks. "Excuse me?"

Farrah explodes: "I said I hate you and I hate this family! You are the worst mom in the whole world!"

"Why do you think you can talk to me this way? Go to your room now!"

When children are rude or even downright defiant, parents have two choices: we can view the behavior through the lens of disrespect for *us* ("My child does not respect me!") or through the lens of emotion dysregulation for *them* ("My child is having a hard time right now").

It's tempting to default to that first lens—it's the easier, often more ingrained route. But think about yourself—why are *you* rude to people sometimes? Why would you talk back to or disobey your boss? I come up with the same reason, every time: I feel misunderstood. I am looking to feel seen and don't. I feel frustrated that someone else isn't really *hearing* me, and my relationship with that person isn't as strong as it could be in that moment. Knowing what would make me act out helps guide my approach to rudeness or defiance in kids.

Let's say you tell your seven-year-old son, Hunter, that he can't play video games this morning. Then, when you walk into the family room after breakfast, you see him playing Madden. When we use a lens of disrespect, we think, "I said no! Do my words hold no weight? Hunter just does whatever he wants, he has no respect for adults!" Feeling *disrespected* can be very triggering, so most of us would have an urge to yell or punish—not because that would necessarily give Hunter a newfound respect for us, but because as adults we cannot tolerate the uncomfortable disempowered feelings in our own bodies, and so we assert ourselves through punishment to make *ourselves feel better.*

But when we look at Hunter's behavior through a lens of emotion dysregulation, we might think, "Hunter really wanted something, I said no, and he couldn't tolerate the feeling of wanting and not having. I have to work on that with him. Also, I wonder if something is off between us, in our connection, that played out in not listening to me."

As we know, kids don't have great emotion regulation skills. The bigger and more intense a feeling, the less able they are to manage it well. So instead of talking through the feeling, or taking a deep breath or a moment to collect themselves—all those things you might want an adult to do when having a big feeling—a child's big feeling might come out in the form of, in Hunter's case, blatant defiance, or, in Farrah's case, an "I hate you" or "I hope you drown!" And the bigger and more intense the feeling, the more likely it is to manifest in these kinds of statements or behaviors, which often lead to a parent's pushing a child away ("You can't say things like that to me!" or "Go to your room this instant!"). Now we're in a vicious cycle: a child's rudeness is met with a parent's reactivity, which leads to the child's feeling more misunderstood and alone, which exacerbates the intensity of the child's feeling (remember: it's not the *feeling* as much as it's the *aloneness in a feeling* that feels so bad) and leads to more dysregulated behavior and words.

As parents, we must try to separate our kids' underdeveloped regulation skills (which, because they are still limited, can surface as rudeness and defiance) from their very real, very normal feelings (anger, sadness). We must learn to look under the expression and see the words as a desperate plea for understanding the bigger picture. And we must unlearn the idea that if we don't punish the original behavior, it will be more likely to happen again. We do not reinforce bad behavior by skipping punishment. The idea that if we "let a child get away with this," they will learn it is "okay to talk to their parents like that" . . . well, this assumes a very negative view of human behavior, one that I don't buy into.

Let's imagine on-the-surface rudeness in our own life: You had a rough day, and your partner asks if you've unloaded the dishwasher. You react: *"I've done a million things. No, I didn't get to the dishwasher. Can you do just one thing by yourself?"* Instead of biting back or scolding you for your on-the-surface rudeness, picture your partner saying, *"Wow, that was rude. But, sweetie, you must be feeling overwhelmed to have reacted that way. That's more important than your tone. So let's start there—what was today like? I want to understand."*

How does this feel? Afterward, are you more or less likely to be rude to your partner? And how would you feel if, instead, your partner responded, *"I won't tolerate your rudeness. No TV for you for a week!"* I think we all know this scenario doesn't end well for anyone. The same principle holds true for our kids; meeting their rudeness with empathy and kindness will make them feel seen and help inspire kindness in return.

Strategies

Don't Take the Bait

Responding to your child's on-the-surface behavior, as if their words are their sole truth, is taking the bait. Seeing your child's on-the-surface behavior as a sign of something deeper and more vulnerable—seeing the *feelings underneath the words*, not the words themselves—is *not* taking the bait. This difference is every-thing.

How does this work?

- Step 1: Put a *boundary* around your child's behavior ("I won't allow . . ." or "I won't let you . . .").
- Step 2: Provide *a generous interpretation*, acknowledging the deeper feelings, worries, and desire to be seen. Sometimes, presence without words is enough (remember, children interpret your presence as a sign of their goodness, because you're showing your child they don't scare you).

Examples:

- "I am turning off the console and taking the controller. Look, something is going on. I said no and you started playing anyway. Let's figure this out later after we each think on it— something about video games makes it really hard for you to listen to me, and also there must be something going on between us for this to have happened."
- "Wow, those are big words . . . You must be really upset to have said that. I know you're mad that your tower fell. I'd feel mad too. I'm here. I love you."
- "I won't allow that tone . . . having said that, you must be upset about lots of things to be reacting to me in this way. I'd

love to get alone time with you. I know it's really hard to be a teenager right now. I want to listen and understand. I love you, even when you're mad at me."

- Sometimes words are too much; always allow yourself to simply take a deep breath and nod, maybe gazing toward the floor. In intense moments, even eye contact can feel like too much, but this simple gesture says, "I heard you. I'm here. I love you."

Embody Your Authority—Without Punishing or Being Scary
In the face of blatant defiance:

1. Take deep breaths. Remember, defiance is not a sign of disrespect or having a bad kid.
2. Embody your authority. Narrate what you're doing as you reassert your role of establishing boundaries (remember to always know your job). You might say, "I am taking you off the couch," as you pick up your son who shouldn't be jumping on the sofa. Or, when you find your daughter hiding in the closet with her iPad after screen time is over, "You can give me the iPad right now or if it's too hard to give it up, I can take it from you." Then, maybe, "I am going to take it from you, honey, I know this won't be pleasant."
3. Maintain the boundary, but remember you are doing so because your child doesn't yet have this impulse-control skill rather than because your child disobeyed you. This might mean staying in the room with your son who clearly wasn't able to listen to your no-jumping rule or putting the iPad somewhere your daughter can't reach. Do not expect your child to suddenly develop impulse-control ability just because she got "caught." Your child is *telling you* that she needs your help with the boundary. Now you need to be the helper.

4. Consider whether there's a way to *sublimate* the urge. In other words, can you help your child express her general desire in a way that doesn't violate your boundary? Language here might be, "You really want to jump. I won't let you jump on the couch. Let's go outside and jump on the grass," or "I think you're telling me we need to make you a list of solo activities that feel fun when I'm busy with work emails."

5. Reflect and act later. What impulse control does your child struggle with? When things are calmer between you, can you help your child practice having that urge and then pausing and breathing and choosing a better option? Do you need more buy-in from your child to have her listen to certain rules?

State the Truth

The next time you're setting a rule you *know* your child won't like, say as much. When you do this, you establish your connection by validating her experience and you provide an opportunity to brainstorm and cope in advance. In this case, you might tell her: "There's no jumping on the couch. I know, what a bummer, right? You love to jump on things and the couch is definitely bouncy. I wonder what you *could* jump on?" or "I have to do some work emails. I know you know our family rule—no iPads until later on. It may be hard for you to think of something fun to do while I'm occupied and I know you wish we could have iPads as an option. I get it. Hmm . . . what could you do while I'm working for a bit?"

Connect and Build Regulation When Everyone Is Calm

When kids talk back or meet us with pushback, parents often want to *disconnect* from them. Yet what our kids need most in these periods are efforts to reconnect. Deep down, a child in a stage full of rudeness and defiance is screaming out: "I don't think you understand something big inside me. I need you to try to understand, to want to be around me, to see me as a good kid inside. This doesn't mean allowing me to behave in any way I'd like; it means wondering with me about why I'm acting this way and trying to find ways to reconnect." PNP Time is key here. You could also try "Did I ever tell you about the time . . . " and the Fill-Up Game.

How Does This Play Out for Farrah and Heather?

When Farrah yells, "I hate you," it's important for Heather to remember, "This is dysregulation, not disrespect," and acknowledge Farrah's feeling. "I understand . . . it's upsetting that you can't go to Amina's." This takes Farrah by surprise, but still she rages back, "You don't understand! You'll never understand!" Then Heather remembers that presence is sometimes enough. She takes another deep breath, looks toward the floor, and nods slowly. "I'm here," she says.

Later that night, after they've both cooled down, Heather sits on Farrah's bed. "I know you hate to miss fun things with your friends. I used to hate that too. Did I ever tell you about the time I had to miss my friend's sweet sixteen party because I had to watch my brother's soccer tournament? It was awful, I was *so* mad." Later, Heather reinforces Farrah's goodness by saying, "You're a good kid who had a hard time earlier. I know that. Nothing you do or say will ever change how much I love you."

CHAPTER 17

Whining

Adeze is doing homework at the table next to her mom, Imani, who helps her while also responding to emails on her phone and getting up to manage Adeze's younger brother, who is crawling all over the living room. Adeze breaks the tip of her pencil and says to her mom—in a major whine voice—"I need a sharp pencilllllll! Can you get me one?!?!" Imani feels like she is about to explode.

If whining gets under your skin, join the club. I'm a founding member. And yet . . . let's look a bit deeper. What gets under our skin and why—these are important clues about ourselves. Even that phrase "gets under our skin" speaks to the way certain behaviors trip circuits in our bodies. Understanding what's really happening when whining drives us crazy will help us figure out what to do about it.

Parents often interpret whining as a lack of gratitude—when our kids whine that they don't like the dinner we cooked or that they really want a new toy, it can feel like they aren't recognizing all the efforts we've made to give them so much. And yet . . . I think this interpretation often misses what's going on for kids in these moments. Here's how I see it: children whine when they feel *helpless*.

I often use the formula *whining = strong desire + powerlessness*. When a child wants to get dressed but the task feels insurmountable, or when a child wants a playdate but you've said no, these are times when the whines come out. So why are we so triggered by whining? It's more than just the high pitch of our kids' voices or the seemingly endless nature of their pleas. If whining represents *helplessness*, then you might be triggered if you grew up in a family where you had to shut down your vulnerability. If phrases like "Get yourself together!" or "Pull yourself up by your bootstraps!" or "Stop being a baby, come on, you can do this!" were common in your family, then there probably wasn't much tolerance for your *own* helplessness. As a result, you may have learned to shut down this part of yourself. Now, when your child whines, it's as if your body is saying, "Oh, I know what to do here, shut this down shut this down!" It reacts to your child as it learned to react to you.

But the truth is, even for adults, that combination of *wanting* and *helplessness* feels brutal. I find myself whining under these conditions. I remember once showing up to a coffee shop before work, only to find the door locked. The manager popped his head outside to tell me, "We're running late today, we won't be opening for twenty minutes." My heart dropped. I was desperate for a coffee because I'd left home early without any caffeine, but I couldn't wait twenty minutes or I'd be late for a meeting. "Pleeeeeeease?" I whined. My voice sounded awful on the outside, and my body felt awful on the inside—desperate and powerless.

Kids also whine when they're looking for connection, to indicate that they feel alone and unseen in their desires. And while our job as parents is to make decisions that we feel are right for our kids even in the face of protest, we can still practice understanding and connecting. Feeling alone and desperate is incredibly difficult, given that humans feel safest when we have connection and hopefulness. This doesn't mean you have to give in to your kids' ridiculous demands, but the more you focus on those feelings underneath the surface and give them the connection they need, the less your children will whine. And when they *do* whine—because they will, at some point—remembering these underlying dynamics is key to getting through the moment without changing your decision. Knowing what motivates whining helps us reduce it but also respond to it effectively when it inevitably does come out.

Let's consider my coffee example. It was not the manager's responsibility to help me feel more emotionally secure, of course, but let's say he had come outside and instead of simply saying, "We're running late," he had said, "I know we usually open at eight, so it makes sense you're here expecting coffee. We're having an issue and can't open until eight thirty today. I know how disappointing that is. Wanting coffee and not getting it is *the worst*!" I'm wondering if I would have collapsed into my desperate "Pleeeease?" whine. Probably not. And let's say I *did* collapse, and the manager said back to me, "I've been there too" (connection) or "I know this stinks and I have a feeling you'll figure it out" (hopefulness). I think I'd have felt a lot better.

There's one final reason kids whine, and it's an important one: children are often looking for an emotional release, and whining is a sign that everything feels like too much—often it's an indicator that a child needs to "let it all out." On a recent Saturday afternoon, my son whined that he wanted water with "nine ice cubes," then whined that the water was too cold, then insisted I make the water warmer while keeping the ice in it. After we survived that, he looked at his lunch and insisted he didn't want his pasta with cheese—he wanted it with no cheese, then actually some cheese, then actually all cheese, then he said he didn't want pasta or cheese at all. I was getting increasingly frustrated, his whines were making my skin crawl, and then I paused and thought, "Huh. My son is actually asking me to hold a boundary so he can let out some feelings. His whining and unreasonableness are his ways of saying to me, 'Mommy, be firm, provide a sturdy container for me. I need a good cry.'" I stopped trying to make things better and just said, "Nothing feels good, huh? Nothing feels like you want it to. I get that, sweetie. Some moments are like that." He didn't look at me in response and say, "Oh, Mommy, you understand me so well." No. He screamed and protested and cried. I took him to his room and sat with him for a while, until it all came out. Here's what I knew: He needed it. His whines were a plea.

Strategies

Channel Your Own Inner Whiner

If you are noticeably triggered by your child's whining and you grew up in a household where vulnerability wasn't tolerated, I want you to try something. Right now, place your hand on your heart and tell yourself, "It's okay to need help and feel powerless. Strong, resilient people feel this way sometimes." Maybe even experiment with whining in front of the mirror. Whine about how many emails you have to respond to, how you don't want to clean your house, how exhausted you feel. Ironically, the more *you embrace* whining yourself, the less you'll be triggered by it. When your kids do whine and you feel your blood boiling? Say aloud: "One moment. I need a deep breath." Then place your hand on your heart and say to yourself, "I am safe. I can get through this," as you breathe deeply.

Humor

The best match for a child's whining is an adult's playfulness. When we respond to a whine with silliness or humor, we offer what a child needs the most: connection and hopefulness, both of which are present in lighthearted moments. (Though, it's important to re-member that playfulness is *not* mockery. The first is intended to connect and add levity, the second is distancing and adds shame.) The next time your child says, "I need you to get me my paja-maaaaaas!" take a deep breath, remind your body you are safe, and then try something like, "Oh no oh no oh no . . . the whines again! How the heck did they" — walk over to the window, look around outside — "get in here again?" Continue with your monologue, and watch your child loosen up. "Okay, I don't know how they got in, but let's get some of those out. Throw them onto some other kids!" Walk over to your child and pretend to "take" the whines out of their body, then throw those whines out the window or door or something else. Then return to your child and say something like, "Okay, sorry, what? Oh, you want your pajamas?" You can get them for your child at this point. You aren't "reinforcing" the whine, you are just adding playfulness and connection.

Restate the Request in Your Own Voice and Move On

A lot of parents believe they must make a child restate their request in a "stronger" voice after a whine, so as not to "reinforce" the whine. There's nothing inherently wrong with this, and it's cer-tainly fine to occasionally say, "Can you ask me that again without whining?" in a way that doesn't feel too pedantic or controlling. But sometimes we get into unnecessary power struggles with our kids when we insist they restate requests in a more "appropriate tone," and all of a sudden a minor moment escalates into an out-right battle. It's just not worth it (nothing is when it ends with two people locked in a power struggle). Rather than demanding a restated request, I find that modeling it myself and moving on is both more humane *and* more effective. What would this look like? When your child says, "Dad, I need my booooooook!" . . . instead of "I need you to say that again in a stronger voice," try *"Dad, can you please grab me that book? Thank you so much."* Then "switch" and reply, *"Oh sure, sweetie, no problem."* Deliver the book, take a deep breath, skip the lecture, trust your child to hear the difference and incorporate the change.

See the Need
When kids are whining, they are asking for some combination of more attention, more connection, more warmth, more empathy, and more validation. There are a number of things we can do in response to a whine that speaks to these unmet needs:

- Place our phones down and say, "I put my phone away because I feel like I've been distracted and you've been noticing that. I'm here now. I'm here."
- Squat down to a child's level and say, "Something doesn't feel good to you. I believe you. Let's figure it out."
- Empathize with the general plight of childhood: "Sometimes it feels really hard to be a kid. I know." Maybe continue, if relevant, "You wish you could make all your own decisions. I get that."
- Allow the release: "Let it out, sweetie. It all feels so bad. I'm here with you. It's okay."
- Play the Fill-Up Game: "I think you're telling me . . . you're not filled up with Mommy. Can I fill you up?"

How Does This Play Out for Adeze and Imani?

Imani is aware that whining triggers her, so when Adeze whines for a sharp pencil, she takes a deep breath and responds, "How did that whine get in here? I can't believe it snuck in, we must have left the door open! Okay, I am going to take these whines . . . and throw them outside!" Imani walks to the window, opens it, and makes a throwing motion before shutting the window again. This allows her to do something with her body so that she feels calmer and buys some time so she can be less reactive. Imani goes back to Adeze and says, "Okay, did it! I hope your buddies Gabby and Raj don't catch them and become whiney for *their* parents . . . eesh!" Then she shifts gears and says, "Okay, sorry, what did you ask for? A sharp pencil? Sure, I'll grab you one." When Imani brings Adeze the pencil, she notices that Adeze seems lighter. They end up having a nice dinner together, avoiding the power struggle or argument that might have happened in the past.

CHAPTER 18

Lying

When Jake gets home from school, his mom, Dara, says to him, "Your teacher called and said you pushed Owen on the playground. What happened?"

"I didn't push anyone," Jake replies. "That's not what happened."

Dara doubles down: "Do *not* lie to my face! You will get in more trouble for lying than just telling me what happened!"

"I am not lying," Jake says. "Why do you believe a teacher more than me? You always blame me!"

Dara and Jake are stuck.

W*hy do kids lie? Well, let's start with what doesn't drive lying before we jump into what does.* When our kids lie to us, we often default to the worst possible interpretation. We think, "My child is so defiant!" or "My child thinks they can pull a fast one on me!" or "My child lied right to my face . . . what a sociopath, something is seriously wrong with them!" But looking at lying through a lens of being disrespected ("Are you lying to me? Do not disrespect me like that!") totally misses the point—it pits us against our children and locks us into a parent-child power struggle where nobody wins. The reality is that lying is almost never about being defiant or sneaky or sociopathic (even when you're only saying that in jest). Like so many of the behaviors addressed in this book, lying is much more about a child's basic desires and their focus on attachment than it is about being manipulative or "pulling a fast one." Now, I'm not saying you should "let your kids off the hook" when they lie. But my approach to dealing with lying is not about eliciting a confession in the moment. It's aimed at getting to the core of what's *driving* the lying, so we can address that head-on and create an environment where truth-telling becomes more possible. We cannot change a behavior we don't understand, and punishment, threats, and rage are never components in environments that foster understanding or change.

Kids lie for a few main reasons. First, the line between fantasy and reality is murkier for them than it is for adults. Kids frequently engage in pretend play, where they aren't constrained by the laws of reality and they enter into different worlds and take on traits of different characters. I'm a big fan of pretend play. It's where children can express and explore the issues they struggle with, because it's a safe world within their control. But when you ask your child if she broke the lamp, knowing full well that she was the one who tipped it over, and she says, "No, I was playing in my room," your child may be *coping* with her guilt, or her fear of disappointing or enraging you in that moment, by entering into fantasy. We can look at this in two ways: that a child is "avoiding telling the truth" or that telling the truth feels so hard and scary that she slips into a world of pretend where she has control and can dictate an ending that feels better to her.

When we start to look at lies in the framework of a child's *wish*— her desire to retain control and change the ending—we see the lie not for its impact on us but as a sign of her need to feel safe and good inside. These are, after all, the needs that drive children all the time, and the ones that drive adults as well. When a child thinks her parent doesn't see her as lovable and worthy, she'll escape into a fantasy where that goodness is preserved. What manifests as lying is truly a byproduct of evolution: our children's survival is dependent on their attachment with us, and their attachment with us is dependent on their feeling secure and wanted. When you ask your daughter if she broke the lamp, I'd guess her first thought is something like: "I wish the lamp wasn't broken. I wish I wasn't playing near the lamp. I wish I had been playing in my room instead." These wishes surface as "I was playing in my room," but characterizing this as a "lie"—and responding with "Don't lie to me!"—misses the essence of what's happening under the surface.

Kids also lie if they believe that telling the truth will threaten their attachment with their parents. Attachment is a system of proximity. It's literally about staying close to your caregivers and feeling that your caregivers want to stay close to you. Kids are constantly monitoring their relationships with their parents with this in mind. They'll wonder, "Is what I'm about to tell my parent going to push me away from them or help me stay close and connected?" If a child anticipates that a parent will interpret their behavior through the lens of their being "bad inside," and thus push them away, that child will lie every single time. After all, the body is designed to protect itself from abandonment, which means that being seen as a bad kid ("I can't deal with you right now, go to your room!" or "What kind of person lies to their mom's face? What is wrong with you?") is the biggest threat in childhood. What we see and label as lying is often a child's body's way of protecting itself—this is far from "manipulation" but rather a form of self-defense.

Finally, it's worth noting that a third big reason kids lie is to assert their independence. All of us—kids and adults—have a basic human need to feel like we can locate ourselves, that we know who we are, and that we exist in our own right. This is why we hate feeling controlled, because it feels like someone isn't acknowledging our separate personhood. People will go to great lengths to rebel in these scenarios, even in ways that work against them, just to have a small slice of life that feels like their own. Kids, of all ages, need to have some part of their lives that is separate from their parents, to access feelings of ownership and sovereignty. For some kids, lying becomes a core strategy to achieve this basic human need. When a young kid growing up in a restrictive food environment sneaks a cookie, she *knows* she's her own person; when a teenager growing up with a ton of academic pressure stops studying for exams, he *knows* he's independent of his parents. So when kids lie—"I didn't take that cookie!" or "I already studied!"—they are trying to hold on to the one part of their lives where they feel a sense of self and separation. Of course, in these situations, a parent is often compelled to respond by tightening control, which only increases the motivation for lying. Now, here's an amazing thing about cycles, even "negative" ones: once we recognize the components of a cycle, we have enough information to change it. Changing the parental control/child lying cycle often starts with (no surprise here!) connecting with our kids about this very pattern. Approach your child in a calm moment, and share something like: "Hey, I want to give you more independence. I know it feels awful, when you're a kid, to be in charge of so little. Where can we start? Where's an area you'd like to have more control?" See what your child says and go from there.

Before we dive into strategies, I want to reiterate something important because it's easy for parents to get fixated on "correcting" or "calling out" a specific lie. When it comes to parenting kids who have a tendency to lie, my approach is designed to increase truth-telling *in the future* rather than increase "confessions" now. The strategies outlined here won't end with your child saying to you, "I lied! It's true!" And that's not the goal. The goal is to change your home environment so your kids see you as a safe adult who can tolerate a wider range of their experiences. This can require that we all take a deep breath and swallow our pride in the moment of a lie—that we allow the moment to pass without demanding acknowledgment and instead focus on the longer-term, higher-impact goal. I promise you it's worth it.

Strategies

Reframe the Lie as a Wish

Seeing a lie as a wish allows us to continue seeing our kid as a good kid—and this is critical in responding to lies. Using the language of wishing in response to a child's falsehoods changes the direction of the conversation, as it allows for more options than just "telling the truth" and "lying." Now there's an in-between place, and your ability to see and vocalize that gray area can soften the intensity of the moment and create a way to connect with your child. When your child says, "I've been on a trip to Florida too!" you might say, "Hmm . . . I bet you wish we vacationed in Florida. It sounds so sunny and warm there. I wonder what we'd do if we went?" When your child says, "I didn't knock down my sister's tower, it just fell!" you might respond, "You wish that tower was still up . . . ," or "Sometimes I do things and then wish I hadn't done them . . . it's so hard when that happens." Seeing the lie as a wish allows us to feel on the same team as our child instead of seeing them as the enemy. This perspective shift makes change possible and might make our child more inclined to tell the truth the next time.

Wait and Provide an Opening *Later*

With my own kids (who of course lie to me sometimes!), my go-to strategy in the moment is to pause—meaning I do nothing and just wait. With my five-year-old, it might look like this:

MY SON: *"Mom, I didn't mess up the puzzle and hide the pieces under the couch. I didn't, I didn't!"*
ME: *"Hmm . . ." Slow nod, not saying anything else.*
MY SON: *"I didn't do it!"*

Why do I say nothing? Because my son is clearly in a state of defensiveness, guilt, and/or shame about this, and that is shutting him down. I know I can't argue my way through this, I don't want to get into a power struggle, and I remember we have to reduce shame first to make change possible later. Hours later, I might give my son a generous interpretation of his "bad" behavior, which I consider an opening to be honest: "I'm thinking about the puzzle I was working on with your older brother . . . how when you came into the playroom and saw it . . . hmm . . . it may have been hard to stay away from it . . . I get that . . ." Now, to be completely honest, my son would likely say: "I didn't do it. I didn't, I didn't!" And then I would have to move on, but I would also, on my own, reflect back on the incident. I'd ask myself: What is this lie really about? Is my son "telling" me through his lie that he wants more independence? That he feels jealous of my time with his older brother? That he feels pressure to be perfect and feels constrained? Once we reflect on the meaning of a behavior ("What is this really about, what is my child telling me he's struggling with or needs?"), we have the foundation for other interventions.

"If It Did Happen . . ."
When a child is stuck in a lie, I find it effective to walk through how I *would* respond if she shared the truth. Let's say you get a call from your daughter's school notifying you that she didn't do her writing homework for the past week. You get home and ask her about it, and she says over and over, "I did do it! I did! I don't

want to talk about it!" After an initial pause, when you feel you have a tiny opening, you might say: "Oh . . . okay . . . well, all I'm saying is that if a kid in this family did have a few days of not doing homework, I would really try to understand. Because every kid in this family, if they didn't do homework, would have some reason for this. It makes me think about when I was seven and didn't do writing homework for a bunch of days. Something about writing felt so tricky and it was so hard for me to work on it. Anyway, if it did happen, I'd sit with you and talk it out. You wouldn't be in trouble . . ." Then play it cool. Don't look at your child and say, "So you didn't do it, right?" Just move on. Trust that this sank in. You can of course return to your child later on and say, "Hey, sweetie. Writing is hard. Or at least it was for me. I'm here. You're a good kid even when you don't do homework. I know that. I love you." I might also add on, "I wonder what you could do if something ever feels too hard to start?" if I felt I had an opening.

Asking a Child What He Needs to Be Honest

If lying is an issue in your home, connect with your child *outside* of the moment to have a larger discussion about what he needs to be honest. This is especially effective with older kids who are more equipped to verbalize these thoughts. You might start like this: "Hey . . . I want to talk for a few minutes. You're not in trouble. I'm just thinking about how sometimes it's hard to tell me the truth. And I'm not blaming you, because I realize there must be things *you* need from *me* in order to tell me the truth. There must be things I'm doing that make truth-telling scary for you, or maybe you think you might get in some type of trouble. Anyway, I'm wondering what you need from me, or if there's something I could do differently. Because I want this to be a house where you can tell me the truth about things even if you think they're not so great."

How Does This Play Out for Dara and Jake?

Dara pauses when she notices Jake doubling down on his lie. "Okay," she says. "I hear you. Let's talk later."

"Do you believe me?" Jake asks. "That I didn't do it?"

Dara shares this: "I am not sure what I believe about that moment. What I believe is that I love you and you're a good kid even when you have a hard time. I believe that all kids *and adults* sometimes do things that they're not proud of—and that my job is to help you understand what happens in these times, not punish you or lecture you. All I'm saying is that if I *did* have a kid who pushed someone, I would bet that something happened before that felt really bad. I would tell my kid that this doesn't make pushing okay but instead gives us a way to think about what felt bad or hard and get to the bottom of all of it. Anyway, I am going to take a few deep breaths here and start cooking dinner . . . I'm here if you want. I love you and we will figure this out."

Jake seems to take some of this in and then walks away. Later, Dara pops into his room and says, "I know what it feels like to be judged or to not be given the benefit of the doubt. It's awful. I know." Jake ends up telling her that Owen called him a loser and a baby and how he got so mad that he pushed him down. Dara knows to work on helping Jake regulate his anger—but stores this data to use later and instead focuses on building her connection with Jake, saying, "I'm so glad we're talking about this. It's so important."

CHAPTER 19

Fears and Anxiety

> Five-year-old Blake is scared of fire. She cries at birthday
> parties when candles are lit, often going from calm to terrified
> in a matter of seconds. On a camping trip with friends, Blake
> returns to the campsite with her dad, Leo, to see that the other
> family has lit a large bonfire. Leo tells Blake repeatedly that
> she is safe and that the fire will stay contained. He then points
> out that the fire is fun, not scary. Blake clings to her dad and
> screams and cries, and Leo feels frustrated and unsure how to
> proceed.

Fear, at its most basic level, is the body's response to a perceived
threat. Think of the last time you were truly frightened—
maybe your heart started pounding or your stomach was twisting
and turning. For all humans, fear registers in the body as a set of
somatic experiences—usually elevated heart rate, chest tightness,
or stomach discomfort. These internal experiences send the message "I am in danger right now," which leads to our emotional experience of fear. These feelings manifest in children's small bodies
just as viscerally as they do for adults. It's important to understand:
Children don't exaggerate their fears or make them up for attention. They experience panicky feelings inside their bodies and need

adult help in order to feel safe again. Our goal as parents should be to recognize when our child is in a fear state and help them move from "I am in danger" to "I am safe."

Though most parents understand this ultimate goal, sometimes their instinct is to take their children *out* of their fears by explaining why they shouldn't feel so worried. When a child says, "This feels scary to me!" it's as if parents have the urge to reply, "No, no, your feeling is totally wrong!"

Trying to rationalize a fear or convince a child they shouldn't be afraid, in the moment, is never a successful strategy. When a child feels fear, his body is experiencing a stress response. In this "I'm in danger" state, the logical-thinking part of the brain turns off so that the brain can focus its energy on survival. This means that when your child is in fear mode, reasoning with them will not deliver a sense of safety. What *will* help your child feel safe is sensing your presence; it's the *aloneness in the fear*, after all, that's the scariest part. In other words, kids need less logic, more connection.

In addition, when we try to convince a child out of her fear, we miss out on helpful information. The "Here's why you don't need to be scared" approach focuses on providing your child a new and different experience; the "Huh, there must be something to this, tell me more" approach focuses on learning more about your child's experience. Asking your child about a fear of dogs, for example, might reveal that they just read a book where the main character was bitten; asking about a fear of being alone might reveal something that happened one afternoon when you were at work; asking about a fear of taking the school bus might reveal that your child just witnessed a fight between two students. Learning the details around a fear gives you more information to help your child.

Finally, we don't want to talk our kids out of their fears because we want them to trust their feelings of threat and discomfort. Down the line, we want our children to trust their feelings when they're in truly threatening situations. We want them to follow their instincts when they think, "Hmm . . . something is off here. My body is telling me this isn't right. I need to leave this situation."

These same principles apply when we're talking about a child's more general *anxiety* rather than one specific fear. When our kids are anxious ("I don't know if I want to go to swim class!" or "I don't think I'm going to do well on my math test"), we often have the urge to tell them why they will be okay ("You love swimming, you'll be fine!" or "Think good thoughts, sweetie!"). But, just as is the case with specific fears, trying to convince a child out of a state of anxiety only makes the anxiety worse. Why? Because children are constantly taking in what we *avoid* versus what we are willing to *name and confront*. We think that by urging a child to think or feel a more "positive" way, we're helping them, but children take in a much deeper message — that they're not supposed to be feeling the way that they are, and that feeling nervous or shy or hesitant is wrong. This wires a child to have anxiety *about the anxiety*. It's as if they're wiring a belief that says, "I shouldn't be feeling this way!"

You cannot just "get rid" of anxiety. Anxiety can only be effectively managed by increasing our tolerance for it, allowing it to exist, and understanding its purpose. This makes space for other emotions to emerge, thereby preventing the anxiety from taking over. When we don't try to fight off a feeling within us but rather acknowledge it while still functioning in our everyday lives, we create the opportunity for more peace within ourselves. A parent's job, then, is *not* to change the feeling itself but to be curious about their children's anxiety and to help them feel at home with themselves when that anxiety emerges.

Strategies

Jump into the Hole with Them

Picture your child feeling anxious about a certain situation. It could be something small, like going to a birthday party, or something big, like the death of a relative. Now visualize your child in a small hole in the ground, with that hole representing the anxiety. Your child is *in* that discomfort. We want our children to feel like we are *jumping into the hole with them*, keeping them company—not trying to pull them out of it. When we jump into the hole with our kid, two powerful things happen: our child no longer feels alone *and* we show our child that this thing that feels so awful to them doesn't feel so awful to *us*, because we are willing to join them. Let's say your child worries at night that you won't be there in the morning, despite the fact that you've never left him without notice. Put logic to the side and "jump in": say something like, "When you go to bed, you have a big worry that I won't be there in the morning, huh? Ugh, that *is* such a scary thought . . ." (Pulling out might have sounded like, "Sweetie. There's nothing to worry about, I have never left without telling you!")

Dry Runs

Parents often don't want to bring up the situations their kids are anxious about; we avoid thinking about them or talking about them, crossing our fingers that our kids will suddenly forget their fears or that things will go differently next time. But believe me, avoidance always increases anxiety. If we aren't willing to name and discuss a situation that our *child* feels anxious about, it tells our child that *we* must be anxious about it as well, and this only adds to his anxiety. *Dry runs* give parents an opportunity to show that we think a challenging situation is conquerable, and they give children opportunities to practice how they will react when the "real thing" happens. Dry runs can help kids feel more prepared for moments of separation, doctor's appointments, sports tryouts, playdates, reading aloud in class . . . actually, as I type, I can't think of any stressful situation that *wouldn't* be improved by a dry run. You can practice dry runs directly with your child or act out the scenario with stuffed animals; using stuffies is especially helpful for younger kids who might not role-play directly, or for kids who are resistant to the idea of rehearsing a scary situation.

A dry run for separation might start like this: "On Monday, you'll have your first day of school. Let's think about how we want to say goodbye and then practice it a few times so our bodies are ready for the moment when it comes!" Then come up with a short routine and practice it, maybe even acting out the walking away or taking a deep breath and using a mantra if a child feels sad. Even if your child becomes distressed, keep in mind that this rehearsal will not make your child *more* anxious; rather, it will allow your child to gain mastery and comfort with a tricky situation.

A dry run for a doctor's checkup, using stuffed animals, might look like this: You have a teddy and your daughter has a stuffed unicorn. You, as the teddy, say, "Hi, Unicorn, welcome to the doctor's office! You and your mom can come back with me to the exam room." From there, walk through the appointment exactly as it will happen, and maybe even act out some challenging moments ("Okay, Unicorn! I need you to sit on your mom's lap while I look into your ear and make sure everything is okay in there! Can you stay super still, Unicorn? Great job!").

Script for Addressing Specific Fears

It can be tempting to avoid talking about fears, as if by not reminding our kids of whatever it is they're afraid of, they might forget their fear altogether. This, of course, is not how it works—the best way we can help a child through their fear is to discuss it head-on, as this is how we show a child that we—the adults!—aren't as scared as they are of this topic. Here's a sample script for addressing fears in a way that is productive for both parent and child.

Step 1: Talk to your child about his fear, aiming only to collect information and build understanding. Start with something like: "Tell me more about what it's like to walk into rooms on your own when it's dark," or "It seems like going into parts of this house, alone, feels tricky to you." Ask more, and tell less—no convincing or explaining, just information gathering. Then restate what you've learned to see if you "have it right." You might say, "Okay, let me see if I have this right. When you walk somewhere alone in the house, and it's dark, it just feels scary in your body. You're not sure why but you know it feels that way. Is that right?"

Step 2: Validate that your child's fear "makes sense." Helping your child understand her fear is key to helping her feel brave enough to confront it. Say something like: "The dark can feel scary because we can't see. And it can feel scary when we don't know for sure what's around us. It makes sense that walking around the house alone when it's dark feels tricky to you!"

Step 3: Tell your child how glad you are that you talked about this fear. Use the word "important." This communicates that the fear feelings within them are worthy of being spoken about, which encourages them to cope with these feelings rather than push them away (which would only make them bigger!). Try, "I'm so glad we're talking about this. This is really important stuff."

Step 4: Engage your child to problem-solve with you. Offer "leading" ideas, but allow your child to experience the aha moment of brainstorming a coping mechanism. Resist the urge to explain the fear away or solve the problem on your own. Phrases like "I wonder" and "I'm thinking about" help engage your child in problem-solving. It might sound like this: "Hmm . . . I'm wondering if we can go to the basement and start going down the stairs one at a time . . . let me know when the scary feeling starts and when it feels like it's getting bigger." As you inquire about the fear in this way, you infuse your parental presence into the moment, and as your child feels less alone in her fear, it won't hold such a strong grip. Next, maybe say, "I wonder what you could say to yourself as you go down one of the stairs . . ." Or maybe you suggest a solution like, "I'm thinking about practicing going down one stair now, then in a few days maybe another stair, and the next day a few more . . . hmm . . ."

Step 5: Create a mantra. For kids who struggle with anxiety, mantras can be very helpful in the moment. Whether spoken out loud or recited internally, a mantra focuses their attention on the calming words rather than the source of distress. Examples of mantras include, "It's okay to be nervous. I can get through this," "I can feel scared and brave at the same time," and "I'm safe, my parents are near." Work with your child to develop a mantra that feels good to them and encourage them to repeat it during scary moments.

Step 6: Share a "slowly coping with a fear" story. Yours might sound like: "This reminds me of when I was about your age, and I was scared of dogs. I still remember how bad those moments felt in my body." Do not offer a quick fix like, "But then I realized that I was safe and it was okay." Instead offer a story of slow coping, something like: "I remember talking to my dad about it, and realizing it was okay to feel scared. I remember that my dad and I would read a lot about dogs, then I'd start to walk closer to dogs with him. And then one day, my dad helped me touch a dog. Little by little, dogs felt less scary. It was such hard work to be brave when I was feeling scared!"

How Does This Play Out for Blake and Leo?

Leo reminds himself, "I know this bonfire isn't scary to me, but it *feels scary to Blake*. My goal is to help Blake understand and feel less alone in this fear, not to convince her out of it." He pulls Blake to the side and says, "There's something about that fire that feels scary to you, huh? I believe you. I'm right here with you." He immediately feels her body release and is surprised that this simple sentence, which felt like nothing to him, made a difference to her. He continues, "I used to be scared of things too when I was your age. I still get scared of things now. Sometimes I tell myself, 'It's okay to feel nervous. It's okay to feel nervous.' I'm going to say that a few times now as I take a few deep breaths." Leo is co-regulating for Blake in this moment. Blake seems to be calming down and Leo tells her, "You can sit on my lap if you want. We can sit right here, far away from it. When you feel ready to move closer or if you want to roast some marshmallows, let me know. You'll know when you're ready, and if you're not, that's fine too."

CHAPTER 20

Hesitation and Shyness

> Jai is a six-year-old who doesn't enjoy playing in large groups.
> At a gymnastics birthday party, Jai hides behind his mom,
> Nala, while the other kids separate and start playing on the
> equipment. In a soft, low voice, Nala says, "Jai, you're six and
> you know every single kid here! You're being ridiculous!" Jai
> starts crying, and Nala gets frustrated. "You're embarrassing
> me!" she says. Then Nala feels overwhelmed with guilt. She
> doesn't know what to do next.

Hesitation and shyness are not problems to fix. In fact, I often think that shyness and hesitation make *parents* more anxious than they do kids, and, as a result, we intervene with the intention of easing our own discomfort rather than seeing what's happening for our children and giving them what they need in the moment. If that resonates with you, it doesn't make you a bad parent—in fact, your willingness to reflect on what your kids' behaviors bring up in *you*, thereby separating what you need from what your child needs, is proof that you are a good parent.

Having a kid who is hesitant—who isn't ready to join the birthday party, who doesn't want to play basketball, who resists talking to adults at a family function—can be one of the more emotionally evocative parent-child dynamics, especially if you're an adult who values independence and extroversion. One of the primary anxieties that drives a parent's reaction to their child's shyness is the concern that he will "be like this forever" or "will never feel comfortable in a group." But we want to avoid falling into a self-fulfilling cycle where a parent's anxiety about a kid's hesitation causes the child to feel even more anxious and hesitant. When that happens, the child internalizes their parent's judgment, which causes them to feel more alone in their emotions and even more stuck in them, which leads to more parental frustration. Then the cycle continues and the hesitance and anxiety intensify. How do we break this cycle? Well, not by changing a child; we start by reflecting on ourselves and doing the work internally.

Let's think about shyness in an adult context: You go to a cocktail party with your partner, you feel nervous, and so you say, "I want to stay near you for a bit, okay?" I can think of two types of responses you might receive. One: Your partner looks at you and says, "You're being ridiculous, you know people here." After seeing you're still hesitant, your partner hisses, "Okay, now you're embarrassing me. For real." Two: Your partner looks at you and says, "Something doesn't feel great for you right now. I see that. That's okay, no biggie. Stay with me until you're ready to talk to people; you'll know when that is."

Think about how each of these responses makes you feel. Has the anxiety eased up? Are you suddenly feeling more capable?

Now let's revisit option one. If, later on that evening, your partner says, "Listen, I responded that way because I can't always be a crutch for you. You have to learn how to be on your own!," does that make any sense to you? Or do you wish your partner would trust that if he gives you what you need *today*, and maybe talks to you about what was happening for you in that tense moment, you might flourish in the way that's right for you, in the time frame that works for you? Whose time line are you on, anyway? Your own or your partner's? And our kids—are they on *our* time line or their own? I think we all know the answer. And while it can certainly be draining to offer the constant emotional support that a shy child might need when struggling to separate or join the crowd—a fatigue that can play a role in our knee-jerk or negative reactions to this behavior—parenting is an exercise in patience. It's about seeing our kids for who *they* are and what they need as separate from who *we* are and what we need.

Most of us, at some point in our lives, were taught that confidence means joining rather than waiting, and jumping in rather than pausing and assessing. I'm not sure why this is. There's a deep irony here, because I talk with so many parents who tell me that their teenagers can't seem to think for themselves and are unwilling to be different from the crowd. I'll never forget the day, in my practice, when I had a consultation with parents of a timid six-year-old followed by a consultation with parents of an impressionable sixteen-year-old. The first set of parents told me: "Chase watches all his friends go play and he hangs back—even when his friends ask him to join, sometimes he says no! He's so timid. I wish he was more confident." Then, in the next hour, the parents of the teenager said: "It's like Alex will just do whatever his friends are doing. It's like he can't think for himself, he's so easily swayed. I wish he was more confident."

So what *is* confidence, and how does it relate to shyness or hesitance? For me, confidence is the experience of knowing how you feel and believing it's okay to be yourself, in that feeling, in that moment. A child who isn't sure they want to join and observes on the side for a while—this can be a form of confidence. And confidence-building for hesitant kids comes from having caregivers who say, "I'm here. Take your time." These messages communicate an understanding that a child knows their feelings better than we do. They tell our kids, "It's okay to be you right now." Confidence isn't necessarily joining a group or engaging in an activity right away. It might be, if a child actually feels prepared internally, but it certainly isn't if a child feels coerced. Confidence isn't *being* ready—confidence is *knowing* when you're ready.

Strategies

Check In with Yourself

Shyness is very triggering for many parents, especially if you're a particularly outgoing person or grew up in a family that valued jumping in, joining, and acting instead of pausing. Right now, imagine that your child is the only one sitting on their parent's lap in a group gathering where the other kids are happily playing independently from parents. Notice how you feel. Do you have an urge to push your child away? There are no wrong feelings or urges here—just important information to collect—so remind yourself, "Noticing how I feel doesn't make me a bad parent. All feelings are allowed, just like I tell my kids. Knowing my own trigger will help me separate my experience from my child's." If you notice that your child's shyness or hesitation or clinginess bothers you, remind yourself that a child's willingness to *not* join the crowd is probably a trait you'll value in her later on. Try to do a 180 on your interpretation of shyness, and experiment with telling yourself: "My child knows who he is and what is and isn't comfortable, even in the face of others' acting differently. How bold, how awesome, how confident!"

Validate + "You'll Know When You're Ready"

When your child is hesitant or feeling shy, start by validating the feeling rather than trying to convince him out of it. Assume your child's hesitation comes from a real place, even if you don't understand it; validating the feelings under reticence is what helps kids feel more at home with themselves, and when kids feel more at home with themselves, they are open to a wider range of responses (this is true for adults too).

Here's a powerful phrase to use with your kids: "You'll know when you're ready to ___." This communicates that you trust your child, which will teach them to trust themself, and self-trust is the essence of confidence. But this phrase also suggests the idea of movement—it implies that your kid will be more comfortable eventually. We want our kids to believe that they are the best feelers of their feelings, because this is what enables them to make good decisions. So if your child doesn't want to talk to neighbors at a block party, this strategy might sound like: "Seems like you need a minute. Take your time. You'll know when you're ready to talk." Or, when you're talking to your child who seems nervous to join a dance birthday party, "You haven't been here before. It's okay to check it out. You can stay near me as you do. You'll know when you're ready to join."

And what if your child never feels ready? Right now you may be thinking, "I do exactly this and still, at every social gathering, my child hides behind me and refuses to join in." This doesn't mean you're employing this strategy "incorrectly." Let's remember our MGI: a child who always stays on the sidelines and struggles to separate must feel incredibly frozen, anxious, and out of their element. They may need a break from larger group gatherings altogether. This isn't collusion, it's not "encouraging" shyness—it might just be meeting your child where they are. Or some other strategies may help in this situation: de-shaming, by telling your child a story of your separation struggles as a child; emotional vaccination, by talking in advance about the feelings that may come up in these situations; and preparation—which I explain below.

Preparation

Kids who feel hesitant do well with preparation for what's to come, in terms of both logistics and emotions. Before you go to, say, a family gathering, share details with your child: "We'll be seeing lots of family later today. We are going to Aunt Marsha's for lunch and you'll see Aunt Marsha and Uncle Rex with their kids Piper and Evan, and then you'll also see Aunt Fiona and Aunt Lauren with their new baby Jasper. Grandma and Grandpa might stop by too. Hmm . . . what will that be like, to be with so many people . . . in a different house . . . with cousins you haven't seen in a while? I wonder if that could feel a bit tricky at first, especially if the adults come to you right away and ask a ton of questions . . ." Then, just wait. There's so much power in predicting feelings: when you name and recognize them in advance, it's as if you give your child permission to feel them, which is half the battle when it comes to regulation. Try preparing your child for a feeling without adding a solution or coping strategy; just pause, as if that really is enough. See what your child does next.

Avoid Labeling

Our kids will always respond to the versions of themselves we reflect back. When we label kids, saying things like "Oh, she's shy" or "He never likes to talk to grown-ups, he's really reserved," we lock them into roles with a type of rigidity that makes growth difficult. Instead of labeling, provide a generous interpretation of your child's behavior, especially if someone else smacks on a label. If a family member says, "Aisha, why are you being so shy?," take a breath, jump in, and share, "Aisha isn't shy. Aisha is figuring out what feels comfortable to her, and that's great. She'll share more about her school year when she's ready." Maybe rub her back as you say this, letting her know you're on her team.

How Does This Play Out for Jai and Nala?

After the party, Nala feels awful about what she said to Jai. She remembers that it's never too late, so she grounds herself in a deep breath; reminds herself, "I am a good parent who had a hard time"; and talks to Jai about his nerves. She apologizes for pushing him to join and calling him ridiculous and embarrassing, and she tells him that the next time they have a group activity, the two of them will talk about it in advance and she'll let him know it's okay to take his time. Before a group playdate the next weekend, Nala talks with Jai about which playground they're going to, how many kids will be there, and how it might feel to be in a group. She pre-validates the feelings, realizing that she can do some of this work in advance, which feels hopeful and efficient. Nala says to Jai, "Some kids like to join in right away. Some kids like to watch first. Both ways are right ways to be a kid. Only you know your body, so only you know what will feel right to you." Sure enough, Jai wants to sit with his mom on the bench for a while, and he is the only kid to do this. Nala sees the bravery and boldness in this and whispers to him, "It's kind of cool you know who you are and that you know when you're ready. Take your time, do what feels right to you. I'm here." Nala feels Jai's body shift a bit and notices his looking around with more curiosity. When his friend Raya invites him, Jai runs off to play.

CHAPTER 21

Frustration Intolerance

Braeden is a four-year-old working on a twelve-piece puzzle. His dad, Ethan, is nearby. Braeden has three pieces connected and is maneuvering another piece, unable to place it. Watching his son, Ethan gets frustrated and says, "Braeden, that one won't work yet. Don't you see, it doesn't fit! They're not even the same color!" Braeden looks to his dad, throws the puzzle piece, and says, "I'm so bad at puzzles! I hate them!" In an appointment shortly after this interaction, Ethan tells me this is one of many examples of Braeden's working well until something becomes challenging—at which point he tends to walk away or insist that a parent has to complete that part for him.

Here's a deep paradox about learning: the more we embrace not-knowing and mistakes and struggles, the more we set the stage for growth, success, and achievement. This is true for adults and kids alike, and it's a critical reminder about the importance of normalizing difficulties, embracing mistakes as an opportunity to learn, and building frustration tolerance. After all, the more a child can tolerate frustration, the longer they can stick with a hard puzzle, work on a tough math problem, or stay engaged while writing an essay. And, of course, these skills translate outside of academics as well, because tolerating frustration is key to managing disappointments, communicating effectively with people with different opinions, and sticking with personal goals.

If we want our kids to develop frustration tolerance, we have to develop tolerance for their frustration. It's an inconvenient truth, I know. Sometimes, when my child is really struggling with something, I remind myself that she's looking at me and absorbing my relationship with her frustration, and this forms the foundation for her own relationship with her frustration. In other words, the more I'm okay with her struggling with a challenge—meaning I let her work it out rather than offering a solution—the more she will be okay with it. If she can tell I think it's fine to struggle with math, she will be okay with struggling with math; if I exude patience for learning to tie one's shoes, she will have patience when practicing this new skill. Beyond any strategy or script I offer in this chapter, the most impactful thing we can do with our kids is to show up in a calm, regulated, non-rushed, non-blaming, non-outcome-focused way—both when they are performing difficult tasks and when they are witnessing *us* perform difficult tasks.

Frustration is, well, frustratingly difficult to manage. It often unravels us, sending both kids and adults into spirals of "I can't do it!" and "I just don't want to try anymore!" and "You do it for me!" What makes tolerating frustration so hard is that it requires us to let go of our need to *finish* and *be quick* and *be right* and *have things done*; frustration tolerance requires us to ground ourselves in what is happening in the moment, to feel okay even when we don't know how to do something, and to focus on effort instead of outcome. This is a lot easier to do when we navigate the world with a "growth mindset"—the belief that abilities can be cultivated through effort, study, and persistence and that failures and struggles are not enemies of learning but rather key elements on the pathway *to* learning.

Growth mindset, a concept first introduced by psychologist Carol Dweck, provides a framework to embrace challenges and build frustration tolerance in kids. It says that anybody can improve at something if they work at it, and that they should do so even in the face of setbacks. People with a "fixed mindset," on the other hand, believe that abilities are innate—you can either do something or you can't, and if you fail at that thing, it's an indication that you'll never be able to do it. Not surprisingly, kids (and adults!) who embrace a growth mindset welcome challenges, learn from mistakes, and stick with hard things for longer, because they believe that hard work leads to growth. A growth mindset teaches us that hard work and improvement are in our control, while specific outcomes are not. The bottom line: the less obsessed we are with "success," the more we'll be willing to try new things and develop and grow, which of course are key elements in all types of success.

One of the best things about a growth mindset is that it builds a tolerance for learning. "Tolerance for learning" might sound like an odd phrase—learning is a good thing, so why would it be hard to tolerate? Keep in mind, our kids are learning all day every day . . . and learning isn't easy. I want you to visualize a time line where the first point is "Not-Knowing" and the end point is "Knowing." All the space in between those two points is "Learning." That space can feel very uncomfortable, especially when we're younger. Often, people find themselves in this learning space longer than they want to be there; it's natural to wish the knowing would just come already, or to have the urge to retreat back to the comfort of not knowing, where we don't have to expend effort or risk failure or embarrassment. Learning exposes our weaknesses and makes us feel vulnerable. It requires us to be brave.

To help our kids become good learners (which I'd argue is more important than being "smart" or "getting things right"), we have to help them sit in the not-knowing-and-yet-still-working-at-it space.

And this comes from how we respond to our children's frustration. I often remind myself that my job as a parent is not to help my kids get *out* of the learning space and *into* knowing . . . but rather to help my kids learn to *stay in* that learning space and *tolerate not being in* knowing! So rather than solving children's problems for them, belittling their struggles, or losing patience with their efforts to understand that which might seem simple to an adult, we have to allow our kids to do the work on their own. The longer children can stay in that in-between space, the more they can be curious and creative, tolerate hard work, and pursue a wide variety of ideas.

Strategies

Deep Breaths

When we get frustrated, one of the best things we can do is to take a deep breath. Deep breaths calm our nervous system, and this sets the stage for accessing all our other coping mechanisms. When you notice your child getting frustrated, instead of telling them, "Take a deep breath," model it yourself. When your three-year-old gets annoyed while trying to get food onto their fork, look off to the side and take a few audible inhales and exhales. When your six-year-old is struggling to learn letter sounds, take a few deep breaths in their presence. Remember: our kids learn to self-regulate through our co-regulation; taking a deep breath allows your child to see that there can be safety and calm around frustration. Not to mention, our deep breathing grounds *us*, which means we are less likely to react with our own annoyance or reactivity.

Mantras

I love mantras. They take moments or emotions that feel big and overwhelming—like episodes of frustration—and give us something small and manageable to focus on. As a result, they can be very grounding for kids. But rather than coming in heavy-handed with a mantra your child should say to themselves, try framing it as something you learned that you just happen to be passing along. This might sound like: "You know, when I was six, I used to get sooooo frustrated when things felt hard! Oh my goodness, it felt so bad! And I still remember something my dad—yes! Grandpa Harry!— told me. He said that when *he* gets frustrated, he places his hand on his heart, takes a breath, and tells himself, 'This feels hard because it is hard, not because I'm doing something wrong.' And so, I started saying that to myself! If you want to try that too, that could be cool . . . it seems kinda silly, but it really helps. Here, I'll show you . . ." For younger kids, a mantra might be "I can do it" or "I like to be challenged" or "I can do hard things" or "This is tricky and I can stay with it."

Frame Frustration as a Sign of Learning, Not a Sign of Failure

Here's something I start saying to my kids early on: "Did you know that learning is hard? I mean it! Every single time any of us learns something—me, you, everyone—it feels frustrating!" If my child seems to be taking in what I'm saying, I'll continue: "And also, listen to this, because this is weird . . . Frustration, that feeling of 'Ugh, I can't do it' or 'Ugh, I want to just be done already!' . . . that's a feeling that tries to trick our brain into telling us we're doing something wrong, but actually, this feeling is a sign that we're learning and doing something right! It's such a tricky thing. Let's be on the lookout for that feeling so we can remind ourselves we are learning and that learning is supposed to feel this way." How might I use this in the moment? Well, let's say my child is getting dressed and I know they can get frustrated while doing this; *before* they begin, I might say: "Oh, you're about to get dressed, huh? Let's get ready for that frustrating feeling . . ." And then, I might mutter to myself, in a way that my child just *happens* to overhear, "Becky, new things feel hard . . . they always feel hard . . . that's okay . . . I can do hard things . . ."

Growth Mindset Family Values

It can be really helpful, as a family, to establish a set of *growth mindset family values* that you can refer to in moments of struggle or challenge (both your kids' moments and your own). Here are four of these values I love, which I often write down in work areas or the kitchen, for my entire family to see:

1. In our family, we love to be challenged.
2. In our family, how hard we work is more important than coming up with the right answer.
3. In our family, we know that not-knowing sits next to learning something new. We love learning new things, so we embrace "I don't know" moments.
4. In our family, we try to remember that sticking with something hard makes our brains grow. And we're big into brain growth.

Once you've established your set of values, talk about them often, especially when *you've* made a "mistake" or don't know something. I've been known to speak growth mindset values aloud while cooking. ("Ugh . . . I think I messed up this recipe! Well, it was a new one and it definitely challenged me. In our family, we do love to be challenged. And I learned how to make it better for the next time, so that's pretty awesome!") Frustration can feel very "alone" and "not good enough" for a child, so the more you let him see your own struggles and model the very frustration-tolerance skills you want him to learn, the more your child will absorb them.

Think in Terms of Coping, Not Success

Frustration tolerance is the ability to sit in the space between not-knowing and knowing, or between starting and finishing, which means we really want to build our child's skills for *coping with hard feelings* rather than building skills for *finding success*. This way, our kids can feel more at home while working hard, *before they've reached success*. But doing this starts with a mindset shift on the part of the parents. Tell yourself, "I don't have to teach my kid how to put his shirt on smoothly . . . I need to teach my kid how to tolerate when it doesn't go on right. I don't have to teach my child how to get the math problem correct, I need to teach my child how to regulate her body while working on the math problem."

Emotional Vaccination, Dry Runs, and "Did I Ever Tell You About the Time . . . ?"

Emotional vaccination is a key strategy for building frustration tolerance, because predicting in advance the frustration to come helps your child's body prepare. Dry runs are also powerful, because you can practice a skill in advance. You can predict the frustration your child will have when beading a bracelet, for example, and then pretend to do it, pause, and practice a deep breath and a mantra ("I can do hard things"). This way you've prepped your child's nervous system for the upcoming difficult moment and also layered on a helpful coping mechanism in advance. Finally, telling your child about a moment where you were frustrated—or even acting out a frustration in the moment—will help your child feel less alone in her struggle. It's incredibly hard to build tolerance for frustration when you're learning in an environment where no one else seems to have had a hard time. More on emotional vaccination and "did I ever tell you about the time . . ." in chapter 11, and you can read about dry runs in chapter 19.

How Does This Play Out for Braeden and Ethan?

Ethan starts by calming his own body. He places his hand on his heart, takes a few breaths, and tells himself he is safe and can start again with his son. He repairs by saying, "Hey, buddy, I had a big feeling right then, and that was my thing, not yours. I'm sorry I reacted like that." After a few minutes, when he senses an opening, Ethan shares with Braeden: "You know something I've never really told you? Puzzles are hard! And they're supposed to feel hard! I don't think I tell you that enough. Sometimes we think if something feels hard it means we are doing something wrong, but it means we are doing something right!"

"I don't care," Braeden says. "I'm not doing it."

Ethan doesn't take the bait and instead remembers to teach *coping*, not *success*. Ethan tries something new: he quietly grabs a few puzzle pieces and starts putting them together himself, off to the side. He models struggling, not getting them together right away, sighing a bit, and saying aloud, "Ugh, this is hard!" Ethan expects Braeden to call his bluff and say, "Dad, I know you're pretending," but he doesn't. Instead, he peeks over with interest. Ethan knows he still can't be too direct, so he continues; he sings a soft mantra song to himself: "If it doesn't fit, put it to the side . . . and try another piece . . ." He models flexibility in placing down one piece and trying another. Braeden eventually moves closer to Ethan and asks to put the last piece of the puzzle in. Ethan considers this a major win.

CHAPTER 22

Food and Eating Habits

Five-year-old Gia loves snack foods, and her parents struggle to get her to eat any real meals. At four P.M. Gia tells her mom, Eva, "I'm starving! I need something to eat. Goldfish! Goldfish!"

"It's best to wait for dinner," Eva says, only for Gia to make a dash to the snack cabinet. Eva hates the idea of Gia's being hungry, so she says, "Okay, okay, but promise me you'll have a good dinner later." Gia promises, calms down, eats a snack, and then at dinnertime refuses to eat. Eva feels exasperated.

Kids' eating habits can cause a lot of anxiety for parents—they may bring up insecurities about our parenting or create power struggles with our children. One reason the feeding process can be so emotionally evocative for parents is that, in some ways, it represents our ability to sustain our kids and fill them up with what they need to survive and thrive. After all, a parent's primary job is to keep their kids alive. In our food-related interactions with our children, it feels like so much is at stake—that in some way, how much and what our child eats is a barometer for how good a job we are doing as a parent. Watching your child reject the dinner you made them can feel like a child is saying, "I won't take in what you have to offer—I am rejecting the food and I am rejecting you—you are a bad parent!" Watching your child eat broccoli, on the other hand, can feel like your child is saying, "I am taking in your effort to sustain me—I am accepting the food and I am accepting you—you are an amazing parent!" When parents around the dinner table start talking about what their kids will or will not eat, what they really seem to be assessing is whether they are doing a good job, whether they are doing enough, whether their kids are willing to "take in" what they want to offer them. Understanding this deeper connection between parenting and feeding is, in fact, the first step to reducing the intensity of mealtime. It helps separate what's actually happening from the deeper feelings that get evoked in our bodies around this issue, and that helps us intervene in a way that's based on what's in front of us, rather than on our fears and insecurities.

Food *interactions* with our kids touch on deeper issues as well: questions of body sovereignty, who is in control, and whether a child can make their own decisions all come up around food-related episodes between parents and children. When kids push back at mealtime and say, "I'm not hungry," or "No, I don't want that," or "I'll only eat if you make me pasta" . . . what they are really doing is asking questions: "What are parents in charge of and what are kids in charge of?" "When can I make my own decisions?" "Do you trust me?" Kids push boundaries, protest parents' choices, and ask for unavailable options in order to feel out their own independence . . . all things they do outside mealtime too, of course.

These two conflicts—the internal issue of parental insecurity and the external issue of body sovereignty—do, ultimately, intersect. As a child pushes a boundary around food or rejects it entirely, a parent feels like a "bad parent," causing her to refocus on controlling her kid in an attempt to feel "good" again. Yet the more a child feels controlled, the more she will cling to rejection or boundary-pushing in order to assert her independence, which leads to increased parental desperation, intensified power struggles, and frustration for everyone.

So what do we do about this? How can we unwind this negative cycle to establish food and mealtime patterns that feel better for the family system? I believe the answer begins with the pioneering work of dietitian, psychotherapist, and author Ellyn Satter, who created what's known as the "Division of Responsibility" around eating. Here's a quick summary of Satter's framework:

- **Parent's job:** decide what food is offered, where it is offered, when it is offered
- **Child's job:** decide whether and how much to eat of what's offered

What's so powerful about Satter's framework is that it allows for the development of healthy eating patterns but it also supports self-regulation, self-confidence, consent, and so much more.

You may have noticed that Satter's division of responsibility sounds quite similar to my family jobs principles from chapter 3. Just as I believe family systems work better when everyone knows their job, Satter believes a healthy relationship with food and with one's body will emerge when there's clarity in every family member's role and when each of us "stays in our lane." Satter says parents should be in charge of the boundaries around eating—this is the what, where, and when. Parents, essentially, come into the picture first. They make the baseline decisions and set the options and limits; after that, a child is in charge. You might even think of parents as a container—they establish the outer edges, but within the container, children are free to explore and express themselves. You've heard me say that a child's job in a family system is to explore and express feelings; in Satter's model, children explore and express themselves through their food decisions—what goes in their mouths, whether they swallow, how much of anything they eat, and what they leave to the side.

Here's something else I love about Satter's division of responsibility: it gives parents a way to feel good about their role no matter what their child does or doesn't eat. Parents can say to themselves: "My job is the what-when-where. Did I do my job well? Okay, I served chicken, pasta, and broccoli. I decided dinner is at five thirty P.M. and that it takes place only at our dinner table. Wow, yes, I did all of that—job well done!" Sure, a parent's mind will naturally wander to questions like "My son only ate the pasta . . . I wonder why he's not eating any veggies? What am I doing wrong?" But hopefully this is when an internal alarm might go off. "Oh wait, that's my child's job! Those decisions are his to make. Let me come back to myself and my role. I will keep doing my job and will trust him to do his . . . I am doing my job well."

Here's what I believe is the most important idea around kids and food: minimizing *anxiety* around food is more important than *consumption* of food. Are there exceptions? Sure. If your child has a medical condition or a doctor has raised health concerns, these are of course special situations. But even then, paying attention to a child's feelings *during* eating is critical. After all, the dinner table is just one more space where we can look at children's behavior (in this case, eating) as a window into how they are feeling; as always, children need parents to set boundaries and exude trust and respect for individuality so that they can explore, experiment, and thrive. Remember, children are in charge of so little—often, the only thing truly under their control is what goes into their bodies. Eating and potty training are areas where parents really have to check in with their own desire to control so that they can give their children the freedom they need.

Strategies

Mantra

I've said elsewhere that mantras help children stay grounded when anxiety swirls around them, but this is true for parents too. If you know that food situations with your kids make you feel anxious, or that it's hard for you to relinquish control when it comes to their eating, use a mantra to remind you of your job and your focus. You might try saying, "My only jobs are the what-when-where. I can do that. I can do that." Or, "What my child eats is not most important. I am doing a good job. My child is going to be okay." Or maybe, "What my child eats is not a barometer of my parenting."

Explain Roles

I love having an honest, direct conversation with my kids about my job and their jobs around food and eating. Share Satter's division of responsibility as a way of holding yourself accountable as well as letting your kids know what they are and are not in charge of. It might sound like this: "Hey, I learned something interesting today and wanted to share it with you. When it comes to food, you have a job and I have a job—and our jobs are totally different. It's my job to decide what we eat, when we eat, and where we eat. And just so you know, I'll always offer at least one thing that you like so that eating never feels stressful. Your job is to decide whether you eat what I serve and how much. That's kind of interesting, right? It means you get to choose what goes into your body, but it also means you don't get to tell me to make something new if you want something I didn't choose that day. I get to choose what we eat that day, but I don't get to make you take more bites of things or tell you what you have to finish. What do you think of that?"

Dessert-Specific Strategies

There's no one right way to do dessert—the key is simply grounding your decision in your role. Remember, you decide all the decisions *around* dessert: whether it's served, what it is, at what time it's offered. After that, it's your kid's job. But this means parents shouldn't link dessert to how much a child eats, because that is the domain of a child, not a parent. I know what you're thinking . . . "But my kid only wants dessert, he wouldn't have dinner at all if I didn't link it to how many bites he has!" This is a good time to reflect and see if the division of responsibility model makes sense to you; if it does, then there are a few things to do about dessert. You can serve a small dessert *with* dinner—as in, at the same time, even on a plate next to broccoli and chicken and pasta. From a practical perspective, I wouldn't make dessert so large that a child could fully fill up on it, but I also don't like the idea of delaying dessert so much that it is set up as a prize to be coveted. Serving dessert with dinner makes dessert less exciting. It exudes a message of trusting your child and sets him up to be less dessert focused over time. Other families I've worked with serve a "dessert" as an afternoon snack so that dinner isn't linked with dessert at all.

Snack-Specific Strategies

Oh . . . snacks. The crunchy, salty, delicious foods we have in our pantry, the ones our kids covet, the ones we vow not to buy anymore but that end up in our grocery bags anyway. There's no right way to do snacks. Some parents choose no snacks, some parents give free access to snacks, and some parents do something in between. There is no moral superiority to decisions about snacks, so take note of any parent guilt you're feeling and then ask yourself this question: "Does my snack approach work for my family?" If you're thinking, "Well, not really, because I want my kids to eat more at dinner," or "Not really, because my kids no longer eat non-snack foods," well, this is the only answer you need. On the other hand, if you don't mind the amount of snacks your kids have, then you have something that's working for you. If you want to make a change, it's critical to remind yourself that your job is the "what, when, where"—you don't have to ask your kids' permission, you just need to announce the change and allow them to have their reactions and feelings. Here's a quick script: "I'm going to make a change to snacks in our house. We have too many snacks, which means we don't eat enough dinner, which is the food that helps your body grow. When you get home from school, the only snacks I will offer are _____ and _____. I know that's a big change and I know it'll take some time to get used to."

Tolerate Pushback

Making food decisions with our kids requires us to assert ourselves, say no, and tolerate children's complaints and distress when they arise. This is a critical piece of implementing Satter's division of responsibility, because after knowing our role, we have to be willing to fulfill it, and that relies on our ability to handle our child's not being happy with us. This sounds easy in theory—"Okay, my child isn't happy with me, that's fine!"—but tolerating an unhappy child who's hungry and tantrumming during meals . . . it's a lot! Here are a few scripts to help:

- Remind yourself what you know to be true: "I know that my child feels safe with one of the foods I offered. It's not their favorite but it's a legitimate option. My job is serving and their job is deciding; this isn't pretty but we are both doing our jobs."
- Remind yourself you don't need agreement: "I don't need my child to agree with me."
- Give permission for your child to be upset: "You're allowed to be upset."

- Name the wish: "You wish we could have ___ for dinner instead . . ." or "You wish you were in charge of every food choice."
- Separate your child's protest from your decision: "My child's protest/tantrum doesn't mean I'm making a bad decision. And it doesn't mean I'm a bad or cold parent."
- Remind yourself and your child of your job: "My job as a parent is to make decisions that I think are good for you, even when I know you're not going to like them."

How Does This Play Out for Gia and Eva?

Eva realizes she has been *asking for permission* rather than *embodying her authority* with Gia around food decisions, so she reminds herself of her job versus Gia's job and talks to Gia one weekend morning when things are calm: "Gia, we are going to make some changes about snacks so our bodies are hungry for dinnertime. You can still have Goldfish—in fact, I'll be putting some Goldfish on your plate for dinnertime so it's right there with the other food we have. For afternoon snack, I will offer you some fruit and cheese, and snack time will end by three P.M. I know these changes may feel tough, and I know we will get used to it." Eva feels nervous yet confident as she asserts this change. That afternoon, Gia has a meltdown at snack time, demanding Goldfish and pretzels. Eva holds strong, saying to Gia: "I know you want those foods now. We can have a few apple slices and cheese now, or if that doesn't work for you, we can wait until dinner to eat. You're allowed to be upset. I know you wish you could be in charge! It's hard to be a kid. I love you. I'm here." Eva reminds herself that if Gia chooses not to have a snack, she can move dinnertime earlier to meet Gia's hunger needs. Eva feels sturdy through this, reminding herself, "Wow, this is how I handle so many other protests, like those around screen time or getting new toys. I hold the boundary and I allow Gia to feel her feelings. It works with food too."

CHAPTER 23

Consent

Four-year-old Kiki and her seven-year-old brother, Lex, are
visiting their grandparents. When they arrive, Kiki's grandfather
hugs Lex and then approaches Kiki. Kiki runs away, saying, "No
hugs!" Her grandfather walks toward her, saying, "I haven't
seen you in months! Give your grandpa a hug! It'll make me so
sad if you don't. Do you want to make me sad, cutie?" Kiki's
mom, Tasha, feels both annoyed and guilty; her father looks
visibly hurt and her daughter is clearly resistant. She doesn't
know how to respond.

S ay this with me: "*I am the only person in my body. I am the only
person* who knows what I want and what I am ready for and
what feels right to me."

Let's continue: "I am in charge of my body. I am in charge of
my body boundaries. I am in charge of who touches me, for how
long, and at what times. I can like something one day and not want
it another day. I can be comfortable touching some people and not
others. I am the only person who can make these decisions."

And one more: "There will be times when I assert myself based
on what feels right to me and other people won't like it. They will
push back. They will talk about what *they want from me* instead

of honoring what I'm telling them *feels comfortable to me*. It's not my job to make other people happy. Their discomfort is a feeling in *their body*, and it's not my fault or my responsibility to make this feeling go away."

Okay, pause. Notice how your body reacts to these statements. What comes up for you? Are they consistent with what you were taught in childhood? Are they in sync with how you currently approach decisions about your body? What about when you were a child or teenager or young adult? Before we can consider how issues of *body sovereignty* play out with our children, we have to check in with our own circuitry and see what these issues evoke in us.

The way we engage with and enforce the idea of body sovereignty—or the notion that we each have the right to fully control our own bodies—will inevitably impact our children. Feeling like you have the right to make decisions about your body doesn't come from a classroom setting or a book; feeling like you have the right to make decisions about your body comes from experience in your early years regarding . . . whether you felt you had the right to make decisions about your body. It boils down to one question, the answer to which kids learn not by our words but by how we handle tricky situations: "Am I allowed to say no to others even if they get upset?"

Personally, I want my kids to have words like "No," "I don't like that," and "Stop it" in their vocabularies. I also want them to have something maybe more important: the ability to use these words. What's the difference? Well, every single one of our children will know the word "no" or the phrase "I don't want to" by the time they enter adolescence, but the confidence to actually hold the boundaries around these words comes from our child's early *experiences with us*. It will depend largely on whether they were encouraged to pay attention to their body's feelings of readiness and comfort, or whether they were encouraged to push these feelings aside in favor of making other people happy.

Please note, I'm not just talking about allowing our kids to decide whether or not they hug their grandparents. Kiki's example is a heightened one, because it epitomizes the conflict between pleasing others and acting in accordance with our body signals, but there are plenty of other moments when we are building the circuitry for body consent. When a child feels hesitant to join a birthday party, or gets upset about a well-intentioned joke, or says she's full even after a small dinner, or claims a dark basement feels scary—all of these are moments for wiring body circuitry.

Remember, kids are always asking questions, and one of those questions is, "Do I know the signals in my body better than anyone else or are other people right about what's happening inside me? Do I interpret the sensations in my body correctly or do I need to rely on others to get things right?" Now consider the examples below and note the two parent responses, one that builds circuitry for consent and the ability to say no, and one that builds circuitry for self-doubt.

A child is hesitant to join a birthday party

- Circuitry for consent: "You're not so sure about playing with the other kids right now. That's okay. Take your time."
- Circuitry for self-doubt: "You're being ridiculous, go join your friends."

A child is hurt by a well-meaning joke

- Circuitry for consent: "I can see that felt bad to you. I believe you. I won't say it again."

- Circuitry for self-doubt: "Oh my goodness, you are so sensitive. Pleeeeeease."

A child says he's full at dinner

- Circuitry for consent: "Only you know your body, so you're the only one who can know if you're full. Here's the thing: once dinner is over, the kitchen is closed. Maybe do one check-in, see what your body is saying, and double-check you're good for the night."
- Circuitry for self-doubt: "You can't be full. You hardly ate. If you want to leave the table, you have to have eight more bites."

A child says she's scared of the basement when it's dark

- Circuitry for consent: "There's something about the dark basement that feels scary to you. You know that. I believe you. I'm so glad you are sharing this with me."
- Circuitry for self-doubt: "You're such a drama queen, come on, it's just the basement."

In each example of circuitry for consent, the adult believes the child's experience. This doesn't mean the adult allows the child to behave in a specific way, but rather that the child's experience is seen as real and as a source of truth. In each example of circuitry for self-doubt, the adult intervenes as if the adult's sense of how the child *should be* reacting is more "true" than the child's actual expressed experience. Children develop self-doubt in response to being repeatedly told "You do not know yourself." This is why I recommend all parents strike the following words from their parenting vocabulary (feel free to strike them from all interactions outside of parenting as well!): "dramatic," "drama queen," "overly sensitive," "hysterical," "disproportionate," "ridiculous." These are gaslighting words that tell a child you don't trust them—which wires them not to trust themself.

Okay, let's pause. Parent-shame check! Note any "Oh no . . . I've messed this all up" or "I'm the worst parent in the world" thoughts that are coming up for you. I've had those thoughts too, I promise, and I know how painful they are. Place a hand on your heart, making sure your feet are on the ground, and take a few deep breaths. Tell yourself: "It's not too late . . . for me or my child. My reaction is a sign that I *care*, not a sign that I'm *bad*. My willingness to reflect and try something new tells me that I am a brave cycle-breaker."

Strategies

"I Believe You"

Building circuitry for consent comes from building circuitry for self-trust. If children don't trust themselves and their feelings, they won't believe in their ability to take charge of personal decisions. When your daughter tells you she's cold even though it feels perfectly pleasant to you, believe her: "You're cold, huh? I believe you. Let's see what we can do about it." When your child tells you he doesn't like to be tickled, believe him: "I hear you. Tickling doesn't feel good to you. I believe you, I'm glad you're telling me, and I won't do it anymore." When your child tells you she feels scared at a cartoon movie, believe her: "This feels scary to you. I believe you."

"There's Something About . . ."

Sometimes we don't know what is happening for our child—we might see that he is upset but we have no clue what's going on or why he's unhappy. Maybe your son is having a meltdown about a red shirt even though red is his favorite color; perhaps your daughter is suddenly devastated when you leave for work even though you've been going to work five days a week for all nine years of her life. These moments often provoke invalidation and gaslighting and all those words I suggested striking from your parenting vocabulary. In these moments, I like to use the phrase "There's something about . . ." It says you believe your child and you validated their experience, even if you don't understand what exactly is happening. It might sound like: "There's something about this red shirt that doesn't feel good to you . . ." or "There's something about my saying goodbye today that doesn't feel good to you . . ." Just because you don't understand your child's experience doesn't mean it isn't real, and this phrase helps bridge that gap.

"You're the Only One in Your Body"

Here's something I say to my kids as often as possible: "You're the only one in your body, so only you could know what you like." Consent, at its core, is about our belief that only *we* know what is happening for us, only *we* know what we want, only *we* know what feels comfortable in any given moment. When your son says, "I like my shirt on backward," maybe say: "You're the only one in your body, so only you could know what you like"; when your daughter tells you, "I don't like pink at all! I like green," build up her confidence by replying, "You're the only one in your body, so only you could know what you like." Maybe even add to it: "It's so cool that you know who you are and what feels good to you," or "You really know yourself, and that's awesome."

Socratic Questioning

I love asking my kids thought-provoking questions around the topic of consent. I do this with other topics too, since kids learn best when *they are encouraged to think and consider*, which comes from *asking questions*. But I find that questions of consent are especially thought-provoking, so this strategy is especially effective in that context. The next time you have an "opening" with your child—a nice quiet moment when you're getting along—explore the topics of decision-making, asserting one's wants and needs, and tolerating other people's distress. I'd start with, "Oooooh, I have an interesting question . . . ," and then share some (but not all!) of the following: "What's more important, doing something that feels right to you or making other people happy? What if you can't do both? When does making someone else happy, instead of doing something that feels right, feel okay to you? When would it be extra-important to choose doing what feels right, even if someone else is super *un*happy? What if you do something that you want and someone else gets mad at you . . . does this mean you're a bad person? Why or why not?"

How Does This Play Out for Kiki and Tasha?

Tasha remembers the circuitry for consent—she wants her kids to be able to assert their wants and needs even if others are upset about it, and she knows these circuits, which are active throughout adulthood, are built during childhood. Tasha says to Kiki: "You don't want to hug Grandpa, huh? That's okay. You're the only one in your body, so you're the only one who could know what feels right to you. And here's the other thing: You see that Grandpa is sad because he wants a hug. That's okay. Other people are allowed to have feelings when we say no. You don't have to change your mind because someone is upset."

Then Tasha approaches her dad and tells him, "It's really important to me that my kids know they're in charge of their bodies. I know you might disagree with how I am parenting in this moment—that's fine. But please don't send her mixed messages about it."

CHAPTER 24

Tears

Abdullah, father to seven-year-old Yusuf, just received an email saying that Yusuf did not make the travel baseball team. Abdullah approaches Yusuf and tells him, "Hey, kiddo. You didn't make the travel team. You're still on the other team, so that's great, right? You can play with all your old friends." Abdullah notices that Yusuf is starting to tear up. He isn't sure what to say or whether to distract Yusuf with something positive to take away the hurt.

ere's a quick multiple-choice check-in: Imagine you're talking to a friend and you notice, totally unexpectedly, that you're about to start crying. How do you feel about your tears? What thoughts come up for you?

A. "There's no reason I should be crying! This is ridiculous."
B. "This is going to make my friend uncomfortable."
C. "I wonder what my body is trying to tell me. It must be something important."

There's no right answer here, only information. What do you notice? Are you feeling critical of yourself for crying? Are you concerned about your friend's reaction? Or you do feel curiosity, respect, and compassion?

We can learn so much about our personal histories from how we feel about our tears. In just that single multiple-choice reflection, we begin to understand how crying was treated in our own families. After all, while tears are universal, our reaction to tears is highly specific and based on the circuitry we developed early on.

Tears operate in our attachment system as a signal that we need emotional support and connection from others. They are a sign of how we feel, and of the sheer strength of that feeling. I sometimes imagine my tears talking to me, saying: "Something so big is happening inside that I am literally a *liquid* coming out of your eyes in an attempt to get you to pause and notice." But tears are also a visceral manifestation of a child's vulnerability, and that can be very triggering for parents. Remember, our triggers tell us what we learned, in our early years, *to shut down in ourselves*, so "shame around crying" is often passed down through the generations: a child cries because they need a parent's emotional support, the parent is triggered because they learned to shut down their own support needs when they were young, the parent then responds to a child the way they were responded to, and the cycle of shaming connection continues. Or, on the flip side, tears may trigger guilt inside a parent, because they assume their child's distress is their fault or a sign of their parental shortcomings. Let's be the generation that changes this. Let's be the pivot point. Let's remind ourselves of this truth: "Bodies never lie. Tears are the body's way of sending a message about how someone is feeling. I don't have to *like* my or my kid's tears . . . but I have to respect them."

Anytime I talk about tears, I'm asked the same question: "But what about 'fake tears' or 'fake crying'?" Let me answer that question with another question: why are we calling these tears fake? We need to zoom out and reflect on how our *framing of a situation* makes us *feel about our child*. When we label something as "fake tears," we are judging it. We put distance between ourselves and our child, and we see our child as manipulative or as "the enemy." I shudder to think about this impact, because as parents we want to do the opposite—we want to approach our child with a compassionate, open-minded curiosity that is grounded in the idea that kids (and adults!) are always doing the best they can with the resources they have available. In other words, kids are good inside . . . so what's going on when they have an escalation in their emotional expression? Now, *that* is a question I want to answer, because it approaches a child with wonder—with an attitude of connecting instead of judging, and seeing our child as a teammate.

Let's think about fake tears for a moment. What would lead me, an adult, to escalate my expression of emotions? After all, none of us are above this. Well, if I want to have the seriousness of my feelings recognized or my needs known, and I sense that someone is responding to me with disinterest, invalidation, or minimization, then my body would undoubtedly escalate into a more intense expression. I would be desperate to feel seen and understood. When we look at fake tears through this lens, we think less about the on-the-surface expression and more about the underlying unmet needs. Words like "I can tell something important is happening for you. I care about that. I'm here," or "I can see how upset you are. I believe you. I really do," are powerful scripts for your toolbox in these moments. Now, remember, this doesn't mean you have to "give in" to whatever your child happens to want in that moment— after all, we know from our family jobs that two things can be true:

we can hold a firm boundary while still approaching a child with empathy and validation.

Strategies

Talk About Tears

Talk about crying with your child *outside of the moment your child is crying*. Maybe you pause while reading a book when you notice a character feeling sad: "She looks sad. I wonder if she will cry. Sometimes I cry when I'm sad. Sometimes I don't. Either way is okay." Or talk about a time you cried: "I still remember when I was your age and I was allowed to get an ice cream from the ice-cream truck. I really wanted an ice-cream sandwich . . . and they were out! OH NO! I cried. I was so disappointed." Here, we are de-shaming the crying experience; after all, when you explicitly share with your child that *you* have cried, even over seemingly "small" things, your child feels less alone with their tears.

Connect Tears with Importance

I tell my kids: "Tears tell us something important is happening in our body." I might continue: "The other day I was watching a TV show and I cried and didn't even understand why! Do you know that sometimes our body knows things before our brain does? My body must have been thinking of something important. Even though I didn't understand why I was tearing up, I knew it was still okay." This is an extremely powerful message to your child: sometimes our body knows things that our mind doesn't yet understand. I've watched so many adults approach their tears with a "This makes no sense, why am I crying, what is wrong with me?"

spiral of self-blame; it's extremely protective of children's mental health to teach them early on that we need patience in understanding our tears and our body's messages.

Socratic Questioning

Take some time to wonder aloud with your kids about tears, encouraging them to think deeply and question the common narrative that tears are a sign of weakness. Here are some starter questions, all of which are meant to promote thoughtfulness, not answers: "What do you think tears tell us? Are tears good, or bad, or neither good nor bad—maybe they just are? Did you know that tears release stress from our bodies? Isn't that interesting? There are some people who don't like to cry. I wonder why? Can boys and girls cry? Can adults and kids cry? Can men and women cry? Is it more okay for girls or boys to cry or okay for both? Why? How did you learn that?"

How Does This Play Out for Abdullah and Yusuf?

Abdullah takes a deep breath and remembers that tears are not the enemy, sadness is not the enemy, vulnerability is not the enemy . . . aloneness in our feelings, this is the true enemy. This is the most painful thing of all. So Abdullah tells the story of what just happened to Yusuf, remembering that his presence, not his solutions, will give Yusuf comfort: "You really wanted to make that team. It's so disappointing, I know." He then pauses and talks to the voice in *him* that learned to judge *his own* tears—he says to himself, "Tears are okay. Tears are important," and then more naturally to Yusuf, "Our tears tell us that something important is happening in our body. In this family, we like to know important things, so let those tears come out. I'm here with you. I'm right here." Yusuf cries and Abdullah himself feels some tears well up inside him as well. This is a powerful father-son moment, the kind that Abdullah wishes he had more of with his own dad.

CHAPTER 25

Building Confidence

> Six-year-old Charlie is running around the backyard with his friends, playing tag. His mother, Clara, notices that he keeps getting tagged and is a bit slower than his more athletic friends. As soon as Charlie's friends leave, he starts crying and says to his mom, "They're all faster than me. And I always get out. I'm the slowest kid in my grade!" Clara hates seeing her child in such pain. She wonders if she should tell Charlie that he just had an off day or remind him that he's great at chess and art.

Kids are often taught that confidence means feeling good, feeling proud, or feeling happy with themselves. It doesn't. I know that might seem like a bold statement, but I firmly believe it's time to reframe the discussion around confidence. When we define confidence as "feeling good about ourselves," we end up trying to convince our kids out of their distress, out of their disappointment, or out of their perception that they are not very good at certain things; this is unfortunate, because I believe this pathway of reassurance and propping up actually destroys confidence.

Hear me out. For me, confidence is not about feeling "good," it's about believing, "I really know what I feel right now. Yes, this feeling is real, and yes, it's allowed to be there, and yes, I am a good person while I am feeling this way." Confidence is our ability to feel *at home with ourselves* in the *widest range of feelings* possible, and it's built from the belief that it's okay to be who you are no matter what you're feeling.

Let's start with an adult example. Say you're in an important meeting with your boss. You nod and try to follow along, only to realize that you have no clue what she's talking about. Confidence in this case is about *self-trust*; it's our ability to sit in that meeting and say internally, "Hmm. I have no idea what she's asking me to do right now. I'm totally confused. I trust my feeling and it doesn't mean anything bad about me," and then say externally, "Wait a second, I am pretty confused and I want to make sure I get it right. Can we start again, so that we can both be on the same page?" Confidence in that meeting doesn't come from trying to convince yourself that you're *not* confused—it's from allowing that feeling and owning it.

It's incredibly common for well-meaning parents to hear a child's pain and then invalidate it—maybe not by saying, "Don't be a baby!" but in a sneakier way, like trying to convince a child to feel happy when she's sad or feel proud when she's disappointed. When we try to convince a child to feel any other way than how they're currently feeling, a child learns: "I guess I'm not a good feeler of my feelings . . . I thought I was upset, but here's my most trusted adult telling me it's not such a big deal. I can't trust my feelings inside; after all, I've learned that other people have a better idea of how I feel than I do." Eesh. That's scary. When we think about the adults we hope our kids will become, I'm pretty sure most of us want our kids to have a strong internal compass, a "gut feeling" they can locate inside their bodies. This is what allows adults to make decisions amid uncertainty—to turn down social plans because they feel exhausted and need a good night's sleep, or to speak up to a colleague who left them out of an important meeting.

This kind of confidence comes from trusting your instincts, from a self-belief that states, **"I have learned to trust my feelings."** And when it comes to kids, I want mine to be able to say, "I know I'm upset about what happened with my friend, but she's trying to convince me I'm overreacting and that it's not a big deal. But wait, how could she know how I feel? I know how I feel! I'm the only one who could know that." Confidence comes when parents allow and connect with the feeling their child is already having. And when you connect about the tougher stuff—emotions like sadness, disappointment, jealousy, or anger—you get an even bigger bang for your confidence-building buck, because you're setting your child up to feel like they can "be themself," no matter what, across a wide range of feelings. What a gift.

Building confidence isn't only about saying the "right" thing when things go "wrong" for our kids. It's also about what we say when things go "right." Because there is one type of commentary we often think will build confidence but actually gets in the way, and that's praise. "Good job, honey!" and "You're so smart!" and "You're an amazing artist!"—these well-intentioned phrases build up a child's reliance on external validation, or approval from other people. Internal validation, on the other hand—which is what we want to encourage in our kids—is the process of seeking approval from oneself. It's the difference between *gazing out* for good feelings rather than *gazing in*. Here's an example: your six-year-old has just drawn a picture; seeking external validation would be finding a parent and asking, "Do you like it, do you like it? Do you think it's pretty?" Seeking internal validation would be pausing and looking at the picture and sharing her own thoughts. Another example: a teenager is angry with her boyfriend for something he said to her; seeking external validation would be asking five friends if they think this is "a big deal"; seeking internal validation would be noticing her own discomfort and deciding to say something.

Now, here's the thing: we all seek external validation, and we all like external validation. This is okay. The goal isn't to make a child impervious to other people's approval or input, but rather to build up a child's *interiority*—meaning who they are on the *inside*—so that they don't feel empty and confused in the absence of outside input. Plus, confidence cannot be built from external validation or praise. Sure, these comments feel good, but they never stick; rather, they disappear almost as quickly as they land, leaving us desperate for the next bit of praise so that we can feel good about ourselves again. This isn't confidence . . . this is emptiness.

Now, a quick praise caveat: commenting on what's happening *inside a child*, or a child's *process and not product*, orients a child to gaze back in instead of out. Comments like, "You're working so hard on that project," or "I notice you're using different colors in this drawing, tell me about this," or "How'd you think to make that?"—these support the development of confidence, because instead of teaching your child to crave positive words from others, we teach them to notice what they're doing and learn more about themself.

Strategies

Lead with Validation

If we remember that confidence comes from knowing it's okay to feel however you're feeling, we can build confidence in our kids by showing them that we see their feelings as real and manageable. When we name feelings and validate them, we show a child that those feelings are okay. Here's what that might look like:

Situation: Your son tells you he was sad when you dropped him off at school.
Lead with Validation: "You felt sad at drop-off, huh? Makes sense,

drop-off can feel hard" (as opposed to: "But the rest of the day was great, right?").

Situation: Your daughter says she doesn't want to go to soccer practice. *Lead with Validation:* "Something about soccer feels kinda tricky right now, huh? Makes sense. Let's think about this together" (as opposed to: "But you love soccer!").

How'd You Think to . . . ?

"How'd you think to draw that?"

"How'd you think to start your story that way?"

"How'd you think to solve that math problem?"

"How'd you think to use those materials together?"

When we wonder with our kids about the "how" instead of praising the "what," we help build up their tendency to gaze in and be curious about themselves, and maybe even to marvel at the things they've done. After all, nothing feels better than when someone around us expresses interest in how we think about things, how we came up with our ideas, or where we want to go next. When we ask our child, "How'd you think to . . . ?," we are letting them know that we're interested in their process and not just their product; this builds up a self-belief inside them that proclaims, "The things inside me are interesting and valuable."

Inside Stuff over Outside Stuff

Circuitry for self-confidence depends on a child's ability to locate *identity* over *observable behavior*; this comes from growing up in a family that focuses more on what's "inside" a child (enduring qualities, feelings, ideas) than what is "outside" (accomplishments, outcomes, labels). In regard to your child's sports team, for example, inside stuff might be her effort in practice, her attitude when winning and losing, and her willingness to try new things; outside stuff might be her number of goals or home runs, or labels like "most valuable player." When it comes to academics, inside stuff might be willingness to try a bonus math problem, spending time on studying, and showing enthusiasm about a subject; outside stuff might be a grade, a test score, or a label like "smartest kid in class." The more our families focus on inside stuff, the more children value inside stuff too—which ultimately translates to valuing who they are over what they do.

"You Really Know How You're Feeling"/"It's Okay to Feel This Way"

If confidence is about *self-trust*, then building confidence in our kids comes from teaching them to trust their feelings. This is something that's hard even for adults. We constantly question ourselves, wondering things like, "Did I overreact?" "Is it okay to feel this way?" "Would someone else feel this way if they were in my shoes?" These are all signs of self-doubt, and they tell us that at some point, our own experiences were met with invalidation, aloneness, or attempts to convince us out of our feelings. As parents, let's wire self-compassion and self-trust next to our kid's feelings. We can do this with phrases like "You really know how you're feeling right now," or "Wow, you really know yourself"—these responses teach a child to look inward with openness, not judgment. When your child clings to you at the park, you can say: "You're not ready to join yet. That's okay. You really know how you're feeling right now." When your child cries about not being invited to a sleepover party, try: "You're so disappointed. It's okay to feel this way."

How Does This Play Out for Charlie and Clara?

Clara remembers that confidence comes from being okay with how you feel, not from erasing or distracting from distressing feelings. She says to Charlie, "Running around playing tag felt really hard today. Getting tagged all the time . . . ugh, that stinks. I know, sweetie. I'm here." She pauses. Charlie moves close to her and cries some more. After a little while, Clara feels an opening and shares, "When I was your age, playing basketball was so tricky for me. The other kids could make baskets and I couldn't even get the ball to the hoop. Ugh, gym class would feel so bad . . ." Charlie takes a few moments, then asks to hear more about his mom's experience, as if her story gives him permission to be feeling the way he does. Clara feels a little unsure after this conversation—it didn't seem to offer any solutions, but she also acknowledges that it just *felt right*, and she decides to trust that.

CHAPTER 26

Perfectionism

Five-year-old Freya is working on a kindergarten writing task; she is supposed to write a four-sentence "How To" story to the best of her ability. Freya's mom, Aislyn, watches as her daughter writes a word; says to herself, "No, that's not how you spell it!"; then erases, tries again, and erases it again.

"Sweetie, just write it how you see it," Aislyn tells Freya. "That's what the teacher said. It doesn't have to be perfect!"

"I hate writing!" Freya says. "I won't do it unless you tell me how to spell each word!"

Aislyn doesn't know how to help.

What's going on for kids who need things to be just right, who can't tolerate "good enough," who shut down unless things go exactly the way they imagined? Well, underneath perfectionism is always an emotion regulation struggle. Underneath "I am the worst artist in the world!" is a child who could envision the picture they wanted to paint and is disappointed in their final product; underneath "I stink at math" is a child who wants to feel capable and instead feels confused; underneath "I let down my team" is a child who can't access all the moments they played well and is mired in their missed layup. In each case, that disappointment—or the mismatch between what a child wanted to happen and what actually happened—manifests as perfectionism. And, because perfectionism is a sign of an emotion regulation struggle, logic won't help—we can't convince a child that her art is great or that math concepts are hard for everyone or that one missed shot doesn't define an athlete. Perfectionism requires us to see our child's big, unmanageable feelings, the ones that live beneath the hyperbole and the black-and-white thoughts, so we can get to the core of what's going on and help our kids build the skills they need.

Kids who are perfectionistic are also prone to rigidity; they have extremes to their moods and to their reactions, so they often feel like they're on top of the world or at the bottom of the barrel. Their self-concept is exceptionally fragile, which means there's a relatively narrow range in which they can feel safe and happy with themselves; anything outside of that range is seemingly bad—this is why these kids shut down after things don't go the way they want. The shutdown ("I won't do it!" or "I'm done!" or "I'm the worst!") isn't a sign that they're stubborn or spoiled but that they can't access good feelings about themselves in that moment. The goal, as parents, is to widen the range, to help perfectionists live in the "gray" so that the highs and lows of their self-worth aren't so extreme. We want to help a perfectionist child feel good enough rather than cling to the need to be perfect.

Part of this inability to live in the gray comes from the fact that perfectionistic kids often can't tolerate—or simply can't understand—nuance. For perfectionists, *behavior* is an indicator of *identity* because they're unable to separate the two; this is true when perfectionists feel good about themselves and when they feel bad about themselves. For example, reading a page of a book perfectly (behavior) means "I am smart" (identity), while mispronouncing a word (behavior) means "I am stupid" (identity); trying to tie your shoe and succeeding the first time (behavior) means "I am great" (identity) while messing up the loops (behavior) means "I am awful" (identity). To help kids with perfectionistic tendencies, then, we want to show them how to separate *what they are doing* from *who they are*. This is what gives kids the freedom to feel good in the gray—to feel capable inside after their first attempt at tying shoes doesn't work or when they're struggling to read. Perfectionism steals a child's (and adult's) ability to *feel good in the process of learning* because it dictates that goodness only comes from successful outcomes. We need to show perfectionist kids how they can find their good-enough-ness and their worth *outside* success.

One more important note on perfectionism: parents should aim to help their kids *see* their perfectionism, not get rid of it. So many parents think they have to make their kids "not perfectionists," but any time we shut down a part of a child (especially when we do so harshly), we're sending the message that the part of them in question is bad or wrong. Instead, we want to help our kids get into a *better relationship with* their perfectionism, so that they can recognize it when it comes up rather than have it take over the control tower and dictate how they feel and what they do. After all, there are *components* of perfectionism—drive and strong-mindedness and conviction—that can feel really good, and we want to help our kids harness these traits without collapsing under the immense pressure perfectionism can add.

Strategies

Make Your Own Mistakes

Kids are always watching their parents and learning what they value and what matters most in their family. If you have kids prone to perfectionism, be mindful of making errors and struggling and "living in the gray" around them. This might sound like: "Oh no! I sent an important email to my boss with so many typos! Oh no no no, I meant to proofread it and I didn't!" Then model self-talk that speaks to the deeper messages your child needs to hear. Place your hand on your heart and say aloud, "I am okay even when I make a mistake. I am safe. I am good inside even when I make a mistake on the outside." This will help you model separating behavior from identity and finding goodness when things are difficult.

Tell the Story of the Feeling Under the Perfectionism

When your child insists on something being perfect or shuts down if things feel flawed, practice seeing the feeling underneath and "telling the story of the feeling," or speaking the feeling aloud. The goal is to take your child's focus on perfection and shift it to the feelings inside his body; this builds self-awareness of one's experience, which is the foundation for regulation. So when your child says, "I'm the only kid who can't do monkey bars. I'm not going to the playground at all, it won't be fun," tell the story of the feeling underneath. That might sound like, "Not being able to do the monkey bars, ugh, that feels so important to you," or "Sometimes one tricky thing feels like it can suck all the fun out of something, huh? It's almost like nothing at the playground feels like it would be fun if you don't feel good at every single part." Here I'm narrating the underlying emotion regulation struggle; I'm showing my child I see what's happening for them. It's tempting to say, "It's okay if you don't want to do that one thing, it's no big deal!" or "Who cares! You can have fun on another part of the playground!" But remember, logic doesn't build regulation, and regulating tough feelings is the core struggle for kids prone to perfectionism.

Stuffed Animal Play

Using stuffed animals or trucks or whatever your child likes to play with, act out a scene involving a perfectionistic character. Maybe you're the excavator truck crying about a hole not being the shape you want; maybe you're the stuffed bear who can climb only halfway up a tree. To start, act out something like, "No no no, I won't do it any more! If I can't do it perfectly, I just won't do it at all!" Then pause. See how your child reacts. If it feels right, whisper to your child, "I've felt like that before. Sometimes when things don't go the way I want, it feels like everything is bad." Or model how to cope—maybe this looks like grabbing a dump truck and coming to the excavator and saying, "It feels so bad to not have things go the way you wished. I know. I'm here." Then showcase even more coping as you, as the excavator, say, "Okay . . . maybe I'll do one more scoop. I can keep going even when things aren't perfect . . ."

Introduce the Perfect Voice

In a calm moment, introduce the idea of you and your child both having a "Perfect Kid" or "Perfect Girl" or "Perfect Boy" inside. It might sound like this: "Do you know that I have a Perfect Girl in me? Yes! She often tells me things have to be perfect or else they're not worth doing! I think you have one too! I think she popped up when you were doing your math homework. Anyway, there's no problem with having a Perfect Voice. A lot of people have them! But sometimes Perfect Girl, for me, she just gets so loud and she makes it hard for me to focus. I've found that talking to her nicely can help . . ." Now pause. See how your child responds. Often a child will take to this immediately and say, "What do you mean?" Continue: "Well, Perfect Girl isn't a problem unless she's so loud that I can't hear the other voices in me. So when she's getting loud,

I just say to her, 'Oh, hi, Perfect Girl. You again! I know, you always say, "Perfect, perfect, must be perfect, if it's not perfect I have to stop." I hear you! And also, I'm going to ask you to step back. I am going to take a deep breath and find my "I can do hard things" voice because I know that's in there too.' Then I can hear a quieter voice telling me it's okay that things are hard and I can do hard things."

You might think there's no way your kid would go along with this scenario of identifying a voice. It's often our skepticism about interventions like these that holds us back from trying them out. Let me assure you, this isn't something I invented out of the blue—the Perfect Voice approach is directly inspired by internal family systems and the idea that we have a multiplicity to our minds (see chapter 4 for more details). Identifying the different "parts" of us speaks to how our mind is organized, and kids often take to this framework because it resonates with what actually goes on inside their bodies. Also, the power of the Perfect Voice strategy is that you're teaching your child how to relate to her perfectionism rather than reject it; after all, rejecting a part of us feels like self-loathing. When we talk about the Perfect Voice, a child doesn't see perfectionism as the enemy; instead, she feels empowered to manage the perfectionism when it arises. Once you've tried it, you might even take it a step further and see if your child wants to describe the Perfect Girl (or Boy or Kid) or even draw her; lots of kids enjoy and benefit from this, because personifying this voice enables them to feel more grounded and capable of understanding themselves.

Do a 180 on Perfectionism

One day my daughter taught me a word she learned in Spanish and I responded, "One–nothing!" She looked at me, confused, and I explained, "Not knowing something means I can learn, and learning new things is awesome. I learned one thing just now so I get one point!" In this game, "winning" isn't equated with being "perfect" or already knowing something, but instead with the process of learning. There's something about making not-knowing into a "win" that gives kids permission to struggle and learn. This is huge for perfectionists. My daughter loves referencing this game when she's learning—"Mom, two points for me, I just learned two state capitals!" There are many ways to do a 180 on perfectionism: make a game of not-knowing, make it a goal to make a mistake, give high fives for errors.

How Does This Play Out for Freya and Aislyn?

Aislyn remembers to help Freya see the perfectionism, not get rid of it. "Spelling is so hard. I know," she says. "It feels like if you can't get each word right, you can't move on, right? I remember feeling like that too when I was six. It was the worst." Freya looks a bit calmer, but she still insists she won't write her story unless Aislyn tells her how to spell the words; Aislyn knows this is a short-term fix and will only reinforce Freya's belief that things have to be "right" to be good enough. She remembers to do a 180 and says, "Freya, you know what? You're in kindergarten and your teacher told me you're supposed to be learning how to spell, not spelling correctly. I have to go check something in my room, but when I get back I'll look at your writing. Don't get ANY words correct. NOT EVEN ONE! If you get even one word correct, I'll have to email your teacher that you're not being a good student. Okay?" She really sells this idea and walks out, anticipating Freya's continued crying or whining. To her surprise, there's silence. When Aislyn returns, Freya has done two sentences. Aislyn sees seven words spelled incorrectly and three spelled correctly. "Freya," she says. "I don't know what to do with you. That's WAY too many words that are spelled just right. Seriously, your job is to learn! And with those words, you didn't learn anything!" Freya and Aislyn laugh, and inside, Aislyn knows that this was a huge moment.

CHAPTER 27

Separation Anxiety

Three-year-old Wesley is going to preschool for the first time. He's excited, especially after years of watching his older siblings leave for school in the mornings. Wesley's dad, Jeff, knows that some kids have a hard time with drop-off, but he doesn't say anything because he doesn't want to put any ideas into Wesley's head. Still, when the moment of goodbye arrives, Wesley is clingy. He refuses to let go of Jeff's leg and screams, "No no no, Daddy, stay! Stay!" Jeff isn't sure what to do or how they got here.

Separation is tough. There's nothing wrong with a child who cries at drop-off or clings when Mom heads off to work or delays leaving the house in anticipation of going to school. Remember, these behaviors are rooted in attachment. Children associate parental presence with safety, because their bodies tell them: "As long as your parent is near, you have protection." In moments of separation, children must try to find feelings of security in a new environment or with a new caregiver or teacher, and that's a tall order. It requires them to hold on to the feelings of safety that come from a parent-child relationship without having that relationship right there in front of them. For separation to feel manageable, children have to *internalize*—meaning, have within them—the feelings that often come in the presence of a parent, to trust that they are safe in this world even when a parent is not right next to them. It's no surprise that there might be tears and tough feelings in the process.

I picture feelings of safety as a ball of light—when a child is near her parent, the ball of light shines on her, giving her a feeling of security that allows her to explore, play, and grow. As our kids get older, we hope that the light doesn't just shine on them in their parents' presence, but that it shines *in* them even when they are separated from their parents—that it has actually entered a child's body and become her own.

The concept of internalization helps us understand what kids need to separate successfully; kids literally have to "take in" something from a parent so they can hold on to the good feelings of the relationship even when a parent says goodbye. English pediatrician and psychoanalyst Donald Winnicott introduced the idea that children create a mental representation of the parent-child relationship so that they can access the feelings of the relationship even when a parent is absent. Transitional objects help children with this process; a blanket or stuffed animal or object from home becomes a physical representation of the parent-child bond, reminding a child that parents still exist and are "there" for you even when they are not right in front of you. I always recommend transitional objects to parents whose kids struggle with separation anxiety—they are a way to help make tricky transitions feel more manageable. After all, to ease separation anxiety, we have to help kids "hold on to us" in our absence.

Reactions to separation vary widely among children even within the same family; it's perfectly normal to have one child who separates easily and one who becomes distressed at the mere thought of an upcoming separation. In predicting how your children might respond to being apart from you, it's helpful to consider their temperament. For example, one of my kids is fairly risk-seeking, eager to try new things, and even-keeled, while another is slow to warm up, cautious, and deeply feeling (meaning that kid's intense sensations get activated easily and can last longer). Even if all the external factors of their preschool separation experience were the same, my husband and I could both predict that the risk-seeker kid would likely separate more easily, have fewer tearful days, and jump into a new routine more quickly. What's key here is that we don't add value judgments—one of my kids doesn't separate "better" than the other, they simply have different experiences. Knowing your unique child is critical in helping you understand what your child's separation might be like, and in setting expectations to keep yourself as grounded as possible in the moment of a tearful goodbye.

Speaking of tearful goodbyes, it's important to remember that parents see only one side of the separation process—the goodbye. We don't typically get to see the recovery or the play that follows as our kids move from upset to regulated to happy. In fact, some of the most engaged kids in a classroom are often the kids who protest the most at separation. A vital part of separation is a parent's ability to believe that their kids can cope. A child's experience at the moment of separation is not predictive of his entire experience at school or daycare. Understanding this will allow parents to project an air of confidence, and that's really important—our feelings about our kids' separation has a huge impact on their experience; if our kids sense that we are hesitant or nervous or doubtful, their separation reactions will be more intense, because they will absorb our anxiety, thereby magnifying their own. In moments of separation, our kids are essentially asking us, "Do you think I'll be okay?" There's nothing scarier to a child than separating from a parent who exudes fear around the separation; it's as if the parent is saying, "You aren't safe here. Goodbye!" This would be terrifying to any child. So remember, you, the parent, set the tone—separating might be hard for everyone, but projecting confidence is key to a smooth transition.

Strategies

Check In with Your Own Anxiety

Notice how you feel about separating from your kid. You might feel sad or nervous, and that's okay! We never have to get rid of our feelings, but we should hold ourselves responsible for understanding what we need so that we can show up to separation moments as a sturdy leader. You might start in the way I often do, by greeting your uncomfortable feelings: "Hi, anxiety, you're allowed to be there!" Or, "Hi there, sad feelings about my child's growing up and being away from me for a bit. You're allowed to be here. I'm going to say hello to you before I do drop-off and then again after when I'm home. I'm going to ask you to step back when I say goodbye to my daughter so I can show her that she's safe going to school." Check out chapter 10 for more strategies that can help you accept your emotions.

Talk About Separation and Feelings

Talk to your child about a separation before it happens. For school drop-off, that might mean that a week before the first day, you discuss all aspects of school: how you'll get there, the teachers' names (show pictures if you can!), what the classroom will look like, and what drop-off will look like. You might say, "In a few days, you'll be going to school! School is a place you can play and learn with other kids and where there are adults called teachers who take care of you while you're there. There are blocks in school . . . and dolls . . . and a circle carpet to sit on while you sing songs! One thing about school is that Mommy takes you there in the beginning and picks you up at the end. I don't stay in the room with you. It may feel a bit tricky at first, because saying goodbye to me and being with new adults and kids is a new thing!"

This same strategy can be applied to older kids when you're preparing for a sleepover at a friend's house or an overnight school camping trip. Talk about the separation in advance—show pictures of where your child is going, and anticipate feelings that may come up. This might sound like, "I'm thinking about your sleepover at Raquela's house tomorrow night—how awesome, your first sleepover! Raquela's mom sent me some pictures of her room so we can see exactly where you'll be sleeping . . . oh, look, a blue comforter, just like the one you have at home! And she has a small lamp she likes to keep on in the corner while she sleeps . . . Hmm, that's different. I wonder what it will feel like to sleep somewhere new?"

Routine + Practice

Come up with a routine that is easy to practice and repeat—something short and sweet. Maybe you say, "When we say goodbye, I'll give you one hug, say 'See ya later, alligator!' and 'Daddy always comes back!,' and then I'll turn around and leave. You'll be with your teachers then, and if any big feelings come up, they'll know how to help you. Let's practice!" Then, act out the scene of drop-off—feel free to be the kid first and have your child be the adult, and then switch roles. Practice will make the whole routine feel more familiar, and eventually lead to mastery, which helps separation feel safer.

Transitional Object

Stuffed animals or blankies can be helpful for kids who struggle with separating, because they literally travel with them between the home and school environments, thereby acting as a link between the two. Your child might want to have a laminated picture of the family (feel free to use clear packing tape!), and you can use this in your separation routine, reminding your child that after you leave, they can look at this picture and say over and over, "My family is near. My family is near." Consider involving your child in a transitional object choice: "Is there anything you want to bring to school to remind you of home?"

Telling the Story

We can ease separation anxiety by talking about the separation after we pick up our child at the end of the day or at the moment of reunion. Especially if a child was upset during the goodbye, be sure to tell the story of the day. In a calm, connected moment at home, share this with your child who had a hard time separating at kindergarten drop-off: "Saying goodbye felt a bit hard today. That's okay. Saying goodbye at school is so new and it's okay to feel sad. Then your teacher told me you took some deep breaths and looked at your family pictures, and then you joined the class on the rug for circle time. Mommy came back—just like I said I would!—and now we are together at home." Or share this when your child returns home from sleepaway camp: "Saying goodbye at the beginning of the summer felt tricky, I know, and we had some tears and some tough moments . . . then you got used to camp and the homesickness got less and less over time. And here you are now, after camp ended, with so many amazing stories to share. We are back together, just like we said would happen." Telling the story reminds a child that the moment of separation was part of a larger story, but it didn't color their entire experience.

How Does This Play Out for Wesley and Jeff?

Jeff remembers that it's okay for Wesley to have feelings about separation and reminds himself to prep Wesley better later that night. For now, Jeff crouches down to Wesley's level and says: "This feels new, saying goodbye to Daddy. I know you're going to have a great day at school even if saying goodbye feels hard." He gives Wesley a big hug and whispers: "Your teacher Terry is going to help you when I say goodbye. I'm going to tell her that you love to hear 'Twinkle Twinkle'—she can sing it to you if you want her to. I am going to give you one hug, remind you that I'll be back, and then I'm going to say bye. Here we go . . ." Jeff takes a deep breath himself, reminds himself that he can do this, and then does just as he said: he gives Wesley a hug; says, "Daddy always comes back"; and then leads Wesley to Terry, who helps him say goodbye. Later that night, Jeff tells Wesley the story of the day and practices a goodbye routine that includes Wesley's favorite stuffie. They also act out the separation routine with Wesley's favorite Lego figures. The next morning, Wesley looks nervous and Jeff tells him, "Some kids cry when they say goodbye to a parent. Some kids don't. You can feel any way. No matter what, Daddy knows you are safe, you'll have fun, and I'll be back to pick you up at the end."

CHAPTER 28

Sleep

Four-year-old Cora has always been a solid sleeper . . . until recently. For the last four weeks, she's been protesting bedtime, insisting on ten books instead of two, crying when her parents leave, and waking at two A.M. demanding that one of her dads sleep in bed with her. Cora's parents, Ben and Matt, are perplexed and exhausted. They've tried reward charts and punishments, and now they're considering the latest advice a friend gave them—to lock Cora's bedroom door—but it doesn't feel right. They don't know what to do next.

There's nothing quite like parenting all day and then having your child protest sleep, procrastinate during bedtime, or wake up in the middle of the night when you're desperate for much-needed rest. If you find bedtime protests difficult to manage, you're not alone, especially since they come at the precise moment when parents are eagerly awaiting the precious child-free moments of their day, when they can finally relax or read or do something for themselves. It's a cruel irony that at the end of a long day, parents want time away from their kids at the same time that kids often want continued connection with their parents.

When considering your child's sleep problems, it's important to remember this truth: sleep struggles are ultimately separation struggles, because during the night children are tasked with being alone for ten(ish) hours and also with feeling safe enough that their body is able to drift off to sleep. And because separation struggles are at the root of sleep problems, sleep "solutions" need to be formulated around an understanding of attachment theory. Remember, the attachment system is based in proximity seeking, because children feel safest when their parents are next to them. Nighttime can feel truly dangerous to kids—it means darkness, aloneness, the slowing down of the body and the speeding up of the mind, the emergence of scary thoughts, and even existential worries about permanence ("Are my parents really there when I can't see them?").

Sleep is also a time when kids might express anxieties and struggles from other parts of their lives. Children perceive changes in their environment as *threats*, so until changes such as the start of school, an increase in marital arguments, the birth of a new child, or the move to a new home are explained and an environment is deemed safe, children will seek proximity to their parents. As a result, these critical moments often lead to sleep disruptions, because kids feel uneasy in their bodies and can't reach the state of relaxation necessary to fall asleep. In fact, it's adaptive for children to stay by their parent's side and maximize the likelihood of attachment and security in times of change. And guess what? The opposite of being by a parent's side is separating at night.

So . . . what can we do? I see sleep change as a two-step process: First, we have to help our kids feel safe. We have to help them develop coping skills *during the day*, when the stakes are lower, before a child will feel safe enough to separate at night. Then, and only then, can we implement strategies to create a smoother bedtime experience. Too often, we become myopic about sleep, missing the larger story of what's happening for a child because we're so overwhelmed with our own frustration. While this response is certainly understandable, unfortunately, it can exacerbate the very issues that contributed to sleep problems in the first place. When parents become cold, punitive, and reactive, kids who are searching for understanding and help with self-soothing feel more alone and threatened. Thus our kids' need for our presence heightens, we become more frustrated . . . and the cycle continues.

It doesn't help that so much guidance about sleep follows a behaviorist mentality, missing the struggle *underneath* a bedtime protest or a two A.M. wake-up. I've heard from too many parents who've been instructed by professionals to ignore their child's fears or lock their bedroom door or do nothing at all while their child screams in terror. My heart aches hearing this guidance, but at the same time, my most generous interpretation tells me that parents are desperate for an approach that will get everyone the sleep they need to feel restored. I understand this; I've been through many difficult sleep stages with my own kids, and I know it can put me into a spiral of utter exhaustion and hopelessness. And that's why I feel so passionately about originating an approach to sleep that feels right, respects a child *and* a parent, doesn't fuel further abandonment fears . . . and actually works to promote more independent sleep.

Let's review what we know about attachment and separation. Kids who struggle to separate have trouble *internalizing* the soothing aspects of a parent-child relationship—they feel safe in a parent's presence but, often, terrified in a parent's absence. Separation starts to feel more manageable when we close this gap, when we help a child take in the parts of the parent-child relationship that provide security so that they can access feelings of safety, security, and trust, all of which are necessary for sleep. If we can help *infuse a parent's presence* into a child's environment, then he can access the soothing function of the parent-child relationship even when the parent isn't right there. This is the goal. When you reflect on interventions to help your child's sleep struggles, consider whether they help your child learn skills to tolerate your absence, or whether they actually *add to* your child's terror in your absence. Beyond the strategies I describe here, considering this binary will help you assess what might help *and* feel good.

Before we jump in, a disclaimer of sorts: my goal is to help build feelings of safety in your child. I don't know exactly when that will "convert" into better sleep. What I do know is that sleep changes can take a while, always longer than we would like. In the meantime, while sleep is still disrupted, it's critical to think about what you need: maybe alternating nighttime wake-ups with a spouse or partner (if you have one), extra screen time for your child during the day so you can get some rest, or taking a mental health day from work so you can nap during the day. I know none of these things will feel like enough. I also know that the accumulation of very small self-care moments can make a difference.

Strategies

"Where Is Everyone?"

Kids don't take parents' permanence for granted; when they go to sleep, they don't know that you're still there. To help your kids understand, talk to them, during the daytime, about where you spend your evening. Walk them around your home to show them. You might say: "When you go to sleep, Daddy goes to the kitchen and eats dinner, and then I read on the couch, and then I go to sleep in my room. When you are sleeping, I'm here the whole time! And then I wake up and come get you from your room when it's morning!" In a time of transition or change, you might also add: "There are so many changes in our life. Here's something that'll never change: when you go to bed, I'll still be here. Even when your eyes are closed and even when you can't see me, I'm here and I will be here when you wake up."

Examine Your Daytime Separation Routine

If sleep is hard for your child, start looking at daytime separation patterns. Is it hard for your child to let you go to the bathroom on your own? Is school separation difficult? Does your child struggle to say goodbye when you run errands or take a walk by yourself? Before tackling nighttime separation struggles (i.e., sleep struggles!), work on these dynamics during the day; nighttime can be filled with extra anxiety, so we need to build separation skills when our bodies are less activated and more receptive to learning. Come up with a separation routine, practice saying goodbye (even just to go to the bathroom!), and assure your child that even when you're not right together, she is safe and you will come back. For more daytime separation strategies, check out the previous chapter.

Role-Play

Get out the stuffed animals, trucks, dolls, or whatever your child likes to play with. Use them to act out a bedtime routine, reviewing feelings that come up and strategies that help with the soothing process. Say to your child, "Let's help Duckie get ready for bed!" Then say to Duckie, "Duckie, I know sleeping isn't your favorite part of the day. It's okay to feel sad at bedtime. Remember, Mommy Duck is right outside your room. You are safe. And Mommy Duck will see you in the morning. Okay, let's get ready for bed." Then go over the nighttime routine—use the same one as your child ("Let's read Duckie her two books and then brush her teeth and then sing one song and say good night!"), and feel free to include the moments that tend to be hard for your child.

If your daughter always asks for an extra book, put that into play, acting out that struggle, empathizing with the wish, and holding a boundary. ("Aw, Duckie, you want another book! I know. You can give me that extra book and I'll take it with me outside and have it ready for us to read in the morning." Or "Aw, Duckie, you want another, I know. It's hard to have only two. I won't read another now . . . I can in the morning!")

Infuse Your Presence

My approach to sleep struggles centers around helping your child feel the soothing function of your relationship without your having to be there the whole time. Think of various ways to infuse your presence into your child's room and bed area. Maybe you put a family photo next to your child's sleep area and a photo of your child next to your bed as well. You can introduce this, during the daytime, by saying: "You know what I've been thinking about? Sometimes I have a hard time falling asleep and I think of you and miss you! I'd love to have a picture of you right next to my bed. Then I can see you and remind myself that you're here and I'm safe, and that I'll see you in the morning! I think it would be good for both of us to have pictures of each other. Maybe we can make picture frames and then put them by our beds." I'd suggest making the frames together—nothing fancy, you can just decorate a piece of construction paper and glue the photo on top. This way your presence is infused into the room in your picture but also in your child's memory of creating art with you, a memory that likely feels safe and connected, which are the feelings we want a child to access at nighttime.

Another way to infuse your presence is to tell your child you'll write them a note or create a drawing with their name on it after they fall asleep and put it next to their bed; this way, kids who wake up in the middle of the night will see proof of your presence and your child's body will feel safer knowing there's a time you'll "be there" next to them. I was in a stage with my daughter where each night, she wanted me to drop off a note that had her name and somewhere between fifty and one hundred hearts (she'd tell me the number each night—a way to feel in control); it always took me a while, but this was the thing that helped her feel safe and sleep without much protest . . . it was totally worth it!

Mantras for You and Your Child

You know by now that I love mantras. They take a situation that can feel big and overwhelming and give a child something small and within their control to focus on. I have used this mantra for years with my own kids: "Mommy is near, [*child's name*] is safe, my bed is cozy." You can introduce your child to a mantra in this way: "Did you know that when I was your age my mom told me this special thing to say when I went to bed? I'd say it to myself over and over and over after she left. She told me to say: 'Mommy is near, Farnaz is safe, my bed is cozy.' Sleep was still a bit tricky for me but it helped make it better! Yours would be, 'Mommy is near, Nahid is safe, my bed is cozy.'" Share the mantra in a singsongy voice so that the rhythm is as soothing as the words. You can incorporate this mantra into the routine so that after you sing your child a song, you say the mantra three times; pretty soon, your child will have *internalized* the mantra and be able to produce it herself. A mantra, especially one that has an intergenerational story, is another great way to infuse your presence into your child's room.

Of course, mantras are also good for adults, and they help us manage our frustration and anger over struggles in the bedtime or sleep process. I generally use this one, which reminds me of the eventual ending: "This will end. There will be a moment when my child is asleep. I can cope with this."

The Safe Distance Method

This method operates on the principles of attachment theory, respecting that children need to feel proximal to parents in order to feel safe. Start out in a child's room, staying close by, then—over the course of many nights—increase the distance until you are farther and farther away (and eventually out of the room). Explain to your child: "I know sleep has felt tricky. I will stay in your room while you fall asleep. I won't always do this, but I will for a little while. While I'm here, I won't be talking, because this isn't daytime. I am here so you know you are safe." Here's a safe distance step-by-step:

1. **Stay in your child's room until they're near asleep or fully asleep.** While in the room, gaze away from your child. Once you're farther away from them, feel free to use the time to do some work or take care of personal matters. You're there for your presence, not engagement. Remember, your child won't need you in their room forever. Once we reduce fear, we can increase a child's tolerance of distance. Independence (separation) is born out of the safety of dependence (togetherness).

2. **For the first night, stay as close to your child as they need to feel safe;** you'll know they feel safe when they are calm. Your starting point may be sitting on their bed and rubbing their back. Stay at this distance for three consecutive nights.

3. **Start to create more distance.** Your second "location" might be sitting on their bed without touch or sitting *by* their bed. A few nights later, you might be on the floor closer to the door. The morning of a new change, announce it to your child: "Tonight you are ready for something new. I won't be sitting on your bed tonight. I will be staying in your room, sitting on your chair. I know you can do it!"

4. If your child becomes scared or dysregulated, **sing the bedtime mantra slowly and softly while gazing at the floor**. If your child is still scared, move closer for a bit. It is normal to go "in and out" as you figure out safe distance.

5. **If you notice your frustration or anger, remember *your* bedtime mantra**: "This will end. There will be a moment when my child is asleep. I can cope with this."

6. **Continue this distancing process** until you're near the door, then in the door frame, then, nights later, outside a cracked-open door.

The Comfort Button

Here's what I consider the ultimate sleep conundrum for kids: how can a child have all the good feelings from a parent being in their room . . . without a parent actually being in their room? This led me to create what I call the comfort button, which helps kids access your soothing presence even when you're on your couch or in your own bed. Here's how it works: Get a recordable button with at least thirty seconds of recordable space (you can purchase inexpensive ones online). Find a time when you're alone and calm. Then, in your regulated, soothing voice, record a message for your child about bedtime. It might be a verse from a bedtime song, it might be the mantra your child uses, it might be a message about seeing you in the morning—whatever your child would find soothing in your absence. Integrate this button in the sleep routine; your child might press the button once to hear your message while you're in the room, once while you walk out, twice when you're outside the door. Or you can even strike a "bargain": "Let's work on using the comfort button—I want to hear you listen to four full rounds before you call for me. I'll know you're using it because I'll be waiting outside your door. If things still feel bad, call for me and I'll come in and rub your back and tell you you're safe and we'll try it all again." The button infuses your presence and the soothing function of your attachment relationship into your child's room even when you're not literally right there; now your child can access you, and has the agency to press the button and hear you rather than feeling alone, helpless, and without any tools to feel safe.

How Does This Play Out for Ben and Matt and Cora?

In the morning, when Ben and Matt are rested and calm, they discuss what is really going on for Cora underneath her bedtime protest. They see her fear and realize they need a plan that helps reduce this fear, not exacerbate it. They start with some daytime strategies—they've noticed that Cora is extra clingy lately, especially with Ben, so they work on more general separation routines. They even practice separating in her bedroom during the day, so it feels silly and playful. Cora loves playing with her dolls, so Matt uses them to introduce themes of sleep protest and also to practice using a bedtime mantra. After this, Cora is amenable to trying it herself. Ben orders a recordable button and records the song they always sing at bedtime and the mantra for sleep; Cora has a visible look of relief when they give her this button, and Ben and Matt see how desperate she is for "access" to them at night. The sleep protests continue for a few more nights, then become less frequent. Ben and Matt are relieved and hopeful. They feel they have an approach that makes sense, feels right, and is leading to noticeable progress.

CHAPTER 29

Kids Who Don't Like Talking About Feelings (Deeply Feeling Kids)

Six-year-old Maura is playing near her four-year-old sister, Isla. She starts tickling Isla's toes and then escalates to pinching and light pushing; Maura's mom, Angie, gets between her kids and says, "Maura, I won't let you hit. You're allowed to be mad, I get that, but I won't let you hit." This is all it takes for Maura to start yelling, "Stop saying that! Stop! Get away from me!" Angie reacts with frustration. "Why do you always freak out at everything?!?" she asks. Maura, meanwhile, continues to rage, kicking her mom and screaming, "I hate you! I hate you and I mean it!"

Angie doesn't know what to do. What does Maura need? What's going on? How did this moment go from playful to violent in a matter of seconds?

*S*ome kids feel things more deeply and get activated more quickly than other kids. Their intense sensations last longer. If this rings true for you—if that description reminds you of your own child— let me be clear: you're not imagining things. Your kid likely *does* tantrum more often, and for longer and more intensely, than other children. And let me be clear about something else too: there's nothing wrong with your child and there's nothing wrong with you. I'm going to write that again because I want you to read it again: *there's nothing wrong with your child and there's nothing wrong with you.*

I'm not usually a fan of labels, but I find that having language to describe this type of child helps parents communicate and find support. For children with these more intense emotions, I use the label "Deeply Feeling Kids" (DFKs)—it reflects the way they experience the world and it also explains why these children often feel overwhelmed and enter more easily into a "threat" or "fight or flight" state. Yes, DFKs are tricky. And yes, parents of DFKs actually do need different strategies—ones that are rooted in an understanding of what these kids' core fears are, what they are looking for in their toughest moments, and why their escalations happen so intensely. The strategies in this book that help other kids, and maybe even help the other children in your own family—strategies like naming the feeling or offering support—can actually further inflame an already combustible situation when it comes to DFKs. These kids often struggle to accept help, yell, "Stop it!" when you talk about feelings, and escalate from zero to sixty over matters that are seemingly very small. So here's another important truth: You're not "doing it wrong"; you're not saying the words incorrectly or missing the tone. DFKs just can't take in the direct support you're offering because they feel so consumed by their overwhelming sensations. I know how frustrating this is, how exhausting, how rejecting; I know that right now you may be remembering some awful moments with your DFK, ones where you said something you regret or reacted in a way that didn't end up feeling right to you or your child. Take a deep breath. Notice your "bad parent" voice popping up. Say hi to it, and then find your self-compassion voice. Listen to *that* voice. The one saying, "You're here, reading this book, reflecting and learning and willing to try new things—how awesome are *you*!" We're back to our ultimate truth: you're a good parent and you have a good kid, and both of you can have a hard time.

Here's the good news: I assure you, DFKs *can* learn how to regulate their emotions, find calm and groundedness, and relate well to others. They just need their parents' help. They need our willingness to learn new approaches and our steadfast belief that they, too, are good inside.

Understanding DFKs requires going all the way back to evolution. For these children, vulnerability sits right next to shame; remember, shame puts humans into a primal defense state, one in which we are taken over by the need to protect ourselves. And we do that by shutting down, attacking others, or closing people out. When a child is in this threat state, the world feels dangerous; even a parent's attempts to help can feel like an assault, which is why DFKs push us away at the precise moments they need our help. On top of that, DFKs are especially vulnerable to feeling "bad" inside; they worry that the feelings and sensations that overwhelm them are also overwhelming to others, and they fear their feelings will push other people away. DFKs have deep fears about their badness and their unlovability—they worry about whether their parents can "stand" them, whether their parents can "handle" them, whether their parents can be sturdy leaders when they themselves feel completely unsturdy.

Of course, none of these fears are articulated. I don't know one DFK who says to a parent, "I often feel overwhelmed by my emotions and I worry that they overwhelm others—that's why I enter into these intense fear/attack states. Please bear with me and hold steady so I can learn that I'm lovable and good and will be okay in this world." No child can truly understand this (and, frankly, it would be hard for any adult to articulate this about themselves, either). And yet . . . remember these words. This is the core truth about our DFKs.

Here's an example of how these intense emotions and reactions might play out: Your deeply feeling daughter is having a hard time sharing. She starts grabbing toys out of a friend's hands and won't give them back. In a situation with a kid who is not a DFK, a parent might intervene and say, "I know, sharing is hard! I'm here, let me help you with this." The child might accept help—in the form of both boundaries and comfort—from a parent. But with a DFK, this offer of help might be met with an emotional explosion. In a DFK's body, the state of vulnerability ("I wanted a toy . . . then I grabbed it . . . I wish I didn't . . .") activates intense feelings of shame ("I shouldn't have done that, I am bad"). So, in this sharing scenario, it wouldn't surprise me if when the parent approached the child, she behaved like a caged animal fighting for survival, maybe yelling through tears: "Get away from me!" or "No, give me that toy, I hate you!" In these moments, a DFK is overwhelmed by how big and scary her feelings feel, yet what's happening on the outside seems simply coldhearted and unwarranted. Remember: logic is never our friend when it comes to understanding emotions, and this is never truer than with DFKs.

Because DFKs' escalations, hitting, or nasty words often come after moments that feel, to adults, quite minor, they often provoke reactions of rejection and invalidation. Parents might find themselves yelling, "Okay, fine, if you don't want me to help you, I won't!" or "Go to your room and come out when you calm down!" or "You're so dramatic!" or "You make everything difficult!" Again, if this all feels familiar, you're in the right place. You're still a good parent, so stay with me. One of the core fears for DFKs is that the feelings that overwhelm them will overwhelm others—that things that *feel* so bad and unmanageable *actually are* bad and unmanageable. All kids, DFKs and non-DFKs, learn what's manageable by seeing how their trusted adults respond to their emotions. When DFKs are met with parental screaming or harsh words or rejection, the patterns of dysregulation only intensify.

Now, let's go back to the example of the DFK who grabbed a toy from her friend. Let's say her response to her parent's attempt at intervention was to yell, "I hate you!" What this DFK is *really* saying is, "I'm overwhelmed. I took that toy because I couldn't manage wanting it and not having it, and now, on top of that, all my internal fears of being bad and unlovable are coming up. This fear puts my body into a threat state and now I must protect myself at all costs." In this moment, the DFK needs her parent to understand that yes, on the surface, she's out of control and maybe even in attack mode, but underneath, she's in a state of threat and fear and overwhelm. This child needs her parent's help, but she will not be able to accept direct help while she's in a threat state or while everyone around her feels like an enemy. Parents of DFKs have to practice "holding space"—meaning literally staying present around the child and taking up space, so that the child sees her overwhelming feelings aren't taking over the world around her and leaving her all alone. Parents of DFKs have to commit to limiting the damage instead of solving the problem. They need to focus on the larger arc of a child's struggle rather than fixating on what's happening on the surface.

Strategies

Move from Blame to Curiosity

When parents are in blame mode, we often vacillate between blaming ourselves for our kids' behavior and blaming our kids. These thoughts might sound like, "Something is wrong with me. I'm messing up my kid forever," or "Something is wrong with my kid. She is crazy and will be messed up forever." Curiosity, on the other hand, sounds like: "I wonder what's going on for my child?" or "My child feels inside the way they're acting on the outside . . . wow, my child feels so out of control and so 'bad'! What's going on there? What does she need?"

Start by looking inward and noticing what mode you're in when something challenging happens with your DFK. Be kind to your blame: "Hi, blame, I see you want to take over now! I'm going to ask you to step back so I can access my curiosity. I know that's here too." Then start asking questions.

Containment First

DFKs have massive meltdowns. They often escalate quickly and are full of flails, kicks, thrown objects, and total dysregulation. When kids are in this state, they need containment first. This requires that a parent take a deep breath and remember that their number one job is to keep their child safe. In times like these, that means removing the child from the current situation, bringing him to a smaller room, sitting with him, and being present for the emotional storm. Now, to be clear, your child won't like this. He will protest and plead: "Wait, don't carry me out, no no no no!!! I'll calm down!" Hear me out: YOU MUST CARRY THROUGH. Not because you want to "win," not because your child is manipulative, not to "show your child who's boss." You must carry through because your child needs to see that you are not overpowered by their dysregulation. They must understand that they have a sturdy leader who can take care of them in times of stress. Your child may be, on the surface, asking not to be carried to his room, but on the inside, imagine they're saying to you: "Please be the sturdy leader I need. I am clearly not in a place to be making good decisions. Please please please show me that my overwhelming feelings aren't contagious."

In the moment, describe to your child what is happening. "I'm picking you up and carrying you to your room. You're not in trouble. I'll sit with you. You're a good kid having a hard time."

"You're a Good Kid Having a Hard Time"

Perhaps more than anything else, DFKs pick up on your *perception* of them in their difficult moments; DFKs feel so overwhelmed by themselves and terrified of their own badness that they are hypervigilant for any sign from a parent that confirms their deepest fears. The "good kid having a hard time" strategy is a complex one—there's not really one thing to "do." Instead, there's a version of your child to keep in mind. So, in your child's difficult moments, the ones that make you want to push them away . . . try to imagine them as a child who is in pain and in fear. Reminding ourselves that we have a good kid having a hard time activates our desire to help, while "bad kid doing bad things" mode makes us want to judge or punish. You can tell your kid, "You're a good kid having a hard time," during a difficult moment, or you can share this idea in the aftermath of a big tantrum. You might say, "Earlier today was tough. I know. You're a good kid and you were having a hard time. I know that. I love you. I always will."

You can also use this as a mantra for yourself, to stay calm when your child is struggling. "I have a good kid having a hard time, I have a good kid having a hard time." Sometimes this is the best thing we can do for our kids—look at them lovingly and know we will help them through their struggles.

Be Present and Wait It Out

If there's only one strategy you remember for your interactions with a DFK, please let it be this: nothing is as powerful as your presence. Your loving, as-calm-as-possible presence, without any words or fancy scripts, is without a doubt your most important parenting "tool." Presence communicates goodness. It's as if, just by being there, you're saying, "I'm not scared of you, you're not bad. I'm right next to you and this shows you that you're good and lovable." We have to show our kids that they aren't "too much" for us, that they don't overpower us. What all kids, and especially DFKs, need more than anything is our physical bodies there with them when they're having a hard time. Our presence communicates better than any words: "You are good. You are lovable. You are not too much. You are not alone. I love you and I am here for you." These are the messages our DFKs are craving and yet also the messages that they have a hard time taking in.

Of course, presence doesn't mean we allow ourselves to be hit or put into danger. And it doesn't mean you can't take time-outs for yourself. For example, if you're sitting with your son in his room while he's having a massive meltdown, a "parent time-out" might begin with you saying to your child, "I love you. I need to give my body space for some deep breaths. I'm stepping right outside your door and then I'll be back." This couldn't be more different from yelling, "I can't be with you when you're like this!" Key elements of taking a break: explaining your need to calm your body, eliminating blame, stating clearly that you'll come back.

Thumbs Up/Down/to the Side

DFKs tend to hate talking about feelings. It feels like too much, too intense, too intrusive. For DFKs, feelings sit too close to their vulnerability. As we know, their vulnerability sits so close to shame that it leads them to shut down. So what are we to do? How can we talk about feelings—helpful in building emotion regulation!— with kids who don't like talking about feelings? Enter the Thumbs Up/Down/to the Side game. The next time you're trying to talk with your child about something feelings related, say, "I want to do something different. Lie down and don't even look at me! No eye contact at all. I'm going to say some things . . . if you agree, give me a thumbs-up. If it's a no, give me a thumbs-down. If something about what I say is kind of right, kind of not, give me a thumbs-to-the-side." If your child wants to hide under a bed while you do this, by all means, allow it! Your child is limiting being seen, which can allow your child to . . . be a bit more seen.

Next, say something ridiculous, something you know you'll get a thumbs-down for; it might be: "Today I got pretty upset with my sister because she came home with five hundred scoops of ice cream and I got only one." You'll likely get a smirk or small laugh, which is great to ease tension and make the space that much safer. Now you have an opening, perhaps for something like this: "Today I got pretty upset with my sister . . . it's so hard to have a younger sister, sometimes I wish it was just me in this family." Pause. Allow some time. If you do get a response, or a thumbs-up, move on—don't verbally process. This is likely a huge change for you, so maybe only say, "I hear that," or "I understand." You are slowly building your child's tolerance for feelings, vulnerability, connection.

How Does This Play Out for Angie and Maura?

Angie remembers, "Containment first." She walks toward Maura and says, "I'm going to pick you up and bring you to your room. You're not in trouble. I'll sit with you there. You're a good kid having a hard time and I love you." Maura is screaming, "No, no!" but Angie remembers that she is showing her child that she's a sturdy leader who isn't scared of her daughter in this moment. They get into her room; Angie closes the door and sits down, and remembers to focus on calming her own body rather than trying to change what's happening with Maura's.

When she feels a bit calmer, Angie tells Maura she's going to check on Isla and then come right back. Before she leaves, Angie says, "I love you. It's okay. I love you." After explaining to Isla that Maura is having a hard time and needs her for a bit, Angie returns to the room and waits out the emotional storm. She tells herself over and over, "Nothing is wrong with me, nothing is wrong with my child, I can cope with this." Later that night, when things are calm, Angie plays the Thumbs Up/Down/to the Side game with Maura; she's shocked that this is something Maura will actually engage in, and she learns during this game that an older kid at school pushed Maura on the playground that day. Angie knows this doesn't make it okay that Maura was aggressive with her sister, and yet having this context helps Angie better understand what happened. Maura, she is reminded, is a good kid having a hard time.

Conclusion

W e've covered a lot here. And while information can be empowering, it can also be overwhelming. After all, when we take in new learning, we're confronted with a wave of emotion about how we've understood or approached things in the past. As soon as we think, "Huh, I've never thought about responding to my child in that way—it makes sense and would probably feel better," we may also be met with guilt or shame that says, "I'm a terrible parent," or "I've messed up my child forever." Often, these feelings and thoughts are so intense that we freeze and look away from what we imagine is the source of the pain—the new information. It's a vicious cycle: we want to do things differently → we judge ourselves for how we've handled parenting issues up until that point → we experience a flood of distressing feelings and thoughts → we turn away from change to escape these negative internal experiences → we continue our old patterns.

But I have some ideas for how to break the cycle, and it comes from my first principle: good inside. Here's something I still know about you: you are good inside. I want to say that again, because these two words are so small—just ten letters!—and yet they hold all the potential to make change possible. *You are good inside.* When you yell at your kids, you are good inside. When you promise you'll be home from work to put your kids to sleep and end up staying too late and missing bedtime, you are good inside. When you show up late to school pickup and, instead of apologizing, end up telling your kid that he doesn't appreciate all you do for him, you are good inside. And when you're here—right here, reading this book, thinking about change, confronting painful feelings . . . you are definitely good inside. You are part of a movement of adults who are reclaiming their good-inside-ness and who are seeing how this allows us to change and become better.

Remember, we have to feel good inside to change. This is a paradox, I know. We have to be kind to ourselves and accept who we are today to be brave enough to make changes tomorrow. We cannot change from a place of guilt or shame—this won't work in parenting or any other area in life. I think we all know this, intuitively . . . after all, most of us have tried changing from a place of self-blame for years! It just doesn't work. Our body cannot tolerate feeling bad inside—feeling bad is synonymous with feeling "unconnectable" to others, and our evolutionary success depends on our ability to attach. As soon as we feel bad, unlovable, or unworthy, all of our energy is diverted toward escaping this feeling. There is no energy available to change and try new things! No wonder change is so darn hard.

The key to change lies in learning to *tolerate* the guilt or shame that comes up for us—seeing these feelings as *part* of the change process, not an enemy of the change process. We need to make friends with these feelings, because they're a signal that we're making progress! How do we do that? The key lies in my second principle: two things are true. We have to hold two seemingly oppositional truths at once. I have done things I am not proud of *and* I am good inside; I feel guilty about my parenting past *and* hopeful about my parenting future; I've been doing the best I can *and* I want to do better. Right now, take a break and come up with one "two things are true" statement for yourself. Write it down, say it aloud, share it with a trusted friend. Feel free to use one of my examples or come up with your own. No need to "get it right" . . . there is no right; the goal is just to practice holding two truths: one that acknowledges your feelings about your parenting up to this point, and one that acknowledges your desire to change moving forward.

Our behaviors do not define us. You are not your latest yell. You are a person—a good person—who has recently yelled. You are not your stubbornness. You are a person—a good person—who can be stubborn in an attempt to protect yourself. You are not your impatience. You are a person—a good person—who can display impatience when you're having a hard time. Finding your internal goodness doesn't absolve you from taking responsibility for behavior; by contrast, grounding yourself in your internal goodness *allows* you to take responsibility for your behavior. Once we ground ourselves in our internal goodness ("I am good inside. I am good inside. I am good inside"), we can look around at our behavior with more self-reflection and honesty.

Let's do this together. Place your feet on the ground, place your hand on your heart, and say this aloud with me: "Yes, I've done lots of things I wish I hadn't. I've behaved in ways I'm not proud of. Those are all things I *did*. That's not who I *am*. This difference doesn't let me off the hook; this difference leaves me *on the hook*, because it is the only way I can hold myself accountable to make changes. I am a good person who has done not-so-good things. I am still a good person. I am good inside, I have always been good inside, I will remain good inside." Allow yourself to take in these words. So many of us have developed enough self-beliefs about not being good enough that telling ourselves that we are good inside, even when we struggle or act out, is, well . . . radical.

And herein lies the power of this book, and, really, this movement you're now a part of. This book isn't so much a guidebook to parenting as it is a guidebook to feeling good inside, in any area of your life. After all, reclaiming our internal goodness is the key to change within ourselves and, after that, the key to intergenerational change with our kids. Once we feel good inside, we start to see the good inside our kids. This doesn't make us permissive parents—no way. It makes us parents who show up as grounded, sturdy leaders, who hold boundaries in challenging moments while simultaneously connecting to our children with empathy. We are establishing a new, revolutionary idea: you are still a good person even when you struggle. Two things are true.

You are an integral part of a greater movement. I hope you take a moment and give yourself credit; self-reflection is brave and difficult, and working on yourself while you're raising young kids is incredibly grueling. It feels hard . . . because it is hard. Remind yourself of that, over and over. And remind yourself of this as well: you're not alone. You are part of a community of millions of parents who are right alongside you, who can relate to and empathize with your journey, who see your goodness and can reflect it back to you when you struggle to find it.

Thank you for inviting me into your home. It has been an honor to get to know so many of you, to hear your stories, to learn about your pains and struggles and successes. My experience in this parenting community is one of overwhelming hopefulness. You have shown me that meaningful intergenerational change is not only possible but is actively happening. You're doing it. You're amazing. I can't wait to see what we will continue to create together.

Acknowledgments

There are so many people I want to thank, who made this book possible because of their encouragement and support.

First and foremost, thank you to my husband. Your belief in me is the motor that put this all into motion. After all, for how many years have you told me to write a book? I finally listened. And it was you who noted my special passion for thinking about children and families and told me that I had to turn my excitement into something bigger. You saw something in me before I saw it in myself, and I feel so strong because of your faith in me. You are, truly, the grounding force in my life. You have an amazing ability to focus on the present, rather than on all the things that need to be done tomorrow. You help me stop "spinning"—in anxiety and in what could go wrong—and to instead keep my feet on the ground and access gratitude and optimism. I love how you're focused on all that can go right—not what could go wrong, how you are able to see the bigger picture, how you bring out the fun in everyone around you, how you know so much about so many things, how quick-witted you are, how you always have my back. Marrying you was the best decision I've ever made. You're the best partner I could ask for, and I love you so much.

Thank you to my kids. There's no job that's more important to me than being your mom. What amazes me so much is how different you are—from each other and from me and your dad. I love watching each of you be your own person, find your own way, figure out what you love. I love playing board games with you, creating art with you, pretending to be a firefighter with you. I love the moments when it's past your bedtime and you want me to sit on your bed and give you a shoulder massage and we talk about the things that happened that day that you didn't want to discuss until just that moment. I love seeing your confidence—you each know who you are, how you feel, what you like, and how to speak up for what you want. Thank you for supporting me in all the things I am doing with Good Inside. I know it hasn't been easy to have me working more or to see me preoccupied with writing and ideas and video making . . . and I love that we talk about all this together, that you remind me to put away my phone, and that you keep me focused on what matters most—family.

Thank you to my parents. Thank you for your unconditional love, which was without a doubt the foundation for my belief that the thoughts I have are worthy to be "put out there" into the world. You've always made me feel good inside, which undoubtedly is the best gift a parent could ever give a child. Thank you for all you've done to support this big career shift of mine—the extra carpools, the extra errands run on my behalf, the extra take-my-kids-for-a-sleepover nights. Your involvement in our kids' lives is so special and allows me to work without the deafening noise of mom-guilt. I love you both so much and will never find the words to adequately thank you for all you've given me.

Thank you to my sister and brother. From the day I started an Instagram account, you two were my biggest fans and promoters, sharing with your communities, offering feedback, cheering me on as I tried new things. As we all know, siblinghood can be tough—and yet, I've felt nothing but support and love from you during this crazy ride. I love you both so much. And thank you to my two sisters-in-law and two brothers-in-law: I have truly lucked out having you as bonus family, and I'm deeply appreciative of your friendship. Thank you to my husband's parents, as well, for your endless love, open-mindedness, and support. And also included in the family section—Jordan. J, thank you for all you do to allow our lives to run smoothly. You are so special to us, and we all love you so much.

Thank you to my Good Inside cofounder, Erica, who is the Jane of all trades around here, doing all of the often-invisible labor that has made Good Inside what it is today. Our coming together was meant to be. You are the yin to my yang—the thoughtfulness to my action, the deliberateness to my urgency, the tying-up-the-pieces to my forging ahead. I admire you, I trust you, I respect you, and I adore being around you. I wouldn't want anyone else right by my side during this journey, and I couldn't be doing what I am doing without you. And thank you to the amazing Good Inside team—for your passion, your energy, your dedication, your openness, your drive, and your belief in our mission to help empower parents.

Thank you to my book team. Amy Hughes, you had me at hello. Literally. I feel like you just "get" me, plus you understood the idea for the book and saw—right away—that Good Inside was not just an Instagram account but was really a global movement. Thank you for your support, your extra texts and phone calls, your strategic planning, your friendship. Rachel Bertsche—my book-writing process was made so much easier and smoother because of you. You seamlessly took what I wrote and made the edits and suggestions that turned this from a book into a true story—a story of goodness, of hope, of practical possibility. To say you were a pleasure to work with is a massive understatement—I feel you always understood what I wanted to express, helped me further develop my writing voice, and added finishing touches that pulled everything together. Julie Will, thank you for believing in me long before we even spoke—when you were a follower of my Instagram account and saw that I had a book in me. Working with you has been a dream. Emma Kupor, thank you for your organization and your enthusiasm and for helping this project get to the finish line. Yelena Nesbit and the Harper sales and marketing team—thank you for believing in me and helping me bring this book to so many people.

Tenley, Sarah, Carolyn, Kristen, and Tiffany: I am forever indebted to you for inspiring so much of my thinking around parenthood and child development and for showing me the power of bringing together meaningful learning and deep connection. Thank you for your candor, your vulnerability, your curiosity, your warmth, for all of the tears and laughter, and of course, for coining the name "Dr Becky." Thank you for allowing me to be a part of your motherhood and self-growth journeys and for the ways you've cheered me on in mine. I have so much love and respect for each of you.

Thank you to my long-term private practice clients. You have taught me so much about how crafty young kids are in the way they adapt to their family systems and about how crafty adults are in the way they can rewire, change, and develop resilience. You have been my greatest teachers. Thank you for allowing me into your lives, for sharing your most vulnerable truths, for your trust in me, for your candor as I've taken on a new professional role that none of us expected. I also want to thank my colleagues who have been mentors and supervisors. I am so grateful for hours of thoughtful conversations that have shaped how I think. And Ron: you have been helpful beyond words in allowing me to get to know myself and manage a new career path and a changing world.

I couldn't do anything without my personal support team—my best friends. I love that basically none of you know anything I'm doing on social media and that I have remained just-plain-Becky to all of you. Thank you for your texts, for coming to my side of town to squeeze in an extra coffee, and all your support.

Last but without a doubt not least, I want to thank each member of the Good Inside community. I really mean this: there'd be no movement without you. You each inspire me daily—with your stories, your bravery, your vulnerability, your passion, your trust. Two things are true: we've already done so much together, and this is just the first inning. So gear up and get ready for what's next, for all of us!

Index

About the Author

DR BECKY KENNEDY is a clinical psychologist and mom of three—named "The Millennial Parenting Whisperer" by *Time* magazine—who is rethinking the way we raise our children. She specializes in thinking deeply about what's happening for kids and translating these ideas into simple, actionable strategies for parents to use in their homes. Dr Becky's goal is to empower parents to feel sturdier and more equipped to manage the challenges of parenting.

Dr Becky has amassed a loyal and highly engaged community of over one million followers on Instagram, created a library of popular parenting workshops, launched a top-rated podcast as well as a newsletter, and published a potty handbook. *Good Inside* is her first book.

Her weekly podcast, *Good Inside with Dr Becky*, immediately went to number one on the Apple Podcasts' Kids & Family chart upon launching in April 2021, was placed on the coveted New and Noteworthy list, landed the twenty-sixth spot on the iTunes Top Podcasts' chart in June 2021, and made Apple Podcasts' Best Shows of 2021 list. Each week, she takes on tough parenting questions and delivers actionable guidance—all in short episodes, because she knows time is hard to find as a parent.

Dr Becky received a BA in psychology and human development, Phi Beta Kappa and summa cum laude, from Duke University, and a PhD in clinical psychology from Columbia University.

To learn more, visit: www.goodinside.com.

Growth requires three things: motivation, learning, and connection. By reading this book, you've shown me you have the motivation and the commitment to learning.

And for the connection . . . I'm excited to offer you a **special discount** to join Good Inside—the only all-in-one parenting platform providing like-valued parents a place to learn, share, and grow together.

Scan the QR code to find out more:

I can't wait to *connect with you* on the inside!